ENTERTAINING THE NATION

ENTERTAINING THE NATION

A SOCIAL HISTORY OF BRITISH TELEVISION

JACK WILLIAMS

SUTTON PUBLISHING

First published in the United Kingdom in 2004 by
Sutton Publishing Limited · Phoenix Mill
Thrupp · Stroud · Gloucestershire · GL5 2BU

British Library Cataloguing in Publication Data
A catalogue record for this book is available from the British Library.

ISBN 0-7509-2181-1

Typeset in 10.5/15pt Photina MT.
Typesetting and origination by
Sutton Publishing Limited.
Printed and bound in England by
J.H. Haynes & Co. Ltd, Sparkford.

CONTENTS

LIST OF TABLES

ACKNOWLEDGEMENTS

I must thank those who have helped me with this book. The financial support from the John Moores University was vital for my researches in London and other cities. The assistance of the staff at many libraries has been essential, but I am particularly grateful to the Inter-library Loans Unit at the John Moores University, which supplied the most obscure materials with such promptness. Wendy Thomas very kindly sought out many items for me from the collection that the ITC has deposited with the British Film Institute Library. I learned a great deal from those who agreed to be interviewed by me and hope that they enjoyed our conversations as much as I did. As some of those I interviewed were speaking 'off the record', I have not been able to identify them but I do wish to record my gratitude to them. The staff at Sutton Publishing showed great patience in waiting for the finished version of the book. My biggest debt, as always, is to my wife, Pat. Without her love and support, this book could not have been completed. While my views have been clarified through the help of others, the interpretations and conclusions expressed in this book are entirely mine.

Jack Williams
January 2004

ABBREVIATIONS

ACC   Associated Communications Corporation
APA   Alan Pascoe Associates
ATV   Associated Television
BAF   British Athletics Federation
BARB   Broadcasters' Audience Research Board
BBC   British Broadcasting Corporation
BET   British Electric Traction
BFI   British Film Institute
BREMA British Radio and Electronic Equipment Manufacturers' Association
BSB   British Satellite Broadcasting
DBS   Direct broadcasting by satellite
GEC   General Electric Company
HTV   Harlech Television
IBA   Independent Broadcasting Authority
IMG   International Management Group
ITA   Independent Television Authority
ITC   Independent Television Commission
ITN   Independent Television News
ITV   Independent Television
LWT   London Weekend Television
MEN   Manchester Evening News
NVLA   National Viewers' and Listeners' Association
RETRA   Radio, Electrical and Television Retailers' Association
TWW   Television Wales and the West

Chapter 1

INTRODUCTION

The growth of television viewing has been one of the major changes to life in Britain since the Second World War. One great difference between today, or any period in the last four decades, and the first half of the twentieth century is the amount of time that so many people spend watching television. When the BBC television service resumed in 1946, only a tiny minority of the population had access to television. By 1960 the great majority of the population viewed television on a daily basis. In the 1950s the time spent watching television overtook that spent visiting the cinema or listening to radio. From the 1960s, people in Britain have spent more of their non-work waking hours watching television than on any other activity, though some dispute that watching television is an activity, and very little attention can be directed to a television receiver that is switched on. Most of those aged over sixty may not remember when they first saw television but can probably recall when their families acquired a set. For nearly all of those born after 1960, television has been a part of everyday life, something taken for granted. This rise of television viewing was not restricted to Britain but occurred at more or less the same time in all developed countries.

This book examines the social and cultural significance of television in Britain. It is based on a conviction that analysis of the leisure interests, of how people choose to spend their time away from work, is vital for understanding a society and its cultural values. The scale of television viewing means that no social and cultural history of Britain since the Second World War can ignore the role of television. Most of the book's emphasis is on the second half of the twentieth century. The BBC's television service started in 1936, was closed during the Second World War, and then restarted in 1946, but it was only in the 1950s that television acquired a mass audience and began to be a key element of popular culture. This book concentrates on how television has represented life in Britain. All television programmes, including those described as fiction, provide viewers with data about the world, but they are only representations of the world. All accounts of a social situation are selective. No one can observe all aspects of an event. Television emphasises some aspects of the world and downplays or omits others.

As the study of television and its social and cultural resonances has to consider who watches what, the next chapter of this book discusses the extent of television viewing and the social profiles of viewers for different genres of programmes, and assesses explanations for the growth of television viewing. The subsequent chapters consider the relationship of television with selected areas of British society and culture. These include analyses of television's economic roles, its relationship with politics, its nature as an organ of mass communication and association with those other major forms of mass communication, namely, radio and the press, television's presentation of gender, sexuality and ethnicity, how far television has been considered an art form and its conjunctions with the 'fine arts', and the links between television and sport. These themes are not an exhaustive list of television's connections with British social and cultural institutions. There are no chapters on television and religion or on television and education. As so much has already been written about whether television has encouraged violent behaviour, a subject on which no consensus has been reached, it did not seem necessary to add to this. Television's relationship with social class does not have a separate chapter but class provides a dimension to most chapters and is also considered in the conclusion. It seemed preferable to treat a number of topics in detail rather than deal with a wider range superficially.

Television and Cultural and Social Change

A crucial question that has to be addressed here is whether television has changed attitudes and behaviour. This is part of the question whether the mass media generally have promoted social and cultural change. There seems to be widespread support among the general public for the view that television has influenced attitudes and consequently behaviour. Politicians and the press have fostered the belief that television has a vital influence in shaping behaviour. Changes in sexual activity or supposed rises in the level of crime have often been attributed to television. The nine o'clock watershed for the broadcasting of sexually explicit material and of strong language suggests a widespread belief that sexual mores can be affected by television. Protests from ethnic minorities about their under-representation by television and about stereotypical images of them on television suggest that many groups believe that television presentation can alter the way they are perceived. The enormous sums – £4.6 billion in 2000 – spent on television advertising each year by commercial organisations controlled by hard-headed businessmen whose aim is to maximise sales, strengthen the plausibility of the view that television can and does change behaviour.

Academic researchers, on the other hand, are far from a consensus about whether television and other forms of the mass media influence attitudes and behaviour. According to the so-called effects model of the mass media, in modern societies the views of those who control the media are imposed on the public. This approach was very much associated with the Frankfurt School of German émigré Marxists, and particularly Adorno and Horkheimer,[1] who moved to the United States between the world wars. Adorno argued that technology such as television, cinema and radio had created a culture industry that overpowered viewers and listeners. Viewers were passive absorbers of television, which manipulated their thinking and behaviour and, by encouraging standardisation and undermining individuality, helped to uphold the political and economic status quo. The expansion of television in the 1960s and 1970s contributed to a reaction against the effects model in the form of what became called the 'uses and gratifications' perspective. In Britain Blumler and Halloran argued that research on television and behaviour should focus on viewers and how they used television.[2] They noted that television viewers were not simply passive recipients of what television presented to them but were selective in their choice of viewing and derived different satisfactions from television. This approach suggested that audiences were not a homogeneous mass and that different viewers did not derive the same meaning from television. The 'uses and gratifications' perspective did not mean that television had no capacity to shape the attitudes and behaviour of viewers but, rather, that it could have a variety of effects. The meanings derived from a television programme or programme genre could be different from those intended by its producers. Studies of the way viewers used television for information during election campaigns suggested that television was more likely to reinforce than to change existing beliefs. A criticism of the uses and gratifications approach was that it tended to underplay how far exposure to television and other media over time influenced the way viewers choose to use television.

In the 1980s, Postman, working in America, argued that the nature of television as an entertainment medium meant that it tended to uphold the established social order by discouraging original and critical thinking. Postman contended that television was not suited to presenting reasoned thought and reflection, that it concentrated on entertaining rather than challenging viewers, and that it was driven by a show business desire for applause. By presenting the world in short, episodic bursts, television was undermining print culture and its opportunities for deeper thought and political activism.[3] But, while television may not often stimulate thought as deep as some forms of print have, political satire and treating politics as a form of entertainment in Britain have arguably aired radical criticisms of the political establishment. In the 1990s television in Britain has often been accused of tabloidisation, of 'dumbing down' and making news programmes more like entertainment, but this can be defended on the grounds that it widens access and engages those who would not otherwise watch news.[4]

Within the past three decades, the preponderant view among those working in the growing field of cultural studies has been that not all viewers draw the same meaning from a television programme or television genre. Cultural texts, it has been argued, whether books, films or television programmes, are polysemic, capable of having many meanings ascribed to them. Different viewers draw different meanings from the same programmes. This approach has been very much influenced by the rise of postmodernism and the view that an objective understanding of social reality is impossible. Roland Barthes had written about the death of the author, claiming that it was not the author but readers who ascribed meaning to a text, that one reading was as valid as any other and that any number of readings of a text could be made. This argument implies that viewers, not authors, give meaning to television programmes. Stuart Hall wrote about television texts having 'preferred' messages, that is those of their authors, encoded within them, but he stressed that they could be decoded in different and contradictory ways.[5] Postmodernist contentions about the decentred subject – that one person can subscribe to different identities in different situations – also imply that one individual may draw differing meanings from a television programme at different times. It would seem that some readings of a television programme or series of programmes could change attitudes and behaviour but others could have the opposite effect. A further strand of postmodernist approaches to cultural texts stressed that the nature, or perhaps the limitations, of language prevents us from forming an objective view of the social world. This would seem to suggest that, if we have no objective knowledge of social reality, we cannot be sure of whether or how television may have changed attitudes and behaviour.

Even if a television programme can be interpreted in many different ways, it does not follow that has always been the case. It is very difficult, indeed virtually impossible, to establish what meanings a large number of viewers may have drawn from any cultural text. Tulloch's recent claims that more research into audience responses to television needs to be conducted through small focus groups emphasise the difficulties of establishing the responses of large numbers of viewers.[6] It seems plausible that differing social situations and experience and differing discourses for imagining and describing the social world would lead individuals to 'read' a programme differently; but, equally plausibly, these differences may not be so very great. Curran has argued that audiences do not have an unlimited range of discourses with which they shape the meanings of television programmes, and Philo found that groups with different social backgrounds and from different parts of the country often derived broadly similar impressions of picketing from the television coverage of the miners' strike in 1984.[7] While viewers can, and perhaps sometimes do, draw different messages from a text, it does not follow that this is always what happens. One can argue that no society could exist unless all of its members attached more or less the same meanings to the same messages for almost all the time. Some messages are misunderstood, of course, but in order to interact with each other the great majority have to draw approximately the same meanings from the same messages. Large numbers may more or less agree on what a television programme means. The fact that over twelve million viewers watch the most popular programmes on most evenings suggests, though certainly does not prove, that many may be deriving the same satisfactions from these programmes and may therefore be understanding them in the same manner. We simply do not know how far viewers attach the same or differing meanings to the same programmes or whether some programme genres give rise to more varied readings than others.

One way in which television may encourage uniformity in attitudes and behaviour is by providing us with data about the world. Our actions are governed in part by what we know about the world but the data that television provides about the world is selective. What it ignores may well affect how we imagine the world. By providing only a mediated view of the world, television may be leading us to think in one way rather than another. In recent decades it has been claimed that we imagine who we are through narratives, that stories organise and shape our self-perceptions. Feminist film theory has emphasised narration – that is, the modes of telling stories – as much as the content of narratives in creating meanings of the world.[8] Largely influenced by psychoanalytical theory, feminist film criticism has claimed that how a film is structured, including its writing, camera work, sound effects and the direction of actors, induces, some might say manipulates, the viewers to adopt a particular interpretation of a film, which is very close to the notion of a preferred reading of a cultural text. Yet other feminist writers have argued that, rather than being manipulated by film-makers, women viewers fashion the pleasures that they derive from watching films. The emphasis on narration in feminist film criticism can be extended to television and has parallels with Marshall McLuhan's argument that television affects how we think, not through its subject matter but through its form of presentation.

Uncertainty about whether television can change attitudes and behaviour is also related to the difficulty of isolating its influence from that of other cultural forces. If television can influence behaviour, other forms of mass communication probably have similar effects. Television and the press, for instance, could both have some bearing on voting behaviour, but it is impossible to determine which may have the stronger impact, and television and the press may well condition responses to one another. Attempts to establish whether viewing depictions of violence on television leads to violent behaviour have found it difficult to distinguish the effects of television from other influences such as home background, the example of peers and exposure to violence in other areas of life. The sheer volume of television and the great variety of programme genres add to the complications of determining how far television can shape attitudes and behaviour. Much more needs to be known about how viewers watch television. The extent of television viewing has been monitored, and much is known about the social profiles of viewers for individual programmes, though little of this data has been made public. Studies have been made of why viewers watch television but far less research has been conducted into how viewers watch television. An experiment in 1986 that filmed viewers as they watched television showed that they often combined television with other activities and paid only cursory attention to television.[9] The intensity of viewing may increase any potential influence of television, though viewers may watch very intently programmes with which they disagree. Less intensive viewing over a longer period may have a stronger cumulative impact than occasional programmes that are viewed with great concentration.

Notwithstanding the doubts surrounding its impact on attitudes and behaviour, a very strong case can be made for the view that television has changed aspects of British society. The start of commercial television provided a new outlet for advertising. In the 1990s television commercials accounted for over a quarter of all advertising expenditure. The sale and renting of television sets became an important form of retailing. Television magazines were among those with the highest circulations in Britain and television material became an increasing part of newspaper content. General elections campaigns became centred around television. By the 1960s leaders of political parties had to have what viewers thought was an effective television manner. Their supposed inadequacies on television were important reasons why Home, Foot and Duncan-Smith were party leaders for such a short time. Television transformed leisure. In the 1950s, much of the time that had been spent listening to radio or visiting the cinema became diverted to watching television. The style and content of radio and film had to adapt in order to face the competition from television. Television broadcasting fees became an increasingly important source of finance for many sports. In soccer, television revenues were the driving force behind the establishment of the Premiership in England and the introduction of the European Champions League. Television income led rugby league to establish the Super League, which plays in summer instead of winter.

Writings on Television

The scale of television makes writing about it daunting. Programmes are the most obvious source for a history of television and of its social and cultural roles, but no one can have watched more than the tiniest fraction of all the programmes that have been broadcast in Britain. In 1952, when there was only one television channel in Britain and viewing hours were limited, television broadcasts exceeded fifty hours per week. In the second half of the 1990s, the five terrestrial channels broadcast for more or less twenty-four hours a day every day. At present, anyone watching terrestrial television for twelve hours every day would see only 10 per cent of its output; and this ignores the dozens of cable and satellite channels. No visual record of many early programmes remains. Even after the adoption of video recording tape in the early 1960s, tapes of many programmes were wiped clean to be reused. Reading the script of a programme is a poor substitute for viewing it and cannot recapture the tone of voice or gestures that do much to shape the nature of a broadcast. Analysing programmes requires vast amounts of time and explains why there has been relatively little textual analysis of television programmes and little that covers more than one decade. *Radio Times* and *TV Times* list the times and dates of broadcasts; but trying to establish when the first programme on a particular topic may have been broadcast is like searching for needles in haystacks. Broadcasting organisations have generated vast archives of documents. The BBC's Written Archives Centre has a quarter of a million files of correspondence and 25,000 reels of microfilms of correspondence. If only a third of these were concerned with television, which is probably an underestimate, this is a staggering number of documents. The British Film Institute has inherited around 500 crates of books and other materials from the Independent Television Commission (ITC) library. Because of the vast scale of the sources concerned with television, conclusions about its significance have to be tentative. The phrases 'probably', 'possibly' and 'likely' occur frequently in this book.

Television has provided subject matter for scholars working in psychology, sociology, the burgeoning fields of cultural and media studies, political science and history. This widespread interest in television brings advantages and problems for those researching the history of television. The variety of disciplines focusing on television has enriched historical studies by providing new approaches to the subject, though it can be hazardous to stray into disputes between practitioners from other disciplines. To a historian, the approach of other disciplines seems to concentrate on very short periods of time, although studies made decades ago provide valuable source material for historians of television. The extent of the academic literature on television is awesome. The search term 'television' brings up more than 10,500 entries on the British Library online catalogue. *The British Humanities Index* for 2000 had more than a hundred entries for television. Those trying to write about television must feel overwhelmed by the flow – perhaps 'flood' is a more accurate term – of new books and articles about it. No author would be able to finish a manuscript if he or she tried to read and assess all that is published about television. Writers about television have no choice but to ignore what is just being published when their own work is close to completion.

So much has been written about the history of television that assessments of it have to be selective. Two works that appeared in the 1990s on the socio-cultural history of television deserve special mention. Cashmore's . . . *And There Was Telev!s!on*, published in 1994, is an admirably clear commentary on theoretical approaches to the nature of television and discusses how television in Britain and America has represented politics, gender, ethnicity and violence.[10] Its comparative approach provides interesting perspectives on British television but, as the main emphasis is on the United States, perhaps dictated by the publisher, the British experience is rather pushed out of the picture. Cashmore argues strongly that economic considerations have done much to shape television in America and Britain. Scannell's *Radio, Television and Everyday Life* provides many arresting insights into how broadcast programmes were constructed to be interpreted in a particular way.[11] His approach concentrates on case studies of programmes but devotes more space to radio than to television.

The administrative structure of BBC television and of the ITA/IBA, and of their relations with government, has been examined in detail,[12] but so far little has been published about the organisation of television in the 1990s. Horrie and Clarke have provided a detailed and hugely entertaining narrative account of the reorganisation of BBC television in the late 1980s and early 1990s;[13] but no detailed examination of the background to the mergers of the ITV companies in the 1990s has been published, though the business dimension to these is discussed in the biographies of Michael Green and Gerry Robinson.[14] An informed assessment of the ITC's supervision of independent television has still to be written. No academic studies of individual ITV companies and of their organisation and programme production exist, although Michael Leapman's *Treachery?* analyses the difficulties of TV-am in the early 1980s.[15] Briggs and Spicer and Davidson have produced monographs which look at how ITV broadcasting franchises were awarded in 1980 and in 1991.[16] *Dished!* by Peter Chippingale and Suzanne Franks is a detailed narrative of the establishment of satellite broadcasting in Britain; but, except for biographies of Rupert Murdoch, little has appeared about the operation of BSkyB.[17] Little has been written about the setting up and limited growth of cable television, although *L¿ve TV* by Chris Horrie and Adam Nathan is a minutely detailed and often highly amusing account of the start and early difficulties of the cable entertainment channel L!ve TV.[18]

The links between television and politics have stimulated much historical writing, though some areas still call for further research. The pioneering studies of television's role in the general elections of 1959 and 1964[19] have been followed by studies of television in subsequent elections. Goodwin's detailed examination of Conservative governments' policies towards television between 1979 and 1997 emphasises the need for similarly detailed studies of the approach of other governments to television.[20] Michael Cockerell's *Live from Number 10* is a largely anecdotal account of the often fraught relationship between prime ministers and broadcasters, but has insights that can be provided only by a broadcaster.[21] Seymour-Ure's *Prime Ministers and the Media* demonstrates how prime ministers tried to manipulate the mass media in the 1980s and 1990s.[22] Studies of television news have concentrated on political news. Since the 1970s the Glasgow University Media Group has been examining the content and presentation of television news and the biases that it may contain; and in the 1990s changes in the content of television news were quantified and assessed by Barnett, Gaber and Seymour.[23] Harrison has shown how in the 1990s the content of television news was influenced by the culture of television journalists and the changing economics of television.[24] Her work emphasises the need for similar studies of earlier decades. Comparisons of how television and other forms of mass media have presented politics and political information have been discussed by Curran and Seaton and by Seymour-Ure.[25] Little attention, however, has been paid to how far newspapers reacted to the growth of television and to how television became a topic of news coverage by the press, although Hargreaves has pointed out the similarities and differences in the outlook and working methods of newspaper and television journalists.[26] The political repercussions of changing television technology in the 1990s have been addressed by Seaton.[27] Curran's *Media and Power* evaluates the theoretical approaches to the role of television and the other media in politics. No study has drawn together and evaluated the scattered work on television's presentation of politics as a form of entertainment.

The economic history of television from its beginnings is waiting to be written. Collins, Garnham and Locksley made an excellent survey of employment in television, the costs of programme production and the international trade in television programmes; but unfortunately their study concentrates on the ten years up to 1988 and there is no equivalent for other decades.[28] The impacts of television on the economy (apart from advertising) have been more or less ignored. The emphasis in the social sciences since the 1980s on the construction of identity has stimulated interest in television and gender identities but, no doubt because of the growth of feminism, much of this has concentrated on female identities. There have been impressive investigations of how programme genres represented women and of how women responded to these, such as Geraghty's *Women and Soap Opera*,[29] but most have concentrated on one moment in time. More attention needs to be focused on how television's representations of men and women have changed over time. The gay and lesbian presence in television grew in the 1990s; but how far television presentation of homosexuals changed over time has not been investigated in detail. The presentation of ethnicity on television has been studied only in recent years. Cumberbatch and others have collected much data about the extent and forms of ethnic minority representation on television in the 1990s.[30] Bourne, Pines, and Cottle and Ismond have explained the absence of black people from television by a biographical approach which highlights the prejudices that black producers, writers and actors have faced in television.[31] *The Colour Black*, edited by Daniels and Gerson, examines ethnic representations in television situation comedies (hereafter sitcoms) and in crime dramas, and includes extensive quotations from contemporary periodicals to show the variety of responses to them.[32] Daniels has also examined how programmes made in the 1980s and 1990s by black producers and black writers and with black actors provoked debate about whether they ought to have promoted a more favourable impression of black people. She also notes that such programmes did not make a great impact on 'mainstream' television.[33] Sarita Malik's excellent *Representing Black Britain: Black Images on Television* discusses the changing representations of blacks in the differing genres of British television. All of these works consider ethnicity in television from a historical perspective. They all point to the need for a chronological study of how whiteness has been depicted on television.

Programmes on classical music, opera, dance, classic plays, painting and sculpture have formed only a tiny fraction of the output of television in Britain, but they have often received critical acclaim and have been praised for making the arts accessible to greater numbers of people. The varieties of television programmes and series concerned with the arts were reviewed by Walker in 1993. He demonstrated how changes in television technology and in the economics of television had influenced the television presentation of the arts. One of the most valuable aspects of his work is the discussion of the evolution of television arts magazine programmes. Unfortunately, there is little comparable material for the period since 1993. Almost all films made for exhibition in the cinema are shown at some time on television. Television dramatists such as Dennis Potter, Alan Bleasdale and Alan Bennett have been accorded an artistic status similar to that of the leading writers for the stage. This book argues that television situation comedy deserves to be classified as an art form. Little has been written about the place of television in Britain's artistic life. There are biographical and critical studies of television writers, such as Carpenter's study of Dennis Potter,[34] and assessments of the nature and making of television drama, such as Brandt's *British Television Drama* and Millington and Nelson's *Boys from the Blackstuff: The Making of a TV Drama*.[35] The collection of essays on television drama in Britain edited by Bignell, Lacey and Macmurraugh-Kavanagh is an especially valuable contribution to writings about television and the arts as it traces and explains the changes over time in a major television genre.[36] The emphasis in writings about soap operas on the representation of women has somewhat marginalised evaluations of the artistic qualities of this form of drama. The dominant theme of the many books on sitcoms is why they are so amusing, though this often includes assessment of their writing and acting.[37] Stokes has examined how television has been treated in British and American films, but she rather sidesteps the issue of whether television has led to changes in film-making.[38] The impacts of television on the artistic output of radio are discussed in Carpenter's history of the Third Programme and Radio 3;[39] but little has been written about the relationship of television with opera, ballet and modern dance. Many regard jazz and pop music as art forms, but little attention has been focused on why they have received such limited coverage on television.

The nature of television's presentation of sport in Britain and of its impacts on sport has been discussed with great clarity in Barnett's *Games and Sets* and in Whannel's *Sport, Television and Cultural Transformations*.[40] The latter was published in 1992 and no subsequent study has examined the repercussions on sport of the vast sums that the more popular sports received in the 1990s from increased competition, stimulated largely by BSkyB, for the rights to televise sport live. Whannel's *Media Sport Stars* does examine the effects of television money on the celebrity of sport's mega stars since the early 1990s and compares these with earlier decades; but his discussion of the construction of sport celebrity concentrates mainly on the role of the press and pushes television to one side.[41] Hill's *Sport, Leisure and Culture in Twentieth-Century Britain* has made perceptive suggestions about how historians and social analysts need to approach the relationship between television and sport.[42]

Entertaining the Nation cannot fill all the gaps that have been highlighted in the history of television's cultural and social roles. No single volume could do that. This book is also very much dependent on the research that has been conducted into the history of television. It attempts to establish those areas of British social and cultural life where television has had a profound impact, while recognising that there are many areas of British life on which any influence from television cannot be traced. It accepts that in many ways we cannot be sure of what impact, if any, television has had on attitudes, but it does try to show that some social and cultural institutions have changed because of television and that others have remained largely unaffected by television. *Entertaining the Nation* will not be the final word on the cultural and social significance of television but one hopes it will have demonstrated that, if we wish to understand post-war Britain, we have to pay due regard to its television.

Chapter 2

THE CENTRALITY OF TELEVISION

Television Viewing

Television has been a central feature of life in Britain since the Second World War. In the late 1930s and late 1940s, when sets were expensive, watching television was a minority interest; but since the 1960s, when there was reasonable reception of television broadcasts in more or less all regions, it has been a national interest. By the end of 1936, the year when the BBC started its television service, only 280 receivers had been sold in Britain. By August 1939, the last full month of transmissions before the BBC television service was closed because of the war, probably no more than 25,000 sets were in use.[1] Watching television grew rapidly after the restoration of the BBC's television service in 1946, and by the end of the 1950s television had dethroned radio as the main home-based entertainment. In 1947, when acceptable television pictures were obtainable only in south-east England, the number of the combined radio and television licences, which owners of television sets were required to buy, was only just over 14,500, but by 1950 this figure had grown to nearly 344,000 though in that year 11.8 million licences for radio use alone were bought. Ten years later, 10.5 million combined radio and television licences were bought, more than double the number of radio licences. By 1970, the last year when radio-only licences were needed, 2.3 million of them were bought but more than 15.6 million for radio and monochrome television.[2] The increase in the number of households with television is a further measure of the interest in television. In 1951 fewer than 10 per cent of all households in Britain had a television set. Ten years later about 75 per cent of all households had a television set and by 1978 over 90 per cent. By 1994–5, 99 per cent of households had a television set.[3] In 1965 only three out of a hundred homes had a second set. By 1979 almost a quarter of all homes had at least two sets and two-thirds by 1994.[4] In 1999 more people lived in households with three or more sets than in those with one set.[5] In 1979 more households had a television than had a telephone, washing machine, refrigerator, deep freezer, car or central heating.[6] Between 1983 and 1990 the number of households with a video cassette recorder rose from a little under 5 million to 14.8 millio.[7]

By the 1960s people in Britain were spending more of their waking hours watching television than on any other non-work activity. In 1961 the average number of hours spent watching television per person each week was over thirteen and over eighteen by 1981.[8] In 2001 average weekly hours spent watching television had reached 24, although this was slightly lower than the weekly average in 1999 of 25.6 hours per week or 3.6 hours per day.[9] In 1955 the average time spent watching television overtook that for radio. *Social Trends* found that, between September 1965 and March 1966 for a sample of the population in England and Wales aged over fifteen years, 23 per cent of leisure time was spent watching television. For men the other leisure pursuits on which most time was spent were gardening (12 per cent) and participating in physical recreation (11 per cent). For women, crafts and hobbies took up 17 per cent of leisure time, and social activities, defined as visiting or entertaining friends and relatives and parties, 9 per cent.[10] In May 1995, a month when the weather would have added to the attractions of outdoor activities and the popularity of television viewing would have been lower than the average for the whole year, those aged over sixteen still spent nineteen of their forty-two free-time hours watching television or listening to radio. Visiting friends, the next most popular activity, took up five hours.[11]

Statistics of television viewing, of course, are all based on samples of viewers, and different sampling techniques have produced different estimates for the numbers watching particular programmes. Until the BBC and ITV set up the Broadcasters' Audience Research Board (BARB) in 1981, they used different methods to calculate audience numbers, and this resulted in conflicting, and sometimes widely differing, estimates of viewing numbers. In 1980 the BBC and ITV broadcast the Scotland–Zaire World Cup soccer match at the same time. The BBC claimed that 16.5 million had watched its transmission and 5.5 million that of ITV. ITV calculated that 5.1 million homes had watched the BBC transmission and 4.4 million that of ITV.[12] The differing techniques of audience measurement have never suggested that television was not watched by vast numbers. Viewing numbers have always been very largely a measure of how many people are in a room where a television has been switched on, and do not register the intensity of viewing. An experiment in the mid-1980s by Peter Collett, who televised viewers watching television, revealed that not all programmes were watched with the same concentration and that viewing was often combined with another activity on which more concentration was focused.[13]

Watching television has been popular across society. Women have tended to watch more television than men, though not very much more. In the mid-1960s the BBC claimed that 55 per cent of the total audience for BBC television was female and 57 per cent for ITV.[14] In February 1978, men in employment watched television on average for seventeen hours per week and women in employment for eighteen hours. Men not in employment watched for 22 hours and full-time housewives and unemployed women for 23 hours.[15] In 1994 females formed a higher proportion of the total viewers for BBC1, ITV and Channel 4, while the two sexes watched BBC2 in equal numbers. ITV was the channel with the widest gap in the proportion of female and male viewers. Nearly six females watched ITV for every four male viewers. Slightly more males than females watched the cable and satellite channels in 1994, though more than two-thirds of the viewers for Sky News and Sky Sports were male.[16] The numbers of men and women watching individual programmes from 1981 can be traced through the BARB statistics of the viewing numbers for each terrestrial channel. For one week in February and another in July 2001, two weeks chosen at random, BARB figures show that the proportion of women viewers of programmes with the biggest audiences was always higher than that of men. A live football match screened on a Sunday in February had more than twice as many men than women viewers, but its total number of viewers, a little over 5.5 million, was not vast by the standards of ITV. Programmes with most viewers were usually broadcast between 6 p.m. and 11 p.m. Sport programmes tended to be those with more men than women viewers, but those with most women viewers – soaps and drama series – were also among those watched by most men. Usually, programmes that most men watched had even more women viewers.

Bigger, though again not very great, differences are found in the extent of television viewing between social classes, and the data compiled by *Social Trends* show that for all classes more non-work time has been spent on television than any other leisure interest. From the late 1960s until the early 1990s, those from social classes A and B watched least television, class C1 had the next lowest viewing figures, while class C2 watched more than C1 and more than classes D and E. In the 1980s classes D and E were spending about a third more time watching television than classes A and B. In 1986 ABs were watching nearly three hours' television per day. In 1994 the proportion of viewers from each social class for each terrestrial channel was more or less equal to its proportion of the UK population.[17]

Tables 2.1 and 2.2 examine the number of hours watched on average by different age groups from 1967 to the early 1990s. Although the age groupings for the two tables are not identical and their sampling techniques varied, the tables do make clear that all age groups spent a lot of time watching television and that their hours of television viewing have increased over time. In the late 1960s and 1970s, those aged 4–15 watched most television, but by 1985 that age group watched least television. From 1985 to 1993 the average number of hours each week spent watching television rose with age.

The audiences attracted to the most popular programmes are a further register of the centrality of television in British life. It was reported to the Pilkington Committee that 22.5 million, about a third of the total population, watched BBC television at some time each day during June 1960.[18] In the mid-1960s the ITA's annual report claimed that on average more than 12.5 million watched ITV programmes between 7.30 p.m. and 10.30 p.m.[19] The

Table 2.1   The age profile of television viewers, 1967–1979

Age group	Average number of hours spent watching television per week (February)			
	1967	1971	1977	1979
5–14	18	21	22	24
15–19	15	17	18	16
20–29	15	17	18	18
30–49	16	18	18	18
50+	16	19	20	–
50–64	–	–	–	20
65+	–	–	–	22

Source: Social Trends 10 (London: HMSO, 1980), p. 227.

Table 2.2   The age profile of television viewers, 1985–1993

Age group	Average number of hours and minutes spent watching television per week (February)				
	1985	1987	1989	1991	1993
4–15	19.59	20.35	19.14	18.20	19.12
16–34	21.36	21.10	20.03	22.20	22.42
35–64	28.04	27.49	27.17	27.38	26.24
65+	36.35	36.55	37.41	37.27	35.47

Sources: *Social Trends 21* (London: HMSO,1991), p. 172 and *Social Trends 25* (London: HMSO, 1995), p. 216.

most accessible guide to television audiences is *40 Years of British Television* by Jane Harbord and Jeff Wright, who calculated the twenty programmes with the biggest audiences each year from 1955 until 1994, though changes in the techniques for sampling audiences mean that exact comparisons of the numbers viewing the most popular programmes are not possible across the whole of the period they examined. In 1955 and 1956 their statistics indicated the percentage of homes in the London area capable of receiving BBC and ITV. From 1957 until 1976 they used the Audits of Great Britain calculations of the numbers of homes across the country watching programmes. From 1977 Harbord and Wright quote the number of viewers for each programme. Their figures show that in the winter months for every fifth year from 1965 until 1990 and in 1994, the last year for which they published data, the twenty most popular programmes each had more than 10 million viewers, approximately a sixth of the UK population. Between 1955 and 1994, 1979 was the only year when all of the twenty most popular programmes each year had more than 20 million viewers.

Statistics of television viewing also show that almost the entire population of Britain has watched television at some time over the week. In the 1980s over 70 per cent of the population watched at least three consecutive minutes of television each day. In the week ending 25 February 2001, over 80 per cent of the population watched television at some time each day.[20] In the same week, by no means unusual for television output, fifteen programmes attracted more than 10 million viewers each. Two had more than 20 million viewers. The thirty most popular programmes on ITV and BBC1 each had more than 6 million viewers.[21] The thirty most popular programmes on BBC 2 and Channel 4 each had more than 2 million viewers. Channel 5 was the terrestrial channel with fewest viewers but it still had twenty-four programmes with more than a million viewers each.

Other Media and Interest in Television

Responses by other media to television are a further measure of its central role in British culture. Press coverage of television was far greater in the 1990s than in other decades, which suggests that interest in television had grown or, perhaps, that newspaper editors considered that readers wanted this form of reporting; but perhaps it reflected the fact that the breaking of the power of the print unions in the 1980s and the introduction of new technology had reduced the real costs of producing larger newspapers. In 1950, when access to television was still limited to a small proportion of the population, most national daily newspapers did not carry the television programmes for the day, but nor did they carry the radio programmes, which did have a national audience; however, this may have been because of the government restrictions on newsprint, which were not lifted until 1956. In 1960, an edition of the *Daily Mirror*, the best-selling newspaper in Britain, usually consisted of twenty to twenty-four pages. Each issue had one page giving the day's television programmes and criticisms of the previous day's viewing. In January 1960 it had only three features and news stories about television. In 1960 the *Mirror*'s coverage of television was roughly equal to that of cinema and far more extensive than that of radio. By 1980 each issue of the *Mirror* usually devoted a full page to the day's programmes and usually two further columns previewing these. The Saturday edition had five pages of television previews and interviews with actors who would be appearing in the following week.

In the 1990s all the national newspapers had weekly supplements that listed and previewed the following week's programmes and often carried articles about those who would be appearing on television. News about television was also providing much more newspaper content. Issues such as the structure, financing and changing nature of programmes were discussed in the weekly media supplement of the *Guardian* and at least once a week in the features section of the *Daily Telegraph* and the review section of the *Independent*. By 2000 the tabloid press was providing more material about television personalities. In January 2000 the *Mirror* had a weekly magazine supplement, the *Look*, which usually consisted of 40 pages giving listings and previews of programmes and also articles of one and two pages on actors who would be appearing on television in the following week. Each other edition of the *Mirror* usually had three pages previewing the day's programmes plus two pages of criticism and gossip about forthcoming programmes. Most days would also have articles about television personalities. The issue of 14 January, for instance, had one page about the *EastEnders'* actor Tamzin Outhwaite looking for a house, one page on Chris Evans and the merger of his Ginger Media Group with the Scottish Media Group, half a page on the pregnancy of the *EastEnders'* star Lindsey Coulsen, a two-page centre-spread on the love life and weight problems of Shauna Bradley, who appears in *Home and Away*, and two further pages on television chefs. In the 1990s the content of television programmes could also be treated as news. Perhaps the most outrageous example of this was in 1998, when Prime Minister Tony Blair was dragged into the tabloid press campaign for the *Coronation Street* character Deirdre Rachid to be released from prison.

The number of magazines concerned with television is also evidence of television's central role in British popular culture. In 1955, the year when time spent watching television first exceeded that for listening to radio, the BBC's *Radio Times* reached recorded sales of more than 8.8 million copies per week, but it is not clear how many would have bought this for details of radio programmes as much as for television. In 1960, when *Radio Times* was still selling over 7 million copies per week, ITV programme-listing magazines – *Scottish TV Guide*, *Television Weekly*, *TV Post*, *TV Times* and *Viewer* – had combined weekly sales of over 5 million copies.[22] By the mid-1970s *Radio Times* and *TV Times*, the magazine owned by the ITV companies and which listed ITV programmes, were each selling over 3.5 million copies per week.[23] The only weekly publications with higher readerships were *News of the World*, *Sunday Mirror* and *Sunday People*.[24] By 1984 average weekly sales of *Radio Times* and *TV Times* had each fallen to around 3.2 million copies.[25] In the 1980s and 1990s their sales dropped, perhaps because newspapers were providing more detailed listings of television programmes. By 2001, the weekly sales of *Radio Times* had fallen to below 1.3 million, though its estimated profits of £80 million made it the most profitable consumer magazine in Britain. In 1998 the ITV companies sold *TV Times* for £250 million to IPC. In 2001 *TV Times* was selling fewer than 700,000 copies per week. *What's On TV*, also published by IPC, was the highest-circulation television programme-listing magazine, selling 1.7 million copies per week. *TV Choice* and *TV Quick* had combined weekly sales of 1.25 million copies.[26] The *Guardian Media Guide 2002* listed forty magazines published in Britain whose content was related to television. Some, such as *Television Business International*, were trade magazines but others, such as *Inside Soap* or the BBC's *Match of the Day*, were designed to appeal to the followers of particular genres of television programme. In 1997 the National Readership Survey estimated that more than half a million women read the fortnightly *Inside Soap*.[27]

Explanations for the Extent of Television Viewing

The most obvious reason why so very many have watched television in Britain since the 1950s is that they enjoy it. Had many been bored by television, viewing figures would have been lower. For much of the period since the war, viewers were not always provided with what they would have most wanted to watch. Many within the BBC still accepted the dictum of John Reith, the Corporation's first Director-General, that the purpose of broadcasting was to 'educate, inform and entertain' but with entertainment very much the third priority, and the quality threshold that the ITA, IBA and ITC considered when awarding commercial television franchises reflected the political and broadcasting establishments' belief that television ought not to seek to maximise audiences by catering to the lowest cultural level. Yet at the same time television had to go some way towards providing what viewers wanted to see. Commercial television needed large audiences to attract advertisers and the BBC, in order to justify the licence fee, required a sufficiently large audience to show that it was providing a national service. The vast expansion in the number of homes with televisions in the 1950s may have owed something to the novelty value of television; but it seems unlikely that the audience for television would have continued to grow had not those who controlled the television channels ensured that a high enough proportion of their programmes were attractive to viewers. The justification for launching BBC2 and Channel 4 was that they would appeal to viewers who were dissatisfied with existing channels.

The rise of the cinema in the first half of the twentieth century had shown that vast numbers were attracted to watching moving pictures. The decline of cinema audiences in the 1950s as more watched television, the high number of films shown on terrestrial television in the 1980s and 1990s, the sums that BSB and Sky paid for cinema film libraries and the expansion in the hiring of videos of films made originally to be shown first in cinemas all indicate that television was meeting needs previously satisfied by visiting the cinema. The relative ease with which television could be watched gave it an advantage over cinema. It can be watched from the convenience of one's home, but in the 1950s, when many families did not have a television, many visited the homes of relatives or friends to watch television. In the late 1940s the *Manchester Evening News* commented that those who acquired a television set quickly found that the number of their friends had increased. By the 1960s many pubs had television sets, which suggests that those in the drink trade feared that not providing television could harm their businesses. By the 1980s television sets were provided in practically all hotel bedrooms.

The expansion in the number of hours of television broadcasting reflects and explains the popularity of television. The growth in the hours of television broadcasting has increased the opportunities to watch television, but it seems unlikely that these would have been raised unless it had been supposed that sufficient viewers would justify the costs of extending viewing hours. In 1946 only thirty hours of television were broadcast each week. By 1952 this had risen to 52 hours per week and in 1961 the government decided that neither the BBC nor ITV could broadcast for more than fifty hours in one week or eight hours per day. The ITV companies were usually eager to increase the number of hours broadcast each week as more broadcasts provided extra opportunities for selling advertising time. In 1972, Christopher Chataway, the Conservative Minister for Posts and Telecommunications, lifted all restrictions on broadcasting hours.[28] The BBC's breakfast time transmissions started a fortnight before ITV's TV-am in 1983. By the mid-1990s the terrestrial channels were broadcasting for virtually twenty-four hours per day. The growth in the number of channels and the rise of cable and satellite seem likely to have encouraged the watching of television by increasing the range of viewer choice. From its start, ITV had to provide programmes different from the BBC channel in order to attract viewers and to persuade them to adapt or buy sets that could receive the ITV signal. With the launch of Channel 5 in 1997, viewers could choose from five terrestrial channels and dozens of cable, satellite and digital channels. Between 1995 and 2000 the combined number of hours broadcast each year by the five terrestrial channels remained a little over 41,000, while that for cable, satellite and digital channels grew from a little over 100,000 to over 350,000.[29]

Controllers of television services seem to have believed that the adoption of technological innovations intended to improve the quality of television reception has been essential for retaining and increasing the interest of viewers, though calls for technological improvements to television may also have been driven by the economic motives of manufacturers and distributors. Viewers were not always enthusiastic about technological innovation. In the late 1940s and 1950s the BBC expanded its network of transmission stations so that reasonable pictures could be obtained in all regions, but many in the north of England bought sets before the relay station at Holme Moss, built to serve the North, was opened in 1951 and had to watch less than perfect pictures from the Sutton Coldfield station. In 1964, 625-line pictures were introduced and, while they gave better-quality pictures, viewers did not rush to acquire sets that took them. The take-up of colour television, which started in 1968, was gradual. Colour sets were more expensive than monochrome sets, but not vastly so. In 1970 the cheapest colour set cost £50 more than a monochrome set. Initially, the licence for a colour set was £11 and that for a monochrome set £6. In 1969, when only a proportion of programmes were broadcast in colour, just under 100,000 licences for colour sets were bought. In 1973, 13.8 million licences were bought for monochrome sets and 3.3 million for colour. Licences for colour sets first exceeded those for monochrome in 1977, when nearly 10 million were bought. Cable and satellite broadcasters offered a far wider range of channels than terrestrial television, but many viewers were reluctant to subscribe to these. In 2001 a little under 10 million of the 24 million homes with television in Britain were subscribing to cable or satellite television, and terrestrial television accounted for around 60 per cent of all television viewing in Britain.[30] Despite the government decision to switch off the analogue signal in 2010, the British public has been reluctant to acquire digital decoding technology. The immediate cause of the bankruptcy of the Granada and Carlton ONdigital service in 2002 was its inability to attract sufficient audiences to cover the costs of its deal to televise Football League matches, but underlying this was the lack of enthusiasm among viewers to buy the ONdigital facility.

The expansion of television viewing has more or less coincided with rising levels of affluence for most groups, but interest in television has been only in part a result of economic prosperity. Since the 1960s social classes D and E have watched more television than classes A and B, even though classes A and B on the whole have had the higher incomes. In the 1930s and 1940s only countries with advanced economies could afford to establish television services. At first, television sets were expensive in Britain. In 1936 a set cost 95 guineas, but the price fell by a third in 1937, and in 1938 the smallest sets cost 21 guineas – though this was still a large sum.[31] In 1948 a set cost around £50, more than seven times the average weekly wage for an industrial worker. In 1947 just under half of all television sets were owned by the wealthiest 12 per cent of the population.[32] Rising real incomes for those in work and falls in the real cost of television sets made television ownership easier, and in the 1950s, the decade when more than half of all households acquired sets, hire purchase and rental schemes were also important. By 1980 the electrical goods chain store Comet was advertising a black and white television set for £62. Its 20-inch colour sets cost between £239 and £267. In 1990 its rival, Currys, was selling 20-inch colour sets for £200. In the 1980s the cost of the cheapest video recorders fell from £569 to £230.[33] While television sets and video recorders were never cheap, they had relatively low running costs and did not need to be replaced each year; but repairs could be expensive. An attraction of renting sets was that rental companies paid for repairs and if necessary provided a substitute set. Many other leisure activities were more expensive than buying or renting a television. By 1993 television and videos accounted for only 2.2 per cent of total household expenditure, less than the total spending on either alcoholic drinks, tobacco or eating out. Yet between 1971 and 1993 households increased their expenditure on television at a faster rate than on other goods and services. Over that period average household expenditure rose by just over 40 per cent, while spending on television and video increased by over 80 per cent. Expenditure on television and video doubled in the 1980s, probably because of the growing demand for video recorders, and the buying and hiring of video cassettes probably explains why television and video expenditure doubled in the 1980s. The expansion of cable and satellite television was perhaps the main reason why television and video expenditure rose by more than 10 per cent between 1990 and 1993.[34]

Explanations of the extent of interest in television have to consider the types of programmes that have attracted most viewers. Harbord and Wright have shown that, from 1956 to 1994, the types of programmes with the highest number of viewers varied very little. In each month the most popular programmes provided entertainment. By the mid-1960s these were overwhelmingly soaps, drama series, quiz shows, variety shows and comedy. News bulletins, current affairs programmes, documentaries and art programmes were rarely among the twenty programmes with most viewers. Football was usually the only sport among the twenty programmes with most viewers in any month, and this was often only for the Cup Final or World Cup matches. The next most popular televised sports were boxing and snooker after the coming of colour television. From the 1980s films made originally for showing in cinemas figured frequently in the twenty programmes of any year with most viewers, but usually these were those shown on bank holidays. The expansion of cable and satellite television and the launch of Channel 5 in 1997 tended to fragment audiences and made it harder for programmes other than soaps to attract very large audiences. The BARB data on viewer numbers for all programmes broadcast in the week beginning 31 January 1983, a week with no remarkable television events, show that twenty-nine programmes had audiences of more than 10 million viewers. Three of these were soaps, but three news bulletins also each had more than 10 million viewers. For the week beginning 12 March 2001, another unremarkable week, fifteen programmes had more than 10 million viewers. Eleven of these were soaps and two of the others, *Heartbeat* and *London's Burning*, were drama series that had much in common with soaps. The other two programmes were editions of *Who Wants To Be A Millionaire?*

By 1960 most homes were able to receive both ITV and BBC. From then until 1994, the last year surveyed by Harbord and Wright, the great majority of the twenty most viewed programmes each month were broadcast by ITV, though often ITV dominated the ratings during the week, with BBC1 having the higher figures on Saturday evenings when its schedules were dominated by entertainment programmes. By the 1990s ITV's domination of the ratings was not so pronounced. In 1960 Harbord and Wright listed the ten programmes each month which were watched in most homes. All but three of these 120 programmes were broadcast by ITV. In 1994, nearly three-quarters of the twenty programmes each month with most viewers were broadcast by ITV. Of the fifteen programmes that attracted more than

10 million viewers in the week beginning 12 March 2001, only the three editions of *EastEnders* were not broadcast by ITV. In 1992 ITV accounted for 41 per cent of all television viewing and BBC1 34 per cent. By 1999, the figures were much closer to each other: ITV accounted for 31 per cent of all viewing and BBC1 for 30 per cent. In the summer of 2002 BBC1 had more viewers than ITV: BBC1 had over 27 per cent and ITV 22 per cent.[35] In the 1990s competition for viewers became more intense with the rise of cable and satellite television and the establishment of Channel 5. The start in 2002 of BBC4, a satellite channel broadcasting a high proportion of arts programmes, was interpreted by some as a sign that the BBC was shunting intellectual and artistic programmes into this slot so that more of BBC1 and BBC2 could be devoted to entertainment programmes in the ratings battle with ITV. In very general terms it can be claimed that, since their inception, BBC2 and Channel 4 have provided more intellectually demanding programmes than either BBC1 or ITV. BBC2 and Channel 4 have consistently had fewer viewers than BBC1 and ITV. What does seem clear from the data gathered about the popularity of programmes is that the main reason most viewers watched television was to be entertained by programmes that were not intellectually challenging.

In the late 1940s and the 1950s part of the interest in television may have been its novelty. By the 1960s watching television was perhaps so extensive because it had become habitual, part of the routine of everyday life. Gauntlett and Hill in the 1990s revealed that some viewers claimed to be addicted to certain programmes and that they would record on videotape editions of programmes when they were not able to view their original transmission. This was even the case with soaps when it would seem that storylines could be quickly picked up if an instalment were missed. Television structured the timetable and the geography of households as other activities were based around particular television programmes. Programmes such as the early evening soaps or news bulletins marked points of the day and often coincided with other household activities such as meals. Often meals are taken so that particular programmes can be watched at the same time. For those who took part in the Audience Tracking Survey for Gauntlett and Hill, the compulsion to watch programmes such as soaps was often a source of annoyance and sometimes almost of shame. An eighteen-year-old female administrative assistant described watching the soap opera *Neighbours* as 'an infectious disease', while a seventeen-year-old female student wondered whether 'one day they'll start up rehabilitation centres to get people off soap operas!!! Some elderly viewers felt their compulsion to watch soaps could be partially excused if they combined it with another task such as having a meal.

Television satisfied psychological needs for some viewers. Studies of the extent of television viewing in the 1980s and 1990s showed that television was watched most often by those who had been marginalised by mainstream society such as the unemployed, the long-term sick, the retired and the poor, but these were also groups with time on their hands. For those with few social contacts outside the home, television may have been an antidote to loneliness. Viewing hours increase during the break-up of a relationship or the loss of a job, which suggests that it could be a coping strategy, though the extended hours of viewing can be accompanied by a sense of guilt. For those who feel marginalised in society, such as the old, the long-term sick, the poor and unemployed, watching television may be an escape from personal anxieties.[37] The elderly watch most television, but very few peak-hour programmes have been made to appeal specifically to them. It has been claimed that the programmes which they prefer reflect a desire to picture the world not so much as it was but as they wish to remember it, as more polite and better-humoured than the present. Coleman has claimed that regarding the past more favourably than the present helps the aged to maintain 'self concept and self esteem in old age'.[38] But some of the aged may possibly watch television because they feel that it helps them to keep in touch with changes in the world. The fact that very large numbers watched the same programmes at the same time and particularly before the expansion of programme choice may have given people a sense of participating in a national culture and a sense of national belonging. Until the 1980s it was often argued that the previous night's television programmes were a frequent topic of conversation at the workplace.

The gradual expansion in the daily hours of television viewing on a per capita basis since the 1950s may mean that programme schedulers have become more skilled in attracting large numbers of viewers. In the 1990s the broadcasting of soaps on terrestrial television was increased partly because these were among the programmes which had consistently achieved very high viewing figures in the 1980s. *Coronation Street* grew from two to three episodes per week in 1989, and from three to four in 1996. *EastEnders* had two episodes each week until 1994, when it became three, and four in 2001. The more popular soaps were also repeated on digital television. The vast sums that BSB and Sky paid in the late 1980s to broadcast Hollywood films suggest they were convinced that the attraction of watching such films would boost subscriptions to satellite television. Higher per capita levels of viewing in the 1990s may have owed something to the more intense competition for viewers, especially in commercial television, with Channel 4 selling its own advertising time and the establishment of Channel 5. Such competition may have led schedulers to plump for programmes which they believed would interest viewers. Equally, the enormous expenditure by BSkyB on live sports events indicates a belief that this could be the means of persuading young men to watch satellite television. The need to boost audience ratings may have led schedulers to stick to programme formats which have been shown to bring in viewers and to experiment with original programmes only where the production costs were likely to be low.

Programme scheduling has never been an exact science and, when planning programmes, schedulers have had to consider factors other than the number of viewers that a programme could attract. The popularity of some programmes surprised schedulers. This was clearly the case with *Coronation Street*, the longest-running fictional television series in the world, which has probably had more viewers in Britain than any other television programme. When it was launched by Granada in 1960 it was planned to run for only twelve episodes. The situation comedy *Dad's Army* that started in 1968 was originally expected to last for one series; but it was so popular that it ran for nine series. In 2000 *Big Brother* turned out to be a far bigger hit than Channel 4 had expected. Station schedulers have scrapped some programmes that were attracting large audiences. The ATV/Central soap *Crossroads*, broadcast nationally from 1972, was axed in 1988 even though it had nearly always been among the twenty programmes with most viewers each month. It was among the twenty programmes with most viewers for six months in 1987 and even in March 1988, the month when it closed. It was relaunched in 2001 but closed in the summer of 2002. It returned early in 2003 but had ceased to be broadcast before the end of the year. In ITV in particular, programme schedulers have had to consider not merely the overall number of viewers but the capacity of a programme to attract viewers aged between sixteen and thirty-four, as these are believed to be the age group whose spending is most influenced by advertising.

It is not difficult to find examples of programmes that failed to match the hopes of schedulers. Before the start of *EastEnders* in 1985, the BBC had not been able to produce a soap opera that attracted audiences to rival *Coronation Street*. It produced the first soap, *The Grove Family*, but this ran only from 1954 to 1957. *Compact* was screened only from 1962 to 1965, *United!* from 1965 to 1967 and *The Newcomers* from 1965 to 1969. Even after the success of *EastEnders*, the BBC's *Eldorado* was axed in 1993 after running for only just over a year. In 1983 the ITV breakfast-time television programme, with its much vaunted 'famous five' big name presenters – Angela Rippon, David Frost, Michael Parkinson, Anna Ford and Robert Kee – had to be restructured after failing to match the BBC ratings. In 2002 the ITV ONdigital closed because audiences were not sufficient to finance its £315 million deal to screen Football League matches for three seasons.

Schedulers have always had to balance the cost of a television programme with the number of expected viewers; but the cost of making or buying a programme has never guaranteed that it would interest viewers. The successful soaps and drama series have very large audiences but, because the same sets can be used repeatedly, they tend to be cheaper than single-production dramas, which have attracted smaller audiences. Some programmes that appeared to have been made cheaply, such as *Crossroads* and *Prisoner Cell Block H*, achieved a cult following partly because of this. Since the mid-1990s 'fly on the wall' documentaries and programmes on terrestrial television concerned with chefs, gardening and house makeovers may have expanded so much because they were relatively cheap to make and could attract high numbers of viewers. There is of course no way of knowing whether interest in television would have been greater had more money been spent on making programmes. Table 2.3 shows how the hourly costs for different programme genres varied for the BBC in the 1990s.

The extent of television viewing probably owed something to how it harmonised with prevailing ideologies of morality and respectability. Apologists for watching television often claimed that, as an activity that all members of the family could pursue together, it strengthened family ties. Those who were particularly worried about the content of television programmes, such as the National Viewers' and Listeners' Association (NVLA), often argued that the family-based nature of the medium meant that its content should not transgress accepted notions of morality and taste. In the early days of television the 'toddlers' truce', whereby the BBC and ITV did not broadcast between 6 p.m. and 7 p.m., was intended to ensure that television would not distract young children when parents were

Table 2.3 Average hourly costs of different genres of BBC television programmes, 1990 and 2000

Genre	Cost per hour 1990 (£000)	Cost per hour 2000 (£000)
News and weather	57	54
Features, documentaries, current affairs	84	105
Light entertainment	157	183
Sport	39	102
Music and arts	91	110
Drama	448	486
Children's programmes	102	90
Religion	72	102

Source: *Guardian*, 20 November 2001.

preparing them for bed. Choosing what programme to watch could cause friction within families. Gauntlett and Hill found that usually the adult male head of the family decided what programme could be watched, though often this was a matter of negotiation within a family.[39] The growing number of homes with more than one television receiver and the rise of video recorders may have perhaps reduced the potential of a programme to promote family conflicts. The BBC and ITV have always broadcast religious programmes, which may have added to the respectable image of television. From the 1960s, however, critics such as the Clean Up TV Campaign, the forerunner of the NVLA, argued that much television drama and comedy was contrary to Christian morality and particularly Christian teachings on sexuality. Although live broadcasts of both Houses of Parliament began only in 1989, the televising of state occasions such as the annual festival of remembrance, royal events and the state opening of Parliament no doubt added to the respectability of television. The televising of the coronation of Queen Elizabeth II in 1953, watched by more than 40 per cent of all adults,[40] demonstrated how state occasions could become television events. The broadcasting of news, educational and arts programmes added to the respectability of television.

The Disparagement of Television

Television has often been disparaged in Britain, despite the vast numbers who spend so much time watching it. Even in the 1950s many broadcasters considered it an artistically and intellectually inferior medium to radio. Reith had little enthusiasm for the introduction of television in the 1930s. Grace Wyndham Goldie, television critic of the BBC's weekly publication the *Listener* from 1936 to 1939 and who became Assistant Head of Talks Television in 1954 and Head of Talks and Current Affairs Group Television in 1963, had a key role in BBC television's coverage of politics. She recalled that in the 1930s and 1940s the leading figures at Broadcasting House, the headquarters of the BBC, accustomed to a world of words, 'distrusted the visual; they associated vision with the movies and the music hall and were afraid that the high purposes of the Corporation would be trivialised by the influence of those concerned with what could be transmitted in visual terms'. For them television could 'be brushed aside; it was not a medium to be taken seriously; pantomime horses and chorus girls were its natural ingredients; it was not suitable for news or current affairs'.[41] Norman Collins, who had been Controller of BBC Television from 1947, resigned from the BBC in 1950 when George Barnes, the Director of the Spoken Word and Controller of the Third Programme, was appointed over his head to the new post of Director of Television. Collins saw this as an indication that the 'vested interest' in radio at the BBC would hamper the development of television. Collins became a leading advocate for the ending of the BBC's television monopoly.[42]

Sir David Attenborough has recalled that in the early 1950s Broadcasting House 'tended to regard the fashions and moral attitudes of yesterday as being eternal. . . . She regarded her young offspring in Alexandra Palace [the BBC television studios] as feckless, irresponsible, and occasionally inclined to naughtiness.'[43] When Sir Bill Cotton joined the BBC in 1956 an older broadcaster told him that television could not last because its cost was using up too much of the licence fee income.[44] Cotton has pointed out that Gerald Beadle did not even own a television set when he was appointed the BBC's Director of Television in 1956 and, aged fifty-five, was looking forward to 'a gentle canter down the finishing straight to retirement'. The BBC's senior management, Cotton has explained, started to take television more seriously when ITV began threatening the BBC's position as 'the main purveyors of broadcasting'.[45]

The popularity of television as entertainment led some critics, or perhaps the more cynical of them, to argue that much of television's appeal was that it made too little demand on viewers. In the 1950s television was already being described as 'the idiot box'. As early as 1950 the poet T.S. Eliot had written to *The Times* that, before television in Britain was expanded, consideration should be given to the anxieties that television was causing in America. In addition to fears about the mental, moral and physical effects of television, especially on children, he was worried about the spread of the television habit, irrespective of the quality of programmes.[46] In the same year, R. Cannell, radio correspondent for the *Daily Mirror*, wanted a royal commission to investigate the effects of television before its broadcasting hours were increased. He condemned television as 'the biggest time-waster ever invented' whose 'real menace' was 'its hypnotic effect. People will sit watching for hours – even when they don't care much for the programmes they're viewing. . . . The human animal is naturally lazy. It's so easy to sink into an armchair and switch on entertainment until bedtime.' His particular fear was that television would create a generation of children incapable of amusing themselves. For him the 'vision of a nation of tiny selfish groups mechanically entertained day after day in semi-darkness is enough to make the H-bomb appear almost innocuous'.[47] In later decades viewers were scorned as 'couch potatoes'. Such criticisms of television viewing may have reflected a snobbish assumption that what was popular could have little merit, that what had mass appeal was culturally degenerate. Linked with this may have been suspicions stemming from the Protestant work ethic that activity is morally superior to passivity and that watching television was not a productive use of time. There were also fears that television discouraged more worthy and uplifting interests, criticisms which had been levelled against the cinema and radio earlier in the century. Although the expansion in the number of channels was justified on the grounds that this would cater for minority tastes, it also increased opportunities to watch entertainment television that was not intellectually demanding.

Many intellectuals and artists tended to look down on television. In 1961 Kenneth Adam, the BBC's Director of Television Broadcasting, wrote about the 'coteries of contempt' for television. In the same year Stuart Hood, the Controller of Programmes for BBC television, was puzzled that 'television – as opposed to radio – awakens in some intellectuals a kind of passionate hatred, which they did not feel for radio even when it was attracting the kind of mass audience now generally reserved for . . . television'.[48] Mihir Bose has pointed out that *Our Age*, the 600-page tome by Lord Annan about the generation that had shaped post-war Britain, contains only three lines that refer to television. Annan, a prominent Oxford academic, had chaired the government-appointed Committee on the Future of Broadcasting that reported in 1977.[49] The television journalist and entertainer John Sergeant, an Oxford graduate, has remembered that in the 1960s it 'was difficult for many people who thought of themselves as members of the educated classes to accept that appearing in television comedy was not demeaning'.[50] Many still look down on television. In 2001 the broadcaster and writer Mark Lawson spoke of 'people who routinely sneer about television' and that 'a confession to having never watched or owned a television set would be taken by many as evidence of a higher mind'. In his view, 'No other powerful and successful creative form has faced the widespread allegation that everything produced within the discipline is irrelevant or secondhand.'[51] Michael Grade believes that in the early days of television 'it was considered a mark of virtue never to watch the small screen, then later on, one might keep a television set but only in the nursery to occupy the children'. He thought that in 1999 it was fashionable for intellectuals 'to declare an irrational weakness for the odd cult programme such as *Monty Python's Flying Circus* or *Blackadder*'. One Nobel Prize winner had thought that admitting to following *EastEnders* was equivalent to owning up to wife-beating.[52] There have always been intellectuals who have been prepared to appear on television. The historian A.J.P. Taylor and the biologist Julian Huxley appeared frequently in the 1950s. More recent television broadcasters have included the historians Simon Schama and David Starkey and the philosophers Bryan Magee and Michael Ignatieff.

Many from the artistic world seem to have thought that television was a lesser art form. In the 1940s and 1950s, the giants of British acting, such as Olivier, Gielgud, Richardson and Evans, rarely appeared on television, though towards the end of their careers they appeared more often. More recently, actors such as Bob Hoskins have moved from television to the cinema. Those who became big stars through the cinema, such as Michael Caine and Sean Connery, have given interviews on television and their films have been shown on television, but they have rarely acted in television dramas. Writers whose stage and film work has received critical acclaim have tended to write for television only at the start of their careers. The relatively small number of ballets and opera shown on television may explain why the stars of these art forms have concentrated on live performances in theatres.

Explaining why intellectuals have so often dismissed television is not easy. Snobbery may be part of the answer. The popular has often been assumed to be inferior. Mass culture has often been assumed to be third-rate, while only an educated elite can appreciate true quality. In the early days of television, disdain for television may have been linked with cultural conservatism and suspicion of the new. Melvyn Bragg has argued that disregard for television, 'this asinine or panic-stricken reaction is, in fact, a tribute to the force of a new medium so strange and yet so ordinary that it is very difficult to grapple with'. He added that 'self-appointed elites' had been so quick to downgrade television because 'they do not like its power, its hold on the people, just as high-born admirals hated Nelson's command of the ordinary seamen – "and yet the whole Fleet loved him, damn their eyes". Television is a force that seems to threaten their hold on the reins.'[53] Attitudes to television may also have been influenced by a dislike of American popular culture. American programmes were popular with viewers but, partly to restrict imports and to encourage programme production in Britain, and also because of suspicions that British culture was becoming Americanised, programmes made overseas were not allowed to exceed 14 per cent of the output of television until 1993, when the threshold was raised to 25 per cent.[54] For some on the political left, distaste for capitalism was probably a cause of their low opinion of commercial television, a feeling that was probably heightened by the vast profits which the ITV companies were making by the 1960s.

One strand in the disdain for television has been the feeling that too many television programmes are of poor quality and too unambitious in the intellectual demands they make on viewers. The Pilkington Committee, which reported on the future of broadcasting in 1962, condemned the quality of many ITV programmes. It argued that the ITA had attached more importance to satisfying the existing tastes of viewers than to encouraging the acquisition of new tastes.[55] The academic Richard Hoggart, a member of the Pilkington Committee, looking back on its work, described the claims of the ITV companies that they were giving viewers what they wanted as 'low populism masquerading as democracy'. He mentioned with approval T.S. Eliot's comment to the Committee that 'Those who claim to give the public what the public want – (pause) begin by underestimating public taste; they end by *debauching* it.'[56] Beliefs that the quality of television programmes was not as good as it ought to have been never disappeared, and resurged with greater intensity in the 1990s with the contention that television was being dumbed down. It was argued that the more intense competition for audiences resulting from the rise of satellite and cable television, the less stringent regulatory powers of the ITC and a more populist approach to audiences by the BBC had reduced the overall quality of programmes. A broader choice of channels had not resulted in a broader range of programmes. It was alleged that the single play had almost disappeared as soaps, with their industrial scale of production and economies of scale, expanded. News bulletins on terrestrial television broadcast more human-interest stories and less detailed analysis of the background to world events. In 1999 *A Shrinking Iceberg Heading South*, a report prepared by the Campaign for Quality Television based at the University of Westminster, concluded that 'There is a distinct feeling that we are seeing the progressive "Disneyfication" of British television culture where bright, safe, glossy and formulaic guaranteed ratings successes are displacing more challenging, stimulating and enlightened approaches to programme making.'[57] A study by the *Observer* claimed that between 1980 and 2000 the share of 'light' programmes on terrestrial television had risen from 17 per cent to 33 per cent while serious ones had fallen from 44 per cent to 29 per cent.[58] By no means all accepted that the quality of television in the 1990s had declined. Mark Lawson, for instance, wrote in 2003 that 'even the trash these days tends to be clever trash' and 'the clever stuff is cleverer than it has ever been'. In his view 'there are three genres in which today's British television could not only go weight-for-weight with the programmes of the assumed golden age of the past, but might even be judged to have won: news, comedy and serial drama'. He concluded that 'Almost all recent TV successes here have prospered because they have carried greater credibility than their predecessors.'[59] There is no objective manner for establishing the standards of television. What constitutes quality is a matter of personal judgement, a question of taste. What is rubbish for one is gold for another. But it is clear that, while vast numbers have watched television and been eager to do so, others have been just as eager to dismiss it as cultural degeneracy.

Chapter 3

TELEVISION AND THE ECONOMY

Since it resumed broadcasting in 1946, television has been an area of economic growth, although its precise contribution to the expansion of the British economy is not known. In 1999 a report prepared for the Department for Culture, Media and Sport calculated that the income for UK television, which it defined as revenue from licence fees, satellite and cable subscriptions, advertising and sponsorship, digital terrestrial television and programme exports and inter-broadcaster programme sales, amounted to £6.7 billion or approximately three-quarters of 1 per cent of the gross domestic product.[1] This statistic underestimates the total input of television to the economy. It does not include, for instance, the production and marketing of television hardware such as television receivers or video players. It also overlooks the role of television in print publishing and how profits from television have stimulated investment in other sectors of the economy. Television may have influenced cultural values that affected economic activity, but there is no means of measuring this.

The Television Broadcasting and Programme Production Sector of the Economy

The BBC has never been a limited liability company with an obligation to make profits for shareholders; and the licence fee, always its major source of income, is, in effect, a government subsidy. The BBC has, of course, sold radio and television programmes and formats, and even before the Second World War was publishing *Radio Times*, one of Britain's best-selling magazines, and the *Listener*. Soon after becoming Chairman of the BBC Board of Governors in 1986, Marmaduke Hussey concluded that the BBC was not strapped for cash but that there were 'rivers of gold running through the corridors of Broadcasting House'. He thought that its 'conduct of affairs was more like the civil service than a commercial organization' but that it was 'being pitchforked into an increasingly commercial climate'.[2] Prime Minister

Thatcher was believed to favour ending the licence fee. In the 1980s and 1990s, the BBC became more concerned with cutting costs and maximising sources of income other than the licence fee. In 1986 BBC Publications and BBC Enterprises were merged. For the financial year 1985/6, sales of television programmes and formats exceeded £35 million but sales of journals and books were worth more than twice as much.[3] In the financial year 1993/4, the BBC's income from magazine and book publishing was over £115 million.[4] In 2001 its income from publishing, including new media publishing, passed £302 million, but this was relatively small when set against the licence fee income of £2,371 million pounds.[5] In 2002 the BBC was publishing four children's magazines, two teenage magazines, four lifestyle magazines, four general interest magazines and one motoring magazine. In 2000/1 BBC Worldwide claimed that it was the UK's ninth largest book publisher. BBC Worldwide published four of the ten titles in the *Daily Telegraph* list of the best-selling books for 2000, and three of these were based on television series. In 2002/3 overseas sales by BBC Worldwide of programmes and other materials accounted for over half of all the UK's programming exports and made a profit of £123 million.[6] In 2001 the BBC was in 118th place of the 1,000 UK companies with the highest sales turnovers. Its sales turnover was stated as £2,481 million, a figure that treated the licence fee as part of sales income and included sales of non-television materials. This was higher than that of any ITV company or for Channel 4, but modest compared with the sales turnover of £68,304 million of BP Amoco, the company with the highest turnover.[7]

The ITV companies were always limited liability companies intended to produce profits for their shareholders. The main profits from their television business came from selling advertising during broadcasts, though some companies diversified into other businesses, which came to provide more revenue than television advertising. The ITV licence holders were not equally profitable and not every business into which they diversified made money. To date no comprehensive economic history of all ITV companies has been published, but fragmentary evidence suggests that they have been highly profitable. No company went bankrupt while it was holding a licence, although in 1964 Wales West and North was on the point of bankruptcy when it was taken over by another ITV company, Television Wales and the West.[8] Those who held the first licences made losses initially, but by their third year average profits before tax were 130 per cent.[9] The disappointing audiences for London Weekend Television (LWT) in the early 1970s and TV-am in the early 1980s led to major changes in their leadership and programme schedules, but they were soon transformed into profitable concerns. Between 1965 and 1976 the pre-tax profits for all ITV companies were over 10 per cent every year except 1970, and above 20 per cent from 1965 to 1968 and in 1972 and 1973. Their average profit of 19 per cent compared favourably with the average return for the manufacturing industry of 13 per cent.[10] Lord Thomson, the newspaper magnate and majority shareholder in Scottish Television when it was set up, called an ITV licence 'a licence to print money'. In 1963 Gerald Beadle of the BBC calculated that the advertising revenue for all of the ITV companies would be about four times higher than their total costs.[11] ITV companies boosted tax revenue by paying corporation tax and also the levy, an additional payment on their income from advertising, and, in the 1990s, through the system of auctioning franchises which committed them to make annual payments to the Exchequer for the right to broadcast.

In most years almost all ITV companies made profits, but the level of these could vary from year to year. Border Television, one of the smaller companies, has held a broadcasting licence since 1961. It has owned four commercial radio stations but has always cited commercial television as its principal business. Between 1961 and 1999 it incurred losses only in 1961 and 1985, and that for 1961 was for the year ending in April, four months before it went on air. Its profits after tax fluctuated wildly from one year to the next. In 1980 these were £135,000, £25,000 in 1981 and £2,445,000 in 1982. Table 3.1 shows that, despite such fluctuations, profits permitted the payment of what would have been considered high dividends in most years. The dividends at Border never attracted attention which suggested they were atypical of ITV companies. The profitability of the big ITV companies is less clear because they had different categories of shares. Their annual reports did not always make clear how much of their profits had been obtained from their non-television business interests.

Profits from selling television advertising allowed ITV companies to diversify into other forms of business. One of the most successful in this respect was Granada. In 2002 the Granada Group PLC was a giant of British business. It had a labour force of over 30,000 in 2001.[12] The D&B guide to the top 50,000 UK enterprises for 2002 calculated its sales as £4,031 million, the eighty-fourth highest of all British companies. Granada has held an ITV

Table 3.1   Before-tax dividends of Border Television, 1963–1999

Annual dividend payment in pence before tax for 10 pence shares

1963	1	1982	1
1964	1	1983	1
1965	not available	1984	2
1966	2	1985	–
1967	2	1986	1.6
1968	1.325	1987	1.4
1969	1.325	1988	1.7
1970	0.25	1989	2
1971	0.5	1990	2.1
1972	1	1991	2.1
1973	0.5	1992	2.7
1974	1.1	1993	3.3
1975	0.5	1994	4
1976	1.8	1995	4.8
1977	2.6	1996	5.8
1978	2.85	1997	7
1979	2.92	1998	7.7
1980	0.875	1999	8.5
1981	0.25		

Note: The figures for the years before the decimalisation of money have been converted to their decimalised equivalents.

franchise in the north of England since the start of commercial television. Although its founders, the brothers Sidney and Cecil Bernstein, already owned sixty cinemas, profits from television seem to have been the basis for the group's expansion, though with diversification these came to have less overall importance. In 1956, the first year of Granada's television transmissions, when the number of sets capable of receiving ITV was limited, the pre-tax profits of the Granada Group were over £218,000 but had grown to £886,000 by 1958 and £1,876,000 by 1959. These growing profits permitted the launch of its television rental shops in 1959. By 1975 it had more than 400 rental shops in the UK and rental businesses in Canada, Denmark,

Sweden, Belgium, France, Germany, Switzerland, Italy and Spain. It bought the Rediffusion rentals group in 1984 and Electronic Rentals in 1987. In 1995 Direct Video Rentals was bought for more than £22 million. In 1999 it established with Radio Rentals the Box Clever television rental group, which became the dominant force in television rental. In 1961 Granada Publishing was established and acquired Rupert Hart-Davis in 1963 and MacGibbon and Kee in 1968. The paperback imprint Panther has been described as giving Granada 'real significance' in publishing,[13] though this was sold to William Collins in 1983. Granada's first motorway service station was opened in 1965, and in 1997 it sold its twenty-one Welcome Break motorway service stations for £476 million. In 1988 it bought fifteen bingo clubs for £16.5 million, but three years later sold seventy-four bingo clubs for £147 million. Its most costly single acquisition was in 1996, when it bought the Forte hotels and catering group for £3.6 billion. In the 1980s Granada invested in British Satellite Broadcasting and after its merger with Sky held an 8 per cent stake in BSkyB. The relaxation of the laws governing the ownership of ITV franchises allowed Granada to take over other ITC companies. In 1994 it paid £670 million for a controlling interest in London Weekend Television. In 1997 the Granada Media Group was formed after it acquired Yorkshire-Tyne Tees Television for £711 million and in 1999 paid £1.75 billion for the television interests of United News and Media, which owned Meridian TV. In 2001 the Granada Group held seven of the ITV franchises and a 50 per cent holding in ITV Digital.[14] In 2000 the Granada Group and the Compass Group merged in a £17.5 billion deal to set up Granada Compass, which soon afterwards sold 20 per cent of Granada Media for £1.3 billion. In 2001 Granada Compass split to form the Granada PLC media group and the Compass PLC food and hotels group. Television broadcasting and production had probably done much to promote the expansion of the Granada Group in the 1960s and 1970s but, as the activity of the group diversified, its significance within the Granada Group declined. In 2000 it constituted less than 8 per cent of the Group's total sales income. Not all of Granada's business diversifications were successful. Its failures included the music business Transatlantic Records and the attempts to sell insurance in its rental shops.[15]

In the 1990s, ITV companies complained about a harsher economic climate but they remained profitable. The rise of cable and more particularly satellite television and of Channel 5 reduced ITV's share of advertising. In the late 1990s the BBC was competing more effectively for the mass audience and by 2001 BBC1 had overtaken ITV as the television broadcaster with most viewers. Between 1997 and the first half of 2002, Channel 3, the ITV terrestrial channel, lost around 10 per cent of the total of all television viewing, but in 2002 it still had very nearly a quarter of all television viewing and delivered more viewers to advertisers than any other channel in Britain.[16] ITV companies were also worried about the costs of establishing a presence in digital broadcasting. In 2002 Granada and Carlton had abandoned the ONdigital venture primarily because its revenue could not finance its £315 million three-year deal to televise Football League matches live. ITV companies argued that, if they were to be able to produce programmes that would make them big players in the international programmes market, they would require more revenue, which in turn would require bigger audiences and more advertising income. This could be achieved through mergers and ultimately a single ITV company and less government regulation. The merger in 2003 of Carlton and Granada in effect created a single ITV company, or at least one big enough to dominate the ITV system.

Despite the growth and profitability of television in Britain, television concerns are not among the giants of British business. It has already been mentioned that the BBC was in 118th place in a list in 2000 of the 1,000 British companies with the highest sales turnovers. The D&B *Key British Enterprises 2002* rankings of companies on the basis of their sales had BSkyB Broadcasting in 277th place, the ITV Network 606th, Channel 4 752nd, the ITV Network Centre 496th and Central Television 977th. No other ITV companies made the top 1,000. London Weekend was 1,127th, Granada Television 1,216th and Carlton Broadcasting 1,303rd,[17] but it needs to be remembered that Granada controlled LWT and Carlton controlled Central. The global giants of multi-media communications – News Corporation, Time Warner, Disney, Berlusconi, Viacom, Sony and Bertelsmann – are not British television concerns, though they have subsidiaries in Britain and control some major British television businesses. News International controls BSkyB and Bertelsmann has a controlling share in Channel 5.

British broadcasters have had a strong presence in the international trading of television programmes, often being the world's second largest exporter of television programmes, though usually far behind the United States, the world's leading programme exporter. Between 1978 and 1985 the value of British television programme exports grew from £37 million to £110 million. Between 40 per cent and 60 per cent of these exports went to the

United States and Canada. For each year between 1978 and 1985 the value of exported television materials exceeded imports, but from 1986 to 1999 imports outstripped exports, even though the value of exports had risen from £110 million in 1985 to over £403 million in 1999. Despite this deteriorating balance of trade in television materials, the value of British exports to the United States was double that of any other country and constituted about a third of all British television exports. By 1999 exports to the European Union were higher than those to North and South America.[18] Until the 1990s Britain had been a bigger force in the international television trade than had British film in its world market. Had the British film industry received an annual subsidy on the scale of the BBC licence fee, it may well have been a stronger force in film production.

A variety of reasons explain why Britain had a favourable balance of trade on overseas programme sales until the second half of the 1980s. Before 1993 British television programme makers were protected against foreign competition. Overseas productions could not make up more than 14 per cent of the output of terrestrial broadcasters. The size of the domestic markets for television programmes in the United States and Britain explains much of their strength in the world market for television programmes. These encouraged economies of scale and, by allowing production fees to be recouped in the home market, made it possible to export programmes at costs attractive to overseas broadcasters. In the 1980s Thames Television assumed that the first transmission in the UK for one of its productions covered production costs.[19] The size of the English-speaking world has encouraged trade in television programmes between Britain and North America and also with other Anglophone countries.

In the late 1980s and 1990s fewer restrictions were placed on cable and terrestrial television, and to boost audiences they invested heavily in American programmes and also feature films. Cheap high-quality imports from the United States undermined British exports to secondary channels in countries where British exports had traditionally been strong; and even in markets where British sales have remained buoyant this was sometimes achieved only by lowering prices. In the late 1990s the sales price of some British exports fell by around 20 per cent.[20] Although mergers and takeovers reduced the number of ITV companies in the 1990s, the federal nature of ITV in Britain had resulted in relatively small companies which found it hard to compete on the international stage. A report for the television industry by

David Graham and Associates stressed that European broadcasters usually wanted ninety-minute television movies, 13- or 26-part one-hour series and 13- or 26-part half-hour comedies, but few of these formats were made in Britain. It argued that British television had evolved 'a literary and theatrical tradition' which was 'out of step with world markets'. Export potential was not usually a priority with programme heads, who were more interested in achieving large audiences in the UK.[21]

Employment in Television Programme Production and Broadcasting

The Department of Culture, Media and Sport calculated that 102,000 people were employed in 2000 in radio and television production and broadcasting,[22] yet when one considers that the total man-hours spent watching television each day is around 150 million, the broadcasting and programme production labour force seems very small. The BBC estimated that 456 were employed by its television service when it restarted in 1946; but within two years this number had grown to 677.[23] By 1971, 15,332 of the BBC's 24,761 employees were engaged in work directly connected with television.[24] The total number of BBC employees peaked at 25,412 in 1985/6, but the exact number who worked in television is not clear. As a result of pressure from the Conservative government for greater cost-efficiency at the BBC, the stipulation of the 1990 Broadcasting Act that 25 per cent of all output had to be taken from independent producers, and the introduction of an internal market and producer choice, the total number of BBC employees fell. By 1996 the BBC Home Services employed 19,882. Peter Goodwin has calculated that, over the ten years from 1985/6, the BBC had possibly pruned 5,000 television jobs.[25] A list of the 1,000 companies in the UK with the largest turnovers gave the BBC staff in 2000 as 20,919.[26]

In 1965 the ITA estimated that the total number employed in commercial television was around 8,000. In 1980, the IBA calculated that commercial broadcasting, including radio, had a permanent staff of around 15,000 employees. The report of the ITA for 1965 listed the numbers of employees for ten ITV companies. Of these ABC Television with a staff of 982 had most employees. Of the others, only Tyne-Tees and Scottish had more than 400, though it is likely that Granada and London Rediffusion, for whom no statistics were included, would each have had numbers similar to that of

ABC.[27] In 1980 the five largest commercial television companies each had between 1,200 and 2,000 employees, the medium-sized ones between 500 and 700 employees and the smallest under 250. The number of employees of the ITV companies fell in the 1980s with new agreements with unions over manning levels and as companies tried to economise in order to have the funds to bid for the renewal of their licences. According to *Televisual*, the ITV companies employed 6,112 people in 1991 and only two companies, Granada and Yorkshire, had more than 1,000 employees each.[28] A ranking of the leading 1,000 UK companies with the largest sales turnovers in 2000 showed that Granada Television had a staff of 1,286. Central Television had 550 staff.[29] Key Note reported in 2000 that 'most industry sources' suggested that as many as 45,000 were employed in the non-terrestrial television industry.[30]

The establishment of Channel 4 as a broadcaster but not a producer of programmes, and the requirement of the 1990 Broadcasting Act for terrestrial broadcasters to acquire a quarter of their output from independent producers, was designed to strengthen independent programme production, although terrestrial broadcasters were able to sell programmes to Channel 4. David Graham and Associates calculated that in 1980 the number of programmes broadcast on British television by independent production companies had been negligible (though this ignores those bought from overseas production companies), but by 1999 560 independent production companies were selling programmes to both terrestrial and non-terrestrial channels in the UK and accounted for 16 per cent of the broadcast hours of terrestrial television. In part this increased role for independent production reflects the growth in the hours of television broadcasting in the 1990s. Between 1994/5 and 2000, the move to 24-hour broadcasting every day and the launch of Channel 5 increased the total number of hours of broadcasting per year on the terrestrial channels alone from 26,500 to 41,000 hours.[31] The survey that Skillset issued in 2001 of the numbers employed in what it called the 'audio-visual industries', which included radio and film as well as television, indicates that on 19 May 2000, the day it took a census of employment, over 19,000 would have been employed in broadcast or terrestrial television and over 6,000 in cable and satellite television. All of these jobs would appear to be involved with programme production, but do not seem to have included actors. Some, though not all, of the 10,000 or so engaged in the production of commercials and of the 11,000 engaged in corporate production would have been employed in television.

Television has always employed freelance workers. Writers and actors have often been engaged to make one programme or a series of programmes. The freelance presence was stronger in some forms of television than others. In 2000 only 10 per cent of those working in programme distribution, transmission and broadcast engineering were freelancers, compared with more than 70 per cent of those in camera work, costume and wardrobe, lighting, make-up and hairdressing.[32] By 1999 the total number whose work was related to programme production and broadcasting would have been around 100,000, but, as has been mentioned above, the value of their output was £6.7 billion or close to £70,000 per head.

Television Receiver Manufacturing in Britain

In the second half of the 1940s and the 1950s manufacturers of television receivers in Britain had many advantages. The development of radar equipment during the war had boosted electronic technology and, in the late 1940s and 1950s, the demand for television receivers in Britain and overseas was growing while quotas restricted imports. Before the adoption of the 625-line picture in the 1960s, the 405-line picture of British television was a form of protection against foreign competition, as most foreign manufacturers had geared their production to the 625 system. Against these advantages it can be argued that, with more than twenty companies producing receivers in the early 1950s, the industry suffered from over-capacity, while the frequent changes made by governments to hire purchase regulations and rental agreements created short-term fluctuations in demand and often left manufacturers and distributors with a glut of sets on their hands. The record sales of 2.75 million sets in 1959, for instance, were followed by a fall of 36 per cent in 1960. Some mergers and takeovers occurred from the mid-1950s, such as Dynatron being acquired by Ekco, which was in turn acquired by Pye in 1960. In 1967 the Dutch-owned Philips company bought 60 per cent of the Pye shares. In 1962 Rank took over Murphy and became Rank Bush Murphy. Despite such mergers, sets were still being made and marketed in the 1970s under the names of companies that no longer existed, such as Cossor, Ekco and Marconiphone.[33]

The introduction of 625 lines did little to help television manufacturing in Britain. While the take-up of 625-line receivers was slow and did not lead to a great surge in demand for new sets, the UK market became more attractive to overseas manufacturers. The tide began to turn against British manufacturers with the growing demand for colour sets in the late 1960s and 1970s. In 1968, the year when colour broadcasts began, British manufacturers produced only 32,000 colour sets. The demand for colour sets sucked in imports and the failure of UK manufacturers to meet this rising demand reflected an underlying weakness of the industry in Britain. In 1969, the value of sets exported, worth nearly £2.5 million, was more than double the total value of imported sets, though virtually no colour sets were exported, which was particularly ominous as the international demand for colour sets was clearly going to grow. In 1970 exports were worth nearly £3.4 million but imports exceeded £9.4 million. In 1971 exports dropped to a little over £3.1 million but the scrapping of all restrictions on credit helped imports to leap to nearly £18 million. Colour sets accounted for around two-thirds of all imported sets.[34] Yet in 1973, the year when the 2.7 million colour sets delivered to dealers equalled the record number of deliveries for monochrome sets that had been achieved in 1959, British companies were still providing three-quarters of all colour sets sold in Britain and two-thirds of all monochrome sets, but the level of imports was causing concern.

The economic recession that stemmed from the oil crisis of 1973 intensified foreign competition. Japan, with the strongest television manufacturing industry in the world, and other Far Eastern manufacturers saw Britain as an export market in which they could expand. Competition from the Far East would probably have been more severe but for the negotiation of quota agreements. Japanese imports were limited to 10 per cent of the UK market, and quotas were placed on imports from Taiwan and South Korea. In the 1970s Japanese companies began opening factories in Britain or engaged in joint production schemes with British manufacturers, partly to circumvent import restrictions on sets and components but also to gain entry into the market of the European Community. Sony opened a factory in South Wales in 1974. In 1978 Rank and Toshiba formed Rank Toshiba, but when this demerged in 1981 Toshiba retained part of the labour force and formed a new company, Toshiba Consumer Products. Hitachi, who had been refused government permission to open a factory in Britain, formed an agreement with GEC in 1978 and bought out GEC in 1984. In 1979 Mitsubishi began producing colour television tubes in Scotland when it took over a factory operated by the Norwegian company Tandberg. The Taiwanese company Tatung took over the Decca factory in 1981. In the same year

Sanyo took over the Pye factory at Lowestoft that Philips had closed. When British and Japanese companies demerged, it was the Japanese companies that continued to manufacture television receivers. Although Japanese competition forced British companies to reorganise their production methods to compete against Japanese-owned companies, British-owned companies collapsed in the 1970s and 1980s. By 1987, when Thorn sold Ferguson, its television-manufacturing wing, to the French-owned Thomson Grand Public, this left Fidelity, which specialised in producing cheap small-screen sets, as the only British-owned manufacturer of television sets. In 1988, largely as a result of Chinese imports coming via Hong Kong, Fidelity ceased production.[35] The parallels between the fortunes of British-owned motorcar manufacturers and television receiver producers are striking.

The strongest explanation for the collapse of the British-owned companies in the face of Far Eastern competition is that the Far Eastern companies were more efficient and cost-effective. In 1979 the National Economic Development Office found that the more efficient use of labour in Japan and the greater use of integrated circuits and automation meant that the direct labour costs of a set produced in Japan were only half those in Britain, even though the hourly rate of pay in Japan was 72 per cent higher than in the UK.[36] Japanese sets had a reputation for being more reliable than sets produced by the British-owned manufacturers. In the early 1970s a buyer for Currys told a Thorn executive that, when he sold a Hitachi set, he never saw it again but, when he sold a Ferguson set on a Saturday, the customer would return on Monday because the set had gone wrong.[37]

While the collapse of British-owned television manufacturing companies can be seen as a spectacular failure of British industry, the Far Eastern takeover of television production in Britain was not necessarily a disaster for the British economy. Far Eastern penetration of UK television manufacturing is an example of inward investment, of overseas companies maintaining employment and trade in the UK. Had Far Eastern companies not established a presence in Britain, it is possible that television receiver manufacturing in Britain could have disappeared entirely, with all sets being imported, which would have had dire consequences for the balance of payments. To some extent, Far Eastern manufacturers saw television manufacturing in Britain as a means of boosting imports of set components, but their factories in the UK have also used British-made components. In 1976 Matsushita rejected as unsatisfactory 90 per cent of the British-made components it tested, but by

1989, 70 per cent of the components it used in its Panasonic colour receivers were made in Britain. In 1988 Philips Components, formerly Mullard, a British-based company though owned by the Dutch company Philips, was exporting 60 per cent of its output and supplying television tubes to all the UK Japanese set manufacturers except Sony. Sony had established its own plant at Bridgend where it was making 1 million Triniton tubes per year.[38] Almost all of the Far Eastern concerns established research and development divisions in the UK. The survival of television manufacturing in the UK has allowed Britain once more to become an exporter of television sets, though imports have remained high. In 2000, 6.2 million television sets were sold in the United Kingdom but only about 16 per cent of these were produced in the UK. Of the 3.2 million sets produced in Britain, over 2 million were exported. Lord McNally, chairman of the British Radio and Electronic Equipment Manufacturers' Association, the organisation that represented television manufacturers, complained that exports and production had declined 'dramatically' and explained that the competitive nature of the electronic consumer market had forced suppliers to source products from central and eastern Europe and the Far East. Between 1998 and 2000 the number of televisions produced in the UK had fallen from 5 million to 3.2 million. Over the same period exports had dropped from 3.2 million to a little under 2.2 million, although in 2000 half the integrated digital television receivers for the UK market had been designed and manufactured in the UK.[39] Video recorder production has been more of a success for manufacturing in Britain. In 1998 2.5 million video recorders were produced in Britain but, although this figure fell in 2000 to 2.3 million, the number exported had grown.[40] Had Britain been one of the major forces in television receiver manufacturing, British electronics manufacturing would have been better placed to take advantage of the global rise of the personal computer. The visual display unit of a personal computer is an adaptation of television technology. Although Alan Turing had developed the first modern computer at Manchester in the 1940s, British-owned television manufacturing concerns were not able to challenge the Far Eastern domination of computer manufacturing.

Manufacturers of television receivers have often manufactured other forms of electronic communication, such as radios and video recorders, and government publications that analyse employment trends have not made clear the numbers employed solely in manufacturing or assembling television receivers and television broadcasting equipment. The *Ministry of Labour*

Gazette showed that in 1965 nearly 260,000 were employed in the manufacturing of radio and other forms of electronic apparatus, the branch of engineering that included the production of television components and receivers. This was the fifth largest labour force for any branch of manufacturing, though far lower than the 465,000 employed in motor vehicle manufacturing, the manufacturing industry with most workers. Employment in radio and electronic apparatus manufacturing had fallen by the end of the 1970s but in 1999 was higher than in 1979, though this does not mean that the numbers employed in television manufacturing had increased. The *Employment & Productivity Gazette*, the successor to the *Ministry of Labour Gazette*, recorded that just over 311,000 were employed in the manufacture of radio and electronic apparatus in 1970, but by 1979 173,000 were employed in radio and electronic component manufacturing and in the manufacturing of radio receiving and sound reproducing equipment. The government publication *Labour Market Trends*, which incorporated the *Employment Gazette*, shows that in June 1999 more than 190,000, 4.7 per cent of all those employed in manufacturing industry, were employed in the two categories of radio, television and communication equipment on the one hand and radio, television and telephone apparatus manufacturing on the other. While these categories of manufacturing employment for 1965 and 1999 may not be identical, they are probably sufficiently alike to indicate that the branch of manufacturing that includes the production of television receivers and other forms of television equipment has declined from the mid-1960s. These statistics from 1965 and 1999 suggest that the branch of manufacturing that includes television manufacturing has shared in the general decline of manufacturing industry as a source of employment in Britain, but they do not specify the numbers employed in television manufacturing.

The rise of cable and satellite television did not bring great benefits to British manufacturing. In the early 1980s the Thatcher government encouraged the growth of cable television, financed by the private sector, in the belief that establishing broadband cable television would promote telecommunications-based services to homes and businesses. In 1982 the Information Technology Advisory Panel, set up to advise the government, claimed that the expansion of cable television, initially stimulated by its subscribers' desire for more entertainment channels, would result in 'the delivery of many information, financial and other services to the home and the joining of businesses and homes by high-capacity data links'.[41] In order to boost opportunities for British business in the provision and operation of cable television and cable programme provision, the Cable and Broadcasting Act of 1984 limited their ownership to European concerns. Peter Goodwin has shown that these hopes of a business expansion led by cable television have not been fulfilled. Take-up of cable television has been disappointing. By 2001 cable facilities passed 12.6 million homes but only around a quarter of them had become connected to cable. Few cable operators have made programmes, with the result that cable subscribers have tended to use the cable service to receive satellite programmes, reinforcing BSkyB's dominance of multi-channel television. British investors were reluctant to invest in cable television franchises and the 1984 Act had to be amended to allow North American companies to acquire them. By 1993, only ten of the 127 cable operating franchises were controlled by UK companies or joint UK-overseas ventures. Over a hundred had been granted to North American companies.[42] Most American investors in cable franchises were more interested in telephone services than television and wished to take advantage of the 1984 Telecommunications Act, which allowed holders of broadband cable franchises to operate telephone services. As a result of mergers and buyouts, more than 99 per cent of the cable operation was controlled by NTL and Telewest in the early twenty-first century. Telephony was providing half the income for cable franchise holders. Cable had helped to create a more competitive but more fragmented telephone market. Establishing the cable network had cost vast sums. In 2000 Telewest lost £701 million and had debts of more than £3.6 billion. In 2001 NTL's debts were over £9 billion and it made 3,000 of its staff redundant.[43]

The hopes of the Thatcher government in the early 1980s that satellite television would promote British manufacturing were also disappointed. In 1982 it was argued that, if a British-based satellite television service using DBS satellites made in Britain could be established by 1986, this would give the British aerospace industry a significant and perhaps leading presence in the world market for satellites and associated business. Alasdair Milne, the Director-General of the BBC, believed that Kenneth Baker, the Minister for Information Technology, saw a quick start to 'DBS as part of the "information technology-led industrial revolution"'.[44] No satellite service was established by 1986, partly because the costs of setting up such a service had caused the BBC and ITV companies to withdraw. In 1987, soon after being awarded the franchise to provide a satellite broadcasting system in the UK, British Satellite Broadcasting announced that it would be buying DBS satellites from the American company Hughes Aircraft and not from the British aerospace industry, effectively crushing hopes of a major British presence in the international television satellite market. In 1989 Rupert Murdoch's Sky television, based outside the UK, began broadcasting programmes delivered via an Astra satellite before BSB had started its service. In 1990 BSB was obliged to merge – in effect it was taken over – with Sky to form BSkyB. One can only speculate whether the fortunes of the British aerospace industry would have been better had the Thatcher government made public funds available in the early 1980s for the establishment of a satellite television service.[45]

Television and Advertising

Advertising is a sector of the economy in which television has had a massive impact. Commercial television created a new medium for advertisers that grew rapidly. In 1956 television received 6 per cent of all advertising expenditure in the United Kingdom. By 1960 this had risen to 22 per cent, reaching 27 per cent by 1980 and 33 per cent in 1986.[46] In the 1990s television's share of total advertising fell slightly, even though its real value rose spectacularly across the decade. In 2000 television's share of all advertising was 1 per cent lower than in 1991, but its real value had risen by 60 per cent. In the same year expenditure on television advertising came to £4,068 million.[47] It is probable that television's share of all advertising expenditure would have been higher but for the ban on television advertisements for cigarettes imposed in 1965. The role of television in the display advertising of goods and services is even greater than the above figures indicate.[48] Television does not carry the classified advertising consisting of box advertisements, financial and legal notices, company announcements and situations vacant that were estimated by the Advertising Association to make up 20 per cent of advertising expenditure in 2001, although from the 1970s teletext services have carried some small ads.

The real costs of advertising on television rose sharply in the second half of the 1990s. In 2000, the net cost for one minute's advertising was more than 40 per cent higher than in 1994.[49] As charges for television advertising have always depended on numbers of viewers, these have always varied widely between commercial broadcasters. In 2001, for instance, Carlton charged

£30,500 for a half-minute advertising slot in the midweek peak evening time, while Grampian charged £870.[50] In 1999 Central's advertising revenue of over £366 million was the highest of all ITV licence holders, but Carlton, LWT, Granada and Meridian each had revenues of over £200 million whereas that of Border was a little over £23 million and that of HTV just over £22 million.[51] During the 1990s the rise of cable and satellite fragmented the television viewing audience and increased the competition for advertising revenue among television channels. In 1999 Sky 1's advertising income of £133 million was the highest of all satellite channels and the eighth highest of all television broadcasting stations. In that year Sky 1 and seven other satellite channels had a combined income from advertising of more than £285 million.[52]

Since the 1950s advertising expenditure has grown more quickly than the national income, but it is hard to be sure how far advertising has promoted economic growth. The expansion of advertising expenditure suggests that the managers of most enterprises believe that advertising benefits business but their faith in its capacity to promote growth may be exaggerated. The expansion of advertising may be an effect as much as a cause of economic growth. The Advertising Association believes that advertising expenditure grows more quickly when household consumption is increasing, but less quickly when profits are under pressure.[53] Had television advertising not been legalised by the Television Act of 1954, much (though exactly how much can never be known) of the spending on television advertising would have been directed to other forms of advertising. Much television advertising is aimed at specific audiences. Indeed, television may be the most effective and perhaps the only means of reaching some groups. Children, for instance, have been more likely to see television advertisements than those in the press.

Barwise and Ehrenberg have argued that most television advertising for items bought regularly is a form of insurance, part of a strategy to defend a share of a market by reminding purchasers of a brand; but for items bought occasionally television advertisements can be intended to stimulate trial purchases.[54] Some television advertising campaigns, of course, are more successful than others. The television advertisements in the 1950s that featured a solitary man smoking a Strand cigarette with the slogan 'You're never alone with a Strand' are remembered as an advertising disaster because they suggested that Strand cigarettes were for lonely losers. The high cost of prime-time television advertising has meant that the age, gender and social background of target audiences have been carefully researched, though advertising campaigns seem to be determined as much by susceptibility to advertising as by levels of disposable income. A sample of viewer responses to advertising in the mid-1990s revealed that the two age groups most likely to admit that their purchases were influenced by television advertisements were those aged 16–24 and those aged 25–34, which may seem to substantiate the suspicion that the prime-time programmes are intended to attract audiences of young adults.[55] The content of television dramas and soap operas in particular may have raised susceptibility to the advertising of certain products or services by creating awareness of what one needs in order not to feel marginalised in everyday society.

Advertisements may indirectly endorse products other than those they are intended to advertise. Car advertisements, for instance, may also indicate what styles of clothing are fashionable with those who imagine that they are among the economically and socially upwardly mobile young.[56] Advertising expenditure can be regarded as a production cost and in this respect may make the cost of a good or service more expensive for consumers, though in theory it is also possible that, where advertising boosts sales and consequently production, this can lead to economies of scale and so reduce costs to consumers and promote growth by permitting more income to spend on other products or services. Advertisements on British television for goods or services from abroad may have an adverse impact on the balance of payments and on employment in the United Kingdom. Advertisers have always contended that advertising keeps down the price of commodities for consumers. Advertising revenue, for instance, keeps down the cost of newspapers, though it can be argued that goods and services advertised in newspapers cost more because producers need to cover the costs of their newspaper advertisements. Because terrestrial commercial television has always been financed almost exclusively by advertising, viewers have never had to pay to watch ITV or Channels 4 and 5, though it has been obligatory to buy a licence for a television receiver. Advertising revenue, in theory, ought to have enabled commercial broadcasters to provide better programmes, but critics have argued that instead companies used this to diversify into other businesses.

Nearly all television advertisements have been brand-specific and have targeted the end-consumers of products or services. Very little television advertising has been directed at producers, wholesalers or retailers or at a general category of goods or services. Advertisements invite consumers to buy a particular brand of baked beans rather than baked beans in general. Directing most advertising at the end-consumers of products and services relieves suppliers of the final market from having to launch extensive advertising campaigns on their own behalf. In effect, suppliers are able to profit from the advertising expenditure of those at the consumer end of the supply chain. In 1968 nearly half of all television advertising revenue came from food, drink and tobacco, over 20 per cent from household equipment and supplies and over 10 per cent from pharmaceutical products, toiletries and cosmetics.[57] An indication of the types of economic interests that spent most on television advertising can be made from a list of the 49 concerns with the highest levels of television advertising in 1999, though these can be only crude indications as some concerns, such as Lever Brothers, were active in more than one economic area. Expenditure on cosmetics, health care, soap and products related to household hygiene came to over £320 million, food over £307 million, cars over £293 million, telecommunications over £140 million and alcoholic and soft drinks nearly £135 million. The spending of over £134 million by Proctor and Gamble was the highest for one concern and that of Johnson and Johnson in 49th place was £16.8 million. No banks or financial institutions were among these 49 concerns, but they included Camelot, the organisers of the National Lottery. The Central Office of Information was in seventh place with an expenditure of nearly £45 million.[58]

Television and Retailing

Television receivers and materials have been an important part of British retailing. The rise of the rental chains probably caused some small electrical goods retailers to collapse, though the Granada Group calculated that the number of electrical equipment shops selling, but not renting, television sets rose from under 2,700 in 1966 to over 2,900 in 1971 in the area that received Granada television broadcasts. While the sale of television sets may have contributed to this, it is not clear whether they were as significant as sales of, say, washing machines or refrigerators.[59] The abolition of resale price maintenance in 1964, by facilitating the rise of discount price warehouses that specialised in the sale of televisions and other electrical goods, must have made life harder for many small electrical retail businesses. The sale of television receivers had a part in the rise of the national electrical goods chains such as Dixons, Currys and Comet, that have done so much to change the style and structure of electrical goods retailing in the UK. In 1967 Comet opened its first discount warehouse, where it sold electrical goods, including television sets, 20 per cent below the manufacturers' recommended retail price, and opened a second similar store in 1970. Its growth thereafter was explosive. In 1984, Woolworth Holdings, which later became Kingfisher, bought Comet.[60] By 1990 Comet had around a quarter of the UK retail market in televisions and other electrical goods and 80 per cent of those were sold at out-of-town retail parks.[61] In 1984 Dixons bought Currys, which had over 600 shops, and relocated this business in 'edge of town' retail parks. By 1999 it was estimated that, in 2000, 26 per cent of bought and rented television receivers would be acquired from the Dixons chain, 12 per cent from Comet and 7 per cent from Box Clever. The introduction of commercial television in 1955 and colour television in 1967 probably stimulated employment in television retailing but complaints about the slow uptake of digital television receivers in the early twenty-first century suggest that technological innovations in receivers and picture quality do not automatically have an impact on retail employment. The sale of videos of television programmes is an important part of the businesses of the HMV and Virgin chains, whose core activity is the sale of recorded music. The expansion of video recorders in the 1980s and 1990s led to the establishment of shops renting videos in all towns. The number of video rental transactions grew in the 1980s, peaking at 289 million in 1989, but fell in the 1990s and dropped to 119 million in 2002, although in that year 57 million DVDs had also been bought.[62]

Renting a television is not a retail purchase but many shops have specialised in renting sets. The level of television rental in the UK has often been higher than in most other Western countries. The National Economic Development Office calculated at the start of the 1970s that about half of all television receivers in use in the UK were rented. Many viewers may have preferred renting because of the expense of buying a set. In the early 1970s, when the lowest retail price for a 19-inch receiver was £235, the weekly rent for a similar set was £1.13. Rental agreements usually included free repairs and provision of another set while repairs were made. Set manufacturers launched rental schemes to increase sales of their products. In the early 1970s tied outlets of manufacturers controlled nearly 60 per cent of the rental market.[63]

The potential of renting televisions had been demonstrated by radio dealers before the Second World War. Radio Rental, which with DER dominated the television rental market in the late 1940s and early 1950s, had been launched in 1930 and by 1936 was renting 50,000 radios. In 1948 Radio Rental began to manufacture for rental what became called Baird television receivers. When Jules Thorn, owner of the Thorn concern, which manufactured the Ferguson receivers, took over DER in 1947, it had only one shop, but under the leadership of Tom Ludlow it expanded quickly. It has been argued that this more regular demand allowed Thorn to introduce more automated production methods.[64] By 1964 DER, which was dependent on the rental outlets, earned 60 per cent of the profits of the Thorn Electrical Industries. Between 1957 and 1966 the number of television rental shops increased elevenfold. Mergers between leading rental companies became common in the 1960s. In 1967 Radio Rental bought Vista, a rental company that Ludlow had set up when he left DER.[65] In 1968 Thorn bought Radio Rental. Around the same time Ludlow set up Spectra, another rental venture in which GEC, the only leading set manufacturer in Britain at that time without a rental outlet, took an 80 per cent share.[66] In 1975, Radio Rentals and DER, both subsidiaries of Thorn, had more than 850 radio and television hire shops. Rediffusion and Granada each had over 400. Six other concerns each had more than 100 shops. The total number of rental shops may have been falling in the late 1960s. In the Granada Television transmission area, the number of rental shops had been 828 in 1966 and 699 in 1971. If the ratio of shops to population had been the same for the whole of Britain as in the Granada area, the total number of shops would have been about 5,300 in 1966 and 4,500 in 1971.[67] In the 1970s, rental companies could make very large profits and in this period Granada Rentals was the most profitable part of the Granada Group.[68]

Television rental in the UK had passed its peak by the 1980s and 1990s. Between 1985 and 1992, consumer spending on renting television receivers and video recorders fell from £1.2 billion to £975 million. The market survey company Key Note described television rental in 1994 as having an 'old-fashioned image'.[69] In the 1980s and 1990s the rental sector was hit by the greater reliability of receivers (perhaps a result of the higher standards of quality control associated with the increased Far Eastern presence in the UK television manufacturing industry), the sale of sets at discount warehouses and the fall in the retail cost of a receiver (nominally by 4 per cent between 1972 and 1987), which, given inflation, represented a far greater price reduction in real terms. It is also likely that the weakening of restrictions on credit also encouraged the buying of television receivers and video recorders. Falling demand for rented sets led to the closure of shops and encouraged further mergers between the chains owning shops. In 1996, EMI sold Fona, which operated a 'rent to own' scheme in the UK. In January 1997 Granada announced that it was selling 100 of its 562 shops, which now sold as well as rented televisions and electrical goods. A month later Thorn announced the closure of 90 Radio Rentals stores. In 1998 the Japanese investment bank Nomura bought Thorn for £980 million, which gave it ownership of Radio Rentals.[70] In 2000 the Granada rental business merged with that of Radio Rentals to form a new rental company, Box Clever. Before the merger these two concerns had approximately 900 shops across the UK and the *Independent* believed that the new company would have a virtual monopoly of the television rental field.[71] Within months the number of their shops was cut to 449.[72]

Martin Dawes showed how a regional television rental business could grow into an international telecommunications company. From a base of fifteen rental shops in the 1960s, it expanded into telecommunications in 1985, when it began to provide cellular services. In 1999 Cellnet, the mobile telephone arm of BT, bought 100 per cent of Martin Dawes Holdings which in turn provided it with an 80 per cent holding in Martin Dawes Telecommunications. Martin Dawes Telecommunications was calculated to have around 800,000 customers and, besides having offices in Europe, Australia and South America, had alliances with Mercury Personal Communications, the Cooperative Bank, Scottish Telecom, Opal Telecom and Sony.[73] In 2000 Martin Dawes Telecommunications Holding Company had a sales turnover of £388 million and 2,250 employees, and Martin Dawes Telecommunications had a sales turnover of £372 million and 1,566 employees. Both were among the 1,000 British companies with the highest sales turnovers.[74]

Television and the Economics of Other Forms of Communication

The effects of television on the economics of other forms of communication were mixed. Chapter 5 will show how the rise of television was part of the context for the changes in the structure of radio in the late 1960s and early 1970s. Had commercial television not been so profitable, there may have been less enthusiasm to set up commercialised radio stations. Chapter 5 also discusses how far the circulations of purchased newspapers declined because of television, but the extensive coverage of television news by newspapers, especially in the 1980s and 1990s, suggests that editors expect that this helps to sell newspapers. Television was probably a prime factor in the closure of popular picture magazines such as *Picture Post*, which closed in 1957, and *John Bull* and *Illustrated*, which merged in 1958 and then closed in 1960. The establishment of ITV led to the launch of *TV Times* and *TV World*. Chapter 2 has already mentioned that forty magazines whose content was based on television were being published in 2002. (The role of the BBC in magazine and book publishing has been discussed earlier and the connections between television and the reading of books are considered further in Chapter 8.)

Television seems to have been the major cause for the decline in cinema attendances between the 1950s and the mid-1980s and for the closure of more than 3,800 cinemas between 1950 and 2000. Television, however, helped to keep cinema film production alive in Britain. The BBC started making films in 1947, though initially for documentary and news programmes. Associated Communications Corporation (ACC), the holding company that controlled ATV and of which Lew Grade was chief executive and chairman, produced or co-produced over 80 feature-length films, mostly intended for cinema exhibition in America and Britain before being shown on television. A few, such as *The Muppet Movie*, *Rising Damp*, *George and Mildred* and *Porridge*, were adaptations of television series and some, notably *On Golden Pond*, received great critical acclaim. Heavy losses on *Raise the Titanic*, which cost £18 million – it was said that it would have been cheaper to drain the Atlantic – was a main reason why Grade lost control of ACC to Robert Holmes à Court's Bell group in 1982.[75] In the 1980s it was claimed that, by financing the co-production and release of films in cinemas, Channel 4 had mobilised the resources of television to support 'a starving but still creative British film industry'. By 1991 Film on Four had made 136 feature films and provided all of the budget for the critically acclaimed *My Beautiful Laundrette*, and made a substantial contribution to the financing of *Another Time, Another Place*, *Paris Texas*, *Rita, Sue and Bob Too* and *A Room with a View*.[76] In 2001, however, financial pressures caused Channel 4 to close its film production arm.[77] In 1987 Euston Films, the film-making division of Thames Television that had made long-running television series such as *The Sweeney*, planned to concentrate on making mid-budget films to be shown in cinemas when it signed an agreement with the American Sam Goldwyn company. In the previous year Euston Films had made five feature films that were being released in cinemas and on video before being shown on television.[78] BBC Films were co-production funding partners for thirty-one feature films made between 1998 and 2001, but what proportion of the finance came from BBC Films is not clear, although in 2000 BBC Films planned to invest £40 million in films over the following five years, not a vast sum by the standards of international film production. The award-winning films that it co-produced included *Billy Elliot* and *Iris*. The prospects of royalties from the showing of feature films on television have been an important aspect of film finance.[79]

The launch of Channel 4, which commissioned programmes from independent producers, was probably a major reason why the number of companies producing feature films, shorts, documentaries, television commercials, trailers, titles, promotion films, pop videos and television films listed in the British Film Institute's *Film and TV Yearbook* rose from 69 in 1982/3 to more than 300 by 1986/7; however, it is not entirely clear whether the lists for these two years were counting exactly the same activities, and this increase could have owed much to the rise of small companies that may not have survived for long. Film-making in Britain would have been in an even more parlous state in the 1980s and 1990s but for the involvement of British television with film finance and production.

Television, Culture and Economic Growth

It has often been contended that culture can have a decisive influence on the performance of an economy. Corelli Barnett and Martin Wiener, for instance, have maintained that Britain's relative decline as an industrial power in the twentieth century can be attributed to the culture of the public schools, which encouraged disdain for manufacturing, but by no means all historians have accepted this view.[80] An underlying conviction of the Thatcher governments was that economic growth would be most effectively promoted by aggressively acquisitive, commercialised values. The time devoted to watching television by the great mass of the British population since the Second World War registers the cultural significance of television, but whether this led to the acceptance of attitudes which in turn influenced the performance of the economy is debatable. It has already been mentioned that the effects, if any, of television on attitudes and behaviour are far from certain. Distinguishing the effects of television from those of other cultural forces is impossible and, if television does have an impact on values, this is likely to be stronger with some groups than with others. The possible influence of a programme may be related to the concentration focused on it and some programmes may have conscious and unconscious influences on attitudes and conduct.

Television programmes have both supported and attacked consumerist, materialist values. As they are very much part of a capitalist economy, television advertisements have rarely been overtly critical of acquisitive consumerism. Although much creative talent and money are devoted to advertisements – one advertisement for Stella Artois lager required 850 extras, hiring an eighty-year-old ship that had to be made seaworthy, a scene shot in Argentina and another for which four blocks of downtown Buenos Aires had to be closed[81] – not all advertising campaigns succeed in boosting sales, defending a market niche or achieving brand recognition. Advertisements that are set in pubs or other convivial milieus may glamorise a hedonistic, insouciant approach to life that is the antithesis of hard work and steady application, and inimical to those values that promote economic growth. Advertisements may have stimulated purchases of goods produced abroad and so made life harder for producers in Britain. In the United States it has often been assumed that minimal government regulation and the adoption of consumerist values are the most effective methods of sustaining economic growth. Some in Britain have shared these views but they have never been able to dominate television. News and current affairs programmes have discussed differing approaches to economic policy but, as they almost always have spokespersons representing conflicting opinions, they may have a stronger capacity to consolidate rather than change views of how the economy should be managed. No terrestrial television programmes have provided on a daily basis the depth of data about the stock exchange and global financial markets that is found in the *Financial Times*, though movements in shares during the day are monitored on teletext. The proliferation in recent years of series about how to renovate property or to maximise the sale value of houses perhaps indicates, and perhaps may have strengthened, materialist tendencies in British culture. Part of the popularity of *Who Wants To Be A Millionaire?* and of *Big Brother* may also have owed something to the scale of their money prizes and materialist values among viewers. Electoral support for environmentalist political groups has always been limited, but one could argue that science documentaries often publicised 'green' values which have been opposed to the unregulated exploitation of natural resources in the pursuit of profit.

The presentation of aggressive economic individualism has often been ambivalent in television drama. Crooked businessmen have always been stock characters of television crime drama. In drama series and soaps businessmen have been presented at least as often as villains as heroes. Highly regarded dramatisations of classic novels such as those of Dickens and the *Forsyte Saga* were often concerned with the world of the wealthy but often presented the rich as morally bankrupt. No television series can match the longevity of the popularity of *Coronation Street*. Until the late 1990s it was often contended that *Coronation Street* harked back to a largely imaginary north of England world where working-class people appeared to be mainly satisfied with their lot in life, respected those who showed concern for others and observed traditions of mutuality rather than full-blown consumerism. Mike Baldwin, the most successful businessman in *Coronation Street*, was presented as an untrustworthy character. Some of the most popular British television comedies such as *Steptoe and Son*, *Open All Hours* and *Only Fools and Horses* derived much of their humour from poking fun at the ambitions of small businessmen and much of their popularity may have stemmed from a widespread antipathy to business values. The highly popular *The Good Life* can be interpreted as a rejection of materialism. On the other hand, American films, drama and comedy series have often attracted large audiences and usually reflected assumptions about the moral worth of acquisitiveness and consumerism. What television can be said to have done is reveal how varied and often conflicting British attitudes to materialist values have been.

Chapter 4

TELEVISION AND POLITICS

Since the 1920s broadcasting has been a vital factor in the political processes of all developed countries. The levels and varieties of political activism and the functioning of political institutions are all dependent on information. Radio, and then television, added to the knowledge about the political world that was provided by word of mouth and by the press. As television provided information about the world as quickly as radio but with the advantage of visual images, it helped to transform the role of other sources of data about politics. As with radio, the law required television to be politically neutral and objective, but the briefest reflection shows that total impartiality on the part of any medium is impossible. All political information that is presented by television to the public is only a selection of what is available; and the choices of what to communicate and what to reject have always been governed by the cultural assumptions of those who work in television. What is political news is very largely what those who work in television believe is political news. What is withheld from the public by the media can have as much impact on political behaviour as what is presented to it. The style in which political data are broadcast can influence the meanings that are drawn from it. The accompanying pictures can transform the interpretations made of a commentary. Indeed, pictures may so engage viewers that the spoken commentary is ignored. Politics is concerned with the exercise of power, with how one individual or group tries to control others, and can take many forms. Struggles for power occur within all social institutions, but this chapter concentrates on the conventional notion of politics as relations between governments, the activities of parliamentary politicians and parties, and reactions to these, and on electioneering.

Governments, Public Service Broadcasting and the Control of Television

Governments in Britain have established the structure of broadcasting and so have done much to shape the role of television in politics. They have never had direct control of the content of television and, despite bitter rows on occasions with broadcasters, have rarely sought it. All three major parliamentary political parties have subscribed to the ethos of public service broadcasting which, though not always defined in the same manner, has tended to assume that it is in the public interest for television programmes to be of high quality and for television to provide political information without editorial comment and in a non-party political fashion. This outlook can also be seen as paternalistic and an inheritance from radio. Until the rise of cable and satellite television and their multiplicity of channels in the late 1980s, the general view among politicians was that, as viewers could have access to only a small range of television services, it was essential for the health of parliamentary democracy that television should not be used to the advantage of government or any political party. No prominent parliamentary politician has ever advocated that television be under government control as it has been in totalitarian states.

Parliament, but in effect governments, have decided who should be allowed to broadcast television in Britain. Government decided in 1936 that the BBC should have a monopoly of television broadcasting in Britain. The charters of the BBC that define its functions have been given legislative force by Parliament, and the licence fee, the major source of the BBC's income, has been set by Parliament. For other television broadcasters in Britain, governments have delegated the decisions of who can broadcast and the nature of their broadcasts to supervisory bodies created by legislation. The Television Act of 1954 ended the BBC monopoly of television broadcasting by permitting the establishment of commercial television to be financed by advertising. This Act created the Independent Television Authority (ITA) and gave it the powers to determine the nature of its broadcasts and how a television service funded by advertising should be organised. In 1972 this body became the Independent Broadcasting Authority (IBA) and its powers were extended to cover commercial radio, which was just being set up. The ITA/IBA awarded broadcasting licences to ITV companies and monitored the range and quality of their broadcasts. The Broadcasting Act of 1980 gave the IBA the powers to decide the nature of Channel 4 programmes, requiring it to encourage innovation and content and to impose a levy on the advertising of ITV companies to finance the new channel, which began broadcasting in 1982. In 1985 the Thatcher government asked the IBA to superintend the establishment of a satellite television broadcasting service for Britain. In 1986 the IBA awarded a licence for a satellite television broadcasting service to British Satellite Broadcasting. The Cable and Broadcasting Act of 1984 set up the Cable Authority, which could award licences permitting companies to introduce cable television and telephone services for areas based on towns. The Broadcasting Act of 1990 scrapped the IBA and the Cable Authority and set up the Independent Television Commission (ITC). Under this Act, the ITC had to auction ITV franchises, though these did not have to go to the highest bidder. The ITC's powers to monitor the nature and range of programmes were not so extensive as those of the IBA. The ITC decided who would have the franchise to operate Channel 5 and that this could start broadcasting in 1997. Until 1971 governments decided for how many hours television could be broadcast each day.

Governments have had indirect powers over the content of television. They have appointed the BBC governors who in turn appoint the Director-General, who is responsible for running the BBC. Governments have also appointed the members of the ITA/IBA and the ITC. Those who have held such positions have usually been from 'the great and the good' and have not included those with extremist political views. These powers of appointment have ensured that, by and large, control of television is exercised by those who share the assumptions of the political establishment. Indirect influence over BBC programmes has been exercised by government control of the licence fee. While this does not dictate the content of programmes, it does affect their range and quality. Governments have less power over the finances of commercial television companies, but taxation – for many years ITV companies had to pay a levy on their advertising revenue in addition to corporation tax – and the restrictions that regulatory bodies can impose on the frequency and content of advertising affect programme making.

Television has rarely been the dominant issue of party political controversy in Britain. Perhaps on account of their ideological commitment to free enterprise, the Conservatives have tended to be more sympathetic to commercial television, but both the Conservative and Labour parties have accepted that it is the responsibility of government to lay down the regulatory framework for television. When out of power, the response of the Conservative and Labour parties to government broadcasting policy has been largely one of opposition for the sake of opposition. Broadcasting policy never seems to have had a decisive influence on the outcome of a general election. In 1954 Labour attacked the Conservatives' proposals to introduce ITV, but this was not at the top of the political agenda, and at the general elections of 1955 and 1959 Labour did not propose to abolish ITV but advocated the establishment of a third public service channel to be run by a new authority, not financed by advertising.[1] The establishment of Channel 4 by the Conservatives and their plans for the development of cable and satellite television in the 1980s, for the more relaxed regulatory policy of the Independent Television Commission, and for the auctioning of the independent television franchises did not provoke very deep or sustained opposition from Labour. When the Labour government proposed in 2002 to allow the Office of Communications to regulate television, Conservative criticisms related to detail rather than principle. Until 1974 the ministers responsible for broadcasting policy – the Postmaster-General to 1969 and the Minister for Posts and Telecommunications from 1969 to 1974 – were not in the Cabinet. Ultimate responsibility for broadcasting was held by the Home Secretary from 1974 until 1992 and by the Secretary of State of National Heritage from 1992 to 1997; the latter also was not a Cabinet position. Since 1997 the Secretary of State for Culture, Media and Sport has had responsibility for broadcasting and has been a member of the Cabinet. The fact that there has been no Cabinet minister with responsibilities exclusively for broadcasting indicates that parliamentary politicians have not considered television policy to be very important.

Television as a Source of Political Information

News bulletins and current affairs programmes have been the television formats designed to provide viewers with data about politics, though other types of programmes could help to shape perceptions of politicians and political institutions. BBC television's coverage of news was limited when its service resumed after the war. Radio news bulletins were broadcast on television in sound only. William Haley, the Director-General, wrote in 1946 that he did not object to newsreels as 'an ingredient in television so long as they supplement and do not supplant the primary [i.e. sound] news bulletin'. He feared that television news would be governed by its visual content rather than its 'real importance', while showing pictures of a newsreader would not keep news impersonal.[2] BBC television began producing its own newsreels in 1948, though its Film Division, not its News Division, made them, and in 1950 there were only three of them each week.[3] In 1954 the News Division was permitted to produce its own *News and Newsreel*, which had pictures but could carry items only when confirmed by a news agency.[4] When BBC news bulletins began to show newsreaders, they seemed to be excessively formal and dressed in old-fashioned suits and ties. Bulletins were read with great seriousness. The introduction of Independent Television News in 1955 showed that news could be presented in a more relaxed but still professional manner. ITN emphasised that it employed newscasters rather than newsreaders and that they were involved in deciding how news should be presented. Humorous items were included. Soon afterwards, BBC news bulletins became more like those of ITN.

The broadcasting of news grew in the 1990s with the expansion in the total number of broadcasting hours for terrestrial television and the rise of cable and satellite channels. In 1997 the BBC launched its News 24, a twenty-four-hour news service provided for satellite and cable viewers and also available on the BBC1 terrestrial channel from midnight until 6 a.m. Each evening BBC4, one of the BBC digital channels, has a half-hour bulletin of foreign news. The ITV's satellite and cable news service started in 2000. BSkyB was also operating a twenty-four-hour news service. While such initiatives appear to indicate a strong commitment by broadcasters for television to be a medium of political information, the more intense competition for audiences led to news and current affairs programmes being broadcast on BBC1 and ITV outside the peak evening spots. *This Week*, made by Associated-Rediffusion and then Thames, which had started in 1956, was dropped in 1992. Granada's current affairs programme *World in Action*, which had run from 1963, ceased broadcasting in 1998. In 2000 the BBC moved its flagship current affairs programme *Panorama* from Monday evening to late Sunday evening, a time often described as a graveyard slot. In 1999 the ITV companies began to screen *Tonight with Trevor McDonald*, a current affairs programme, but by 2002 this was shown only once a week. Changes to the timing of the late evening news also showed that terrestrial television schedulers considered the timing of news programmes secondary to attracting viewers through entertainment programmes. The ITN news was moved from its 10 p.m. spot to 11 p.m. in 1999 to avoid interrupting films to screen the news. The BBC in 2000 moved its main evening news to 10 p.m. By 2002 the ITN late evening news had been reduced to twenty minutes and was screened at different times on most evenings. In the week beginning Saturday 4 May 2002, the ITN news started at the following times:

Saturday	8.40 p.m.
Sunday	10.30 p.m.
Monday	11.00 p.m.
Tuesday	10.00 p.m.
Wednesday	10.45 p.m.
Thursday	10.00 p.m.
Friday	11.00 p.m.

These varied times for the news were designed to make way for entertainment programmes, though broadcasting the news immediately after a highly popular entertainment programme could have attracted a larger number of viewers to the news. Channel 4 and Channel 5 have usually screened their news programmes at fixed times on midweek evenings, when the Channel 5 news overlaps with the second half of the Channel 4 news.

Jackie Harrison has argued that the content and style of terrestrial television news and current affairs programmes became more varied in the first half of the 1990s. In order to attract viewers, news programmes began covering more items but in less depth, background analysis was reduced, more emphasis was placed on political items from the UK and less on overseas politics and more human-interest stories were included. Political issues were presented more from a party political perspective and with more stress on political personalities.[5] When Channel 5 began broadcasting in 1997, its newsreaders sat on rather than behind desks. Harrison has also shown how differences in the content and running order of stories became more pronounced between the news programmes at different times of the day, a process highlighted in the BBC's Programme Strategy Review of 1998, which envisaged that different news programmes would have different formats and emphases in content with the most detailed analysis being restricted to the late evening bulletin and *Newsnight*. Underlying this policy was a belief that differing content and style of news programmes at different times of the day would appeal to different categories of audience. On the other hand, impressionistic evidence suggests that even in the 1990s differences in the content and presentation of television news were not so great as those between, say, the *Guardian* and *Sun* newspapers.

Occasionally news bulletins could attract very large audiences. Jane Harbord and Jeff Wright have shown that only in four years of the period 1955 to 1994 were news broadcasts among the ten single broadcasts with most viewers.[6] BARB data for a sample week in February 1983 and for another February week in 2001 suggest that the numbers who watch the main evening national news bulletins on terrestrial television fell between 1983 and 2001. In 1983 the ITV early evening news had an average of 8.4 million viewers and the 10 p.m. news 7.4 million. The averages for BBC1 were 8.7 million and 8.2 million. In 2001 the averages for ITV had dropped to 5.6 million and 4.8 million and for BBC1 to 6.1 million and 4.9 million. Over the same period Channel 4 early evening news had trebled its audience on midweek days from 350,000 to 938,000 and, while that for Channel 5 had an average of over 370,000, these did not compensate for the falling numbers watching ITV and BBC1 news. In July 2002 viewers for the satellite news channels Sky News, BBC News 24 and ITN News only just exceeded 1 per cent of all television viewing in the UK. For current affairs programmes in the sample week from 1983 *Panorama* had 5 million viewers, *World in Action* 8 million and *TV Eye* 5.6 million. *Panorama* was not broadcast for the sample week in 2001, but *Tonight with Trevor McDonald* had nearly 4 million viewers. *Breakfast with Frost*, though screened at 9 a.m on Sunday, had over 1 million viewers. The children's news programme *John Craven's Newsround* had an average audience of over 5 million in 1983 but *Newsround*, its successor in 2001, had on average fewer than 3 million viewers. The numbers watching television news appear to have fallen since the early 1980s. The rise of cable and satellite television has increased the amount of news being broadcast but it has also expanded the number of entertainment programmes that can be watched as an alternative to news programmes. It is not clear whether the numbers who never watch news programmes have increased or whether less attention is focused on news programmes.

Whether television has caused the public to become better-informed about politics depends on whether television provides political data that cannot be obtained so easily from other media. Much of the factual content of news and current affairs programmes is broadly similar to that of the press and radio. Some forms of political information can be communicated only by television. By giving viewers close-up views of politicians, television allows viewers to make their own assessments of their characters, although such images can be manipulated and an impression based on a television appearance of a few seconds may lead to a false assessment of a politician's personality. Viewers can also see the body language of politicians. Pictures of a situation can heighten emotional responses to it. Oral reports and still photographs may not have the same impact on the public as television footage of, for instance, the war in Kosovo. But television has not been a rich source of information for some forms of political news. Television news and current affairs programmes have tended to be weak in investigative journalism, though there have been some notable exceptions, such as Thames's *Death on the Rock* in 1988, which showed that the SAS had shot unarmed members of the IRA in Gibraltar. Although the BBC and the ITV regional companies have regional news bulletins which may mention the affairs of town and county councils on occasions, they have never provided the regular coverage of the affairs of one council similar to that of weekly local newspapers.

The content of television news programmes has been largely determined by what television producers and journalists consider is newsworthy. The visual nature of television has perhaps meant that news editors were more likely to include material which could be presented with a visual impact. In 1975 John Birt and Peter Jay complained about the tendency for current affairs programmes 'to work to film imperatives rather than to journalistic concepts'.[7] In 1980, Robin Day, whose experience of television's reporting of politics went back to the start of ITN in 1955, said he had become aware of

the limitations and dangers of television . . . a medium of shock rather than explanation . . . a crude medium which strikes at the emotions rather than the intellect. And because of its insatiable appetite for visual action, and for violence very often, it tended to distort and trivialise . . . I think our presentation of news and events has become affected by television's appetite for violence and action. Our news bulletins, I think, have become too much a kaleidoscope of happenings, visual happenings, rather than explanations of issues.

He thought that the television presentation of the political world had 'contributed to the spate of unreason and violence and conflict in our society'.[8] Geoffrey Cox, the editor and chief executive of ITN from 1956 to 1968, accepted that television had 'undoubtedly magnified the histrionic element in politics' but claimed that Churchill's use of props such as cigars and hats in the age before television showed that television had not created this histrionic element.[9] In the early 1990s Jackie Harrison found that television journalists were keenly aware of how the visual aspect could add to the meanings of their reports. Visual effects and graphics can also facilitate understanding of political issues. As early as 1950 Grace Wyndham Goldie claimed that television had shown that it was superior to radio in presenting the results of a general election.[10]

Birt and Jay also argued that, while television news was effective at conveying factual material, television was not providing the detailed background material necessary for an informed understanding of political events. Television news, they alleged, had tended to 'produce stories which feature Mr Benn and Sir Keith Joseph in struggles for power rather than attempts to understand the ideas they espouse'. This criticism could have been exaggerated. Current affairs programmes such as the BBC's weekly *Panorama* that had started in 1953 as a general interest magazine but in 1955 became a current affairs programme, and the nightly *24 Hours* that started in 1965, and ITV's *This Week*, starting in 1956, and *World In Action*, starting in 1963, examined political issues in depth. In the 1990s there was much debate about whether the content of television news, and its coverage of politics, had been 'dumbed down' as competition for audiences has intensified. Barnett, Seymour and Gaber have carried out a content analysis of terrestrial television news over the period 1975 to 1999.[11] They divided television news items into the categories of broadsheet (serious) including political affairs and social policy, tabloid (light), and foreign news. They concluded that 'Many of the premises of increased tabloidisation of television news – that an emphasis on the sensational, the shallow and the parochial is driving out the complex, serious and outward-looking – cannot be applied to British television news.' Even Channel 5, 'unapologetically rooted in entertainment and the lighter touch', produced a bulletin in which broadsheet and foreign material exceeded tabloid material. They did find, however, that between 1975 and 1999 the political coverage in the evening news broadcasts had dropped by about a third, whereas that on social policy, an area governed by political decisions, had risen by more than a third.

Jackie Harrison reached somewhat different conclusions. She found that in the 1990s the number of stories carried on news bulletins had increased but less background explanation was included. More stress was placed on human-interest stories, and the coverage of local and foreign news had declined. Only Channel 4 *News* and BBC2's *Newsnight* regularly devoted to a story the five minutes needed for background analysis. In the early 1990s ITN had closed some of its foreign bureaux and in 1991/2 made 400 staff redundant.[12] Harrison argued that different news programmes do have different levels of commitment to explanation of complex issues, with programmes such as the *Big Breakfast Show*, *GMTV News*, and ITN's *12-30 p.m. News* and *5-40 p.m. News* telling the story straight, without elaboration or diversification. This causes some concern for the informational quality of these television news programmes and for their lack of contribution to empowering their viewers to participate competently in the public sphere.[13]

BBC television journalists have argued off the record that highlighting human-interest stories at the start of a news bulletin but delaying their details until near the end of a bulletin is a strategy for retaining the interest of viewers and exposes viewers to more serious news in the middle of a programme.

Has Television Been Politically Objective?

Whether the public has become better informed about politics because of television depends in part on how far viewers have believed what was presented to them by television. The legal requirement to avoid party political alignments in the television presentation of political news and to report political news without editorial comment explains in part why viewers have regarded television as a trustworthy source of political information. In the mid-1960s Jay Blumler and Denis McQuail found that viewers considered that television was by far the least biased and most trustworthy media source of political news,[14] and in 1990 Andrew Goodwin wrote that for 'most people in Britain, television remains the . . . most trusted source of information about the world'.[15] While television is not allowed to mix political news with editorial comment as occurs so often in newspapers, the differences between the content of political news and comment on television may not be so very far removed from those in the press. The main political events covered by broadsheet newspapers and television news programmes are broadly similar on most days, perhaps because newspapers and television journalists share the assumptions about what the public want to know. Many television journalists began their careers with newspapers. The first jobs in journalism of more than half of a sample of 261 television journalists in 1989 had been with newspapers.[16]

How far viewers ought to accept what is presented to them by television depends on how far it is possible for television, or any other medium, to present political information in an objective manner. Objectivity is not easy to define. Objectivity may not always be the same as fairness and impartiality. Psychological theories of perception have stressed that no observer can ever be sure of having compensated for his or her subjective prejudices; and aspects of a situation can always evade even the most keen-witted observers. The rise of postmodernism and the associated linguistic turn in the social sciences have emphasised that conceptions of the truth are conditioned by cultural assumptions and inevitably can only ever be relative and conditional. Deciding what to include or exclude from a broadcast is a form of editorialising and can influence how a situation is perceived and understood. McQuail has pointed out that reporting can contain unwitting or unintended bias.[17] Very largely, television producers and journalists decide what is included in news and current affairs programmes.

In practice, television journalists and producers have tended to assume that presenting political news objectively involves striking a balance between the stances of the three major parliamentary parties. This was largely how radio had treated political affairs, and BBC television inherited this approach. Stuart Hood has pointed out that in practice this approach meant that the BBC and the ITV companies interpreted 'impartiality as the acceptance of that segment of opinion which constitutes parliamentary consensus'.[18] Charles Curran, Director-General of the BBC from 1969 to 1977, said that he treasured the comment of one of his senior editors: 'Yes, we are biased – biased in favour of parliamentary democracy.'[19] Greater access to television has coincided with a slight decline in the domination of the House of Commons by the Conservative and Labour parties. The proportion of the Conservative and Labour MPs was greatest after the general elections of 1945, 1950, 1951, 1955 and 1959, but the great majority of the electorate had regular access to television only in 1959. As most television political reporting has tended to concentrate on the Conservative and Labour parties, this may mean that television has not been a major factor in the revival of the Liberal Party or in the rise of the Scottish National Party and Plaid Cymru, though television could have added to disillusionment with the two major parties. The election of Martin Bell, the television broadcaster, as an independent MP at the 1997 general election may have owed something to his television fame, but in 2001 Richard Taylor, a consultant physician who was not a nationally known television personality, was returned as an independent standing in protest at the closure of units at a NHS hospital. The television newscasters and journalists Ludovic Kennedy in 1958 and 1959 and Robin Day in 1959 were not elected when they stood as Liberal candidates, though the television journalists Geoffrey Johnson-Smith and Christopher Chataway became Conservative MPs in 1959 and Austin Mitchell was returned for Labour in 1977.

Those at the extremes of politics in Britain have seen equating the political mainstream with impartiality as bias. Arthur Scargill, leader of the National Union of Mineworkers, declared 'What the BBC and ITN present as news is not news at all: it is pure, unadulterated bias.'[20] In the 1980s the Glasgow University Media Group made one of the most trenchant criticisms of bias by television against trade unions and the political left. The Group argued that its analysis of television news bulletins showed that negative images and language were often used to describe trade unions, which were rarely mentioned other than in a context of strike. Not all students of media bias accepted the findings of the Glasgow Group. It was pointed out that words such as 'demand' and 'threat' used in news reports, which the Glasgow Group regarded as depicting trade unionists unfavourably, are the sort of language that trade unionists used in confrontation with employers, while others speculated whether the Group was too selective in its choice of evidence of bias. Complaints about bias have not been restricted to trade unionists and the political left and, as Andrew Goodwin has commented, suspicions of bias can be self-delusions and also self-fulfilling prophecies.[21] Any group can probably find what it imagines is prejudice against it in television news or current affairs programmes. Harold Wilson and Margaret Thatcher, prime ministers with very different political views, both believed that the BBC treated them unfairly. If there can be no dispassionate and totally impartial view of a political event, then it follows that all television coverage of politics must have been biased. In the early twenty-first century the far right British National Party has expressed strident dissatisfaction with how it has been portrayed on television. Complaints about biased treatment from television may often have been a tactic by politicians to ensure that television presented them as they wished to be presented. What television may be able to do, and has probably tried to do, is to report the views of those who appear to be the leading figures in a political dispute. The environmentalist lobby has never had any MPs but many television science programmes concerned with issues such as global warming could be described as indirect propaganda for the environmentalists.

Friction Between Politicians and Television

Politicians and television journalists have often had differing expectations of how television should present the political world. Governments have tended to assume that television criticism of their policies is not in the national interest, whereas television producers and journalists have believed that their function is to report political issues objectively and without favour to any particular group. The comments made by the television producer Stuart Hood in 1967 have been true across the past half-century. He wrote that the 'nexus between them [politicians and television] breeds an odd brand of love and hate'. The aim of politicians was to 'present their own version of the truth, which is not unnaturally designed to conceal awkwardness and to put the best possible face on things'. Politicians, in Hood's view, had a 'general ambivalence towards the medium. They recognise that they must live with it and the men who work in it . . . It is no uncommon experience to find a politician who has simulated rage, surprise and pain at a well-aimed question peacefully discussing the programme with the interviewer afterwards.'[22] John Sergeant, when looking back in 2001 over thirty years of television reporting, argued that politicians were careful not to be caught lying, but were 'often guilty of the sin of omission'. Common ploys were to withhold relevant information, encouraging investigations into false trails and only slowly or not at all correcting 'misleading impressions when they benefit from the false picture that has been created'.[23] Bernard Ingham, Margaret Thatcher's Chief Press Secretary, notes the wariness with which politicians regarded television journalists. He believed that television and 'quality' newspapers often attracted journalists 'who have a highly developed suspicion, if not conviction, that what must be going on around them is bad and must be exposed . . . They want to change the world . . . As a result, they will cheerfully falsify the account by selective use of facts while, at the same time, accusing the Government of sundry malpractices.' He knew of no government departmental head of information 'who would trust current affairs television producers any further than he or she could throw them. It was impossible to have confidence in any agreement reached with them.' Ingham also thought that BBC television was motivated to demonstrate its independence of government and to be anti-government, regardless of which party was in power, because it was financed by the licence fee that the government set.[24]

The first major clash between a government and television occurred over Britain's invasion of the Suez Canal in 1956. Suez was the first occasion when a prime minister used television rather than the press or radio as the main means of addressing the population. Eden, the Conservative Prime Minister, seems to have thought that the BBC's policy of political neutrality was dividing the nation. Michael Cockerell has argued that Eden wanted the BBC to be an arm of the government in his campaign against Nasser, the Egyptian leader, and saw criticism of his policy as treason and sabotage. In his study of the mass media and Suez, Tony Shaw argues that it is 'indisputable that during the Suez crisis the BBC's editorial independence was subjected to a most severe test'. Eden told Churchill that 'The BBC is exasperating me by leaning over backwards to be what they call neutral and to present both sides of the case, by which I suppose they mean our country's and the dancing major's.'[25] During his first broadcast on Nasser, Eden felt that the BBC deliberately shone lights in his eyes. At the time of the British and French invasion of Egypt, Eden felt that his television broadcast was not controversial and that as Prime Minister he had a right to present the national interest. He objected to the BBC allowing Hugh Gaitskell, the Labour leader, to broadcast on television the following evening. In his broadcast Gaitskell called for Eden's resignation. Eden complained that, by televising demonstrations opposed to the military intervention in Egypt, the BBC had undermined national unity. Conservative MPs claimed that the BBC's coverage of Suez was distorted and did not reflect public opinion.[26]

Harold Wilson was keenly aware of the electoral potential of television and at the 1964 general election had shown that he was more at home with the medium than the Conservative leader Sir Alec Douglas-Home. Yet after Labour had won the election by the narrowest of margins, Wilson's relationship with the BBC soon cooled. Hugh Greene, the Director-General of the BBC, claimed that Wilson thought that he 'had money in the bank with the BBC. But when he came to cash his cheque, it bounced.'[27] Wilson preferred to talk directly to the viewers whereas the BBC wanted Wilson to be interviewed. Wilson complained that the BBC's coverage of the 1965 Labour Party conference concentrated too much on those within the party who were dissatisfied with the government. In the 1966 general election campaign Wilson clashed with the BBC over who should have decided what parts of his speeches were broadcast, and Greene refused Wilson's request for *The Man from Uncle*, an American spoof secret service series, to be re-scheduled on election night. Cockerell believes that Wilson and his circle felt that Paul Fox and John Grist, the head and deputy head of current affairs at the BBC, and the television journalists and commentators Robin Day, Ian Trethowan and Robert McKenzie were all against the Labour government. Wilson felt that during his first government the BBC was too eager to allow the Conservatives to reply to Labour broadcasts. Grace Wyndham Goldie, the BBC current affairs producer, was reported to have said that the 'right to reply is a rational safeguard against a kind of dictatorship and a hogging of the microphone by the party in power'.[28] Wilson felt that the ITV was more impartial between the two parties. In 1967 Wilson's appointment of Lord Hill, the former Conservative Cabinet minister and chairman of the ITA, as chairman of the BBC governors was widely seen as his retaliation against what he imagined was his mistreatment by the BBC. Hugh Greene was initially outraged by Hill's appointment and thought that it was intended to influence the BBC's reporting of party politics.

The BBC reporting of Northern Ireland and foreign policy issues caused friction with the Thatcher government. In 1985 the BBC proposed to show a fly-on-the-wall film featuring Gregory Campbell, a staunch Unionist, and Martin McGuinness, the Sinn Fein politician who was widely believed to have been a high-ranking figure in the IRA. After Leon Brittan, the Home Secretary, complained that the programme would aid terrorists, the BBC governors took the unusual step of viewing the film before its scheduled transmission date, and by nine votes to one decided that it should not be broadcast. On the BBC's *Newsnight* programme Margaret Thatcher said that she did 'not believe that any great body like the BBC should do anything which might be construed as furthering the objectives of terrorists. And I feel extremely strongly about it.' A few days later it was claimed that a retired brigadier was working inside Broadcasting House in unison with MI5 to vet all senior journalistic appointments.[29] Norman Tebbit, the Conservative Party chairman who had described the BBC as having an 'insufferable, smug, sanctimonious, naïve, guilt-ridden, wet, pink orthodoxy', established in 1986 a research panel to monitor television for bias against the Conservatives. In 1986, when American bombers from bases in Britain attacked Libya, Tebbit condemned the BBC coverage as 'a mixture of news, views, speculation, error and uncritical carriage of Libyan propaganda'.[30] He issued these complaints to ITN before sending them to the BBC. Some suspected Tebbit of trying to pressurise the BBC before the forthcoming general election.[31]

In 1987 Marmaduke Hussey, the former managing director of *The Times*, widely recognised as a Thatcherite sympathiser who had been appointed chairman of the BBC governors in 1986, took the unprecedented step of sacking the Director-General Alasdair Milne. Hussey has always contended that the governors made an independent decision to dismiss Milne, but many at the time suspected that the governors had been carrying out the government's wishes. Before Milne's dismissal, the BBC had decided to screen the film *Secret Society*, which alleged that the Thatcher government had hidden from Parliament details of the £500 million Zircon spy-satellite deal. The film was not shown and after Milne's departure Thatcher admitted in the Commons that the government had prevented the film being shown for reasons of national security.[32] The Thatcher government also clashed with ITV companies, though less often. In 1988 the IBA was criticised for allowing *This Week* to show the film *Death on the Rock* about the killing in Gibraltar of an unarmed IRA cell by the SAS. The film's commentary had said that Thatcher 'must have had on her desk the details of how an IRA unit had been detected in Spain'. Thatcher said that her reaction to the programme was deeper than furious and that 'If you ever get trial by television . . . that day that freedom dies.'[33] The editor of *This Week* was Roger Bolton, who had been at the centre of the Thatcher government's first major row with the BBC. In 1979 he had been the editor of the BBC's *Panorama*, when it proposed to show an interview with Irish National Liberation Army masked gunmen at a roadblock at Carrickmore. In the face of government criticism the BBC sacked but then reinstated Bolton, though the film of the roadblock interview was not broadcast.[34]

Television and the Presentation of Party Leaders

Television required politicians, and party leaders in particular, to develop new skills. To rise to the top of the parliamentary system, politicians have had to be effective performers in Parliament, and front-bench politicians have to be able to deliver platform speeches at party conferences. Aspirants for the higher reaches of parliamentary politics must also be able to withstand with good temper aggressive interviews by television political journalists and to hold their own in television studio debates with representatives from other political parties. In interviews, ambitious politicians have to express their views in memorable sound bites that are more likely to be included in news bulletins. To a degree these skills can be learned and the major parties have long coached their members in how to perform before television cameras.

The television journalist John Cole, commenting in 1995 on how George Woodcock, the General Secretary of the TUC, answered questions in the 1960s, emphasised his 'honesty which has quite gone out of fashion, since politicians were taught to "use the medium", to their supposed advantage'.[35]

Until the mid-1950s leading parliamentary politicians were suspicious of television, but this may have been because of their age. Some had begun their political careers even before radio. Churchill first made a television broadcast when he said a few words at the end of a programme to mark his eightieth birthday.[36] Attlee's replies in television interviews were little more than monosyllabic. Television performance scarcely figured in the public responses to the choice of Eden and Macmillan as Conservative prime ministers or of Gaitskell as the Labour leader. In 1953 R.A. Butler was the first Chancellor of the Exchequer to be interviewed on television about his budget. In 1954 the Conservative Party agreed that its conference could be televised, but the Labour Party refused a similar request. Because of the small number of licence-holders, television had little impact on the general elections of 1950 and 1951. Television had realised more of its potential to influence elections by 1955, when the Conservatives hired Roland Gillett from Associated-Rediffusion as their television adviser. Christopher Mayhew and Anthony Wedgwood-Benn, rising young politicians, superintended the Labour broadcasts, but these were described as ranging from the 'soporific to the chaotic'. The final television election broadcast of Eden, the Prime Minister, was considered highly successful.[37]

Harold Macmillan is usually credited with being the first prime minister to have realised the potential of television to shape public perceptions of politicians, though Grace Wyndham Goldie recalled that neither Eden nor Macmillan appeared to take television very seriously; rather, it was for them 'a peripheral activity, sometimes useful, sometimes a nuisance; sometimes – especially and latterly for Macmillan – rather fun'.[38] Macmillan was reputed to have said, 'Coming into a television studio is like entering a twentieth-century torture chamber but we old dogs have to learn new tricks.'[39] In his first television appearances as Prime Minister he appeared stiff and somewhat unkempt, but it was often said that he soon had his teeth fixed to improve his television image. Michael Cockerell has argued that Macmillan developed an effective television style by looking at the interviewer instead of the camera and adopting a conversational tone that emphasised his skill as a raconteur and wit. He made a point of giving brief interviews at airports, where he posed as a world political figure. By the general election of 1959, a third consecutive victory for the Conservatives, the majority of homes had a television set and television was becoming more important as a source of information about politics. At the Rochdale by-election in February 1958, Granada had taken the unprecedented step of allowing the three candidates to discuss the election and then of having them interviewed by journalists. The turnout of 81 per cent at Rochdale showed how television could stimulate interest in elections, but at the general election neither Macmillan nor Gaitskell was interviewed on television, although the daily news bulletins concentrated on their speeches.[40]

The general election of 1964, at which Labour won an overall majority of only four seats, is usually regarded as the first British general election in which television had a decisive influence. The televised debates between Kennedy and Nixon in the American presidential election of 1960 emphasised that television could be the crucial medium for deciding the outcome of elections; and Harold Wilson, who had become leader of the Labour Party in 1962 when Gaitskell died suddenly, is thought to have studied the role of television in this presidential election with great care. In the twenty months between his becoming party leader and the general election, Wilson showed that he was a highly effective television performer. He could read an autocue without letting his eyes roll. When he started to insert in his speeches outside Parliament pithy statements tailored to what editors wanted for news bulletins, he may have been the first prominent politician to demonstrate the sound bite. In television interviews he tried to be reassuring by appearing relaxed, and presented himself as in touch with 'ordinary people' while portraying Macmillan and Home as members of an outdated elite. Sir Alec Douglas-Home, who had had to renounce his peerage when he became Conservative leader and Prime Minister in 1963, never seemed at ease on television despite extensive coaching to improve his television image. A television make-up artist told Home that his face was like a skull and clearly meant that this was to his disadvantage. He was once described as looking 'like a ventriloquist's dummy' when he spoke directly to a camera. Wilson's more effective televisual manner may have tipped the balance in such a close election. Wilson, however, suggested that the impact of television had been decisive in another manner. At his insistence, the BBC moved the start of its situation comedy *Steptoe and Son* from 8 p.m. to 9 p.m. Wilson claimed that this was worth twelve seats. Had Labour won twelve seats fewer, the Conservatives would have had a tiny overall majority.[41] Michael Cockerell describes Wilson as the first prime minister to regard 'the small screen as a central instrument of government'.[42]

After the 1964 general election all the major parliamentary politicians recognised that television had become vital in shaping perceptions of party leaders; but not all party leaders were effective television performers. Michael Foot, who was elected leader of the Labour Party in 1980, seemed unsuited to the demands placed on politicians by television. He appeared dishevelled, which led to him being nicknamed 'Worzel Gummidge' after a scarecrow in a children's television programme. His wearing a duffle coat at the Remembrance Day service in Whitehall in 1981, which was broadcast live and shown on news bulletins, was widely condemned as unsuited to the dignity of the occasion. Foot was not able to display on television his humanity, erudition and oratorical skills. His inadequacies on television may have been a major factor in Labour's crushing defeat at the general election in 1983. The choice of Neil Kinnock to succeed Foot seems to have owed something to Labour's realisation of the need for a leader whose positive qualities would be emphasised by television. John Sergeant thought that the television cameras seemed to like Neil Kinnock and Kinnock himself was reputed to have said 'I got to be leader of the Labour Party by being good on television',[43] though some have thought that television coverage of his exultant manner at a Labour Party rally in Sheffield a few days before the 1992 general election caused Labour to lose key marginal constituencies and with them the general election. When John Smith succeeded Kinnock as the Labour leader in 1992, he was known to have an effective parliamentary manner but was also noted as having an imposing television presence. Tony Blair's personable manner on television was probably one reason why he was chosen as Smith's successor. Ineffectual television appearances were no doubt a factor in the Conservatives deposing Iain Duncan-Smith as party leader in 2003.

Margaret Thatcher was the only party leader in the twentieth century who won three successive general elections, all with clear majorities, and she never lost a general election. Cockerell believes that Thatcher had a keener appreciation of television than her predecessors but was not by nature an effective television performer. Thatcher received intensive coaching to improve her television appearance. Although she had been opposed to the televising of Parliament, John Cole thought that televising Parliament helped rather than damaged her because 'she handled the new medium with her usual assiduous competence'.[44] She altered the tone of her voice to make it less hectoring and strident, and took advice about image creation. While many admired her political toughness, and Thatcher herself seemed to glory in appearing strong and unmovable, delighting in being called 'the iron maiden' and the lady who was 'not for turning', she agreed to soften her image by being interviewed in a television documentary about English women and clothes after her advisers suggested that an impression of harshness could antagonise voters. The advertising agency Saatchi and Saatchi was employed to improve her television image for the 1979 election. Callaghan, the Labour Prime Minister, complained that 'in this election the Tories are being sold as though they were Daz or Omo [two brands of soap powder]'. Thatcher said in a television interview after the election that 'you've really got to have your professional cameramen and people who know something about television'. For her television appearances Thatcher was advised by a television producer Gordon Reece. The *Guardian* described his influence thus: 'There was once a warrior Leaderene who frightened her followers almost as much as the enemy. Her tongue was a lash, her eyes chips of ice, her hair as stiff as an aardvark's bristle. Then one day she met a humble TV producer and a miracle occurred.' During the election campaign, Thatcher told journalists that the cameramen 'are the most important people on this campaign'.[45] Thatcher was careful to ensure that television did not present her to her disadvantage. As Prime Minister she refused to appear in televised debates with the other party leaders.

Television interviews with politicians in the early 1950s reeked of deference. The journalist Bernard Levin recalled that if

a politician in a fix took refuge from a question in a labyrinth of verbiage, the interviewer simply went on to the next question. If the politician in answer to the next question, told an obvious lie, the interviewer behaved as if it was the truth. If the politician behaved as though the interviewer should have used the tradesmen's entrance, the interviewer made it clear that he thought so too.[46]

The development of video recording film in the late 1950s and greater use of outdoors cameras resulted in sharper questions being directed to politicians when they were invited to make public statements. By the late 1950s and early 1960s, the rediscovery of political satire and the television show *That Was The Week That Was* reflected and perhaps helped to create a less respectful attitude to politicians. The launch of daily current affairs programmes such as *24 Hours* in 1965 increased the opportunities for politicians to be interviewed and for interviewers to hone their skills. Ministers who could not hold their own in television interviews did not survive long. An interviewer such as Robin Day, noted for his pugnacious style, was probably more widely known than any newspaper political journalist. By the 1980s and 1990s it was taken for granted that television journalists and interviewers would give politicians a hard ride and try, though often without success, to ensure that politicians gave direct answers to questions. Though objective measures of how the public viewed politicians cannot be made, impressionistic evidence suggests a widespread suspicion that by the end of the twentieth century politicians were considered more self-seeking, devious and evasive than was the case in the 1950s. The much greater exposure of politicians on television and the more aggressive techniques of interviewing have contributed to this.

The more aggressive manner of interviewers may have reflected, and possibly provoked, a growing public disregard for politicians. In 1968 Gerald Kaufman, the Labour Party's Parliamentary Press Liaison Officer who had written for *That Was The Week That Was* and who was to become a Labour MP, compared newspaper and television journalists. He argued that newspaper journalists did 'not have the urge to hold the stage during . . . interviews. Their aim is to get the information they require by skilled questioning, and thus equip themselves to turn lethally on the politicians whenever they decide to write a considered piece.' Some broadcasters, he claimed, 'cannot resist turning their interviews into confrontations, during which they endeavour to score points and even to browbeat them – though any politician who falls victim to this technique is not up to the job of being a politician. The broadcaster will sometimes explain that he does this because he represents his viewers and is speaking on their behalf.'[47] Robin Day argued that the value of the television interview 'to our democracy should not be underestimated'. Television was one of the very few sites outside Parliament where a politician's performance could not be 'completely manipulated or packaged or hyped'. The televised interview allowed viewers to form 'some impression of the politician's credibility, candour and character'. Unlike a written report of an interview with a politician, the television interview in Day's opinion placed a politician's personality under public scrutiny without a writer's 'embroidery or embellishment'.[48] Geoffrey Cox believed that, before the televising of Parliament, television 'could provide for the first time a chance for the citizen and the voter to scrutinize closely those who would be their leaders. People could not only look at politicians, they could stare at them in close-up, could have their means of forming their own opinions about them on the evidence of their own eyes', but to do this there had to be 'an informed, questing, challenging interview, capable of testing and portraying the politician's personality as well as his policies'.[49]

Oliver Burkeman in 2000 claimed that the 'first truly aggressive interruption' of a prime minister was by Reginald Bosanquet in his interview with Macmillan following a Conservative by-election defeat in 1957.[50] John Humphrys, the radio interviewer noted for his strong questioning of politicians, said of Robin Day that 'At one stage we were all totally obsequious and a difficult question was, "What else do you wish to say to a grateful nation, minister?" Robin changed all that. He recognised . . . politicians were just like the rest of us. He broke the taboo, and we were all his beneficiaries.'[51] Another commentator described how Day 'puts his blunt, loaded questions with the air of a prosecuting counsel at a murder trial. As he swings back to face the cameras, metaphorically blowing his knuckles, one detects the muffled disturbance as his shaken victim is led away.'[52] In the 1990s, Jeremy Paxman was usually regarded as the interviewer with the most forceful attitude to politicians. He is reputed to have decided, after reading H.L. Mencken's opinion that 'the correct relationship of a journalist to a politician was that of a dog to a lamppost', that there was only one choice of career open to him.[53] When interrogating politicians, he has said that he is 'always asking myself why is this bastard lying to me?'[54] Before the 1997 general election he asked the Home Secretary Michael Howard the same question fourteen times when he thought that Howard was not giving a direct answer to it. The former American Secretary of State Henry Kissinger walked out of an interview with Paxman and it was alleged that William Hague, when leader of the Conservatives, refused to be interviewed by Paxman after what the *Guardian* called 'a particularly gruesome mauling'.[55] Robin Day felt that by the 1980s party leaders were transforming televised interviews to their advantage. He claimed that Thatcher and Kinnock had determined to make the television interview their own platform. They treated the interviewer's questions as 'tiresome interruptions to the statistical hammering of a Thatcher, or the repetitive rhetoric of Kinnock'.[56]

Television, Politics and Entertainment

Television has encouraged politics and politicians to be seen as a form of entertainment. Cartoons from the late eighteenth century show that making fun of politicians has a long history in Britain, but in the first half of the twentieth century political satire that lampooned politicians was not strong in Britain. Newspapers printed political cartoons but no magazine that tried to ridicule parliamentary politicians sold enough copies to last for very long. *Punch* survived but its focus on politics rarely exceeded gentle mockery. In the first half of the twentieth century cinema and radio avoided satirical criticism of the political establishment and parliamentary politicians, though by the 1940s radio comedy often featured issues with a political dimension such as rationing or the idiocies of military life. The BBC's *Variety Programmes Policy Guide for Writers and Producers*, issued in 1948 and unchanged in the 1950s, stated that variety programmes could 'in moderation . . . take a crack at the Government of the day and the Opposition so long as they do so sensibly, without undue acidity, and above all funnily' but also specified 'We must bar altogether . . . anything that can be construed as personal abuse of Ministers, Party Leaders, or MPs' and 'derogatory to political institutions'.[57] Humphrey Carpenter has shown that political satire resurfaced in student reviews and at the Establishment Club which opened in 1961, but that this was also related to cultural changes in the second half of the 1950s including the rise of rock'n'roll and young dramatists such as John Osborne whose work condemned the self-satisfaction of the upper and middle classes. It was television that brought biting, personalised political satire to something approaching a mass audience.

That Was The Week That Was, launched in 1962, was a landmark change in television comedy and political satire. It was the first programme to ridicule politicians on either radio or television in Britain. Ned Sherrin, the producer, had proposed that it would be a late night show, 'a new sort of revolutionary programme . . . a mixture of News, Interview, Satire and Controversy'.[58] Ian Trethowan, later to be the Director-General of the BBC, claimed that *That Was The Week That Was* 'swept through British broadcasting as a cleansing agent, scouring away the last of the bland and the banal' and that 'in the longer term, the programme contributed to a feeling among politicians that the BBC was not so much hostile to any one party as contemptuous of the whole parliamentary process'.[59] A vital ingredient of the show was political satire, often highly personalised, but this was mixed with sketches, song and fiercely combative interviews of public figures, though not all were politicians. Twelve million viewers watched the programme on 27 April 1963.[60] *TW3*, as it was soon called, was fortunate to coincide with misfortunes of Macmillan's government such as the Profumo affair, in which the Defence Secretary was forced to resign after lying to the House of Commons about his sexual relationship with a woman who was also involved with a Russian diplomat, incidents that probably meant that a large proportion of the public was disposed to laugh at and think the worst of politicians. *TW3* reflected and helped to fashion attitudes to politicians, though many objected that its satire was too savage, disrespectful and laced with too many double entendres. The playwright John Mortimer, who wrote sketches for *That Was The Week That Was*, claimed that 'nobody had really laughed at politicians before, and it liberated us all from having to be respectful'.[61] In the 1960s and 1970s television programmes such as *Not So Much A Programme, More A Way of Life* and *The Frost Report* mocked politicians and showed that they could be the subject of comedy; but these programmes are usually thought to have lacked the sharp edge of *That Was The Week That Was*. Macmillan had written to Reginald Bevins, his Postmaster-General, that 'I hope you will not, repeat not, take any action about *That Was The Week That Was* without consulting me. It is a good thing to be laughed over – it is better than to be ignored',[62] but its second series ended prematurely, ostensibly because 1964 would be a general election year.

Savage political satire reappeared in 1984 with the start of ITV's *Spitting Image*, which used latex caricatures of politicians and other public figures, including royalty. It lasted until 1996. Many felt that the dialogue of the sketches did not match the grotesque savagery of the latex caricatures. Among the more memorable models were Norman Tebbit as a skinhead and Prince Charles with massive ears. While it could be argued that the satirical edge of *Spitting Image* was cruder and more insulting than that of *That Was The Week That Was*, it provoked less hostile comment, which could mean that public expectations of politicians were lower than in the early 1960s. *The New Statesman*, the Yorkshire Television comedy series that ran from 1987 until 1992, starring Rik Mayall as a young Conservative MP, was a situation comedy which ridiculed the values of Thatcherite Conservatives and indicated how it had become accepted that parliamentary politicians could be the subject of comedy. *Have I Got News For You*, the BBC satirical political quiz show that has run from 1990, has allowed its contestants to make what have often been amusing (but what would once have been regarded as highly offensive) comments about politicians and other public figures. Despite the appearances as contestants of leading political figures such as Neil Kinnock, Cecil Parkinson, Charles Kennedy and Ken Livingstone, the general tone of the programme has suggested that politicians are totally unprincipled self-seeking careerists. The programme's longevity suggests that there is no great public dissatisfaction with such representations of politicians.

Not all of the presentation of politicians as the subject of entertainment and of comedy has been satirical. In the 1960s and 1970s the impressionist Mike Yarwood, who pioneered the impersonation on television of leading politicians and of Harold Wilson in particular, was one of the biggest names in light entertainment. His peak-time shows indicated the popularity of his comedy, but it was affectionately mocking rather than acerbic. Leading politicians did not hesitate to be associated with Yarwood, and it could be that they saw his act as a means of adding a more human dimension to their political personas. In the 1990s Rory Bremner's impersonations of politicians, though displaying a staggering ability to look like as well as sound like his subjects, poked fun at politicians but rarely ridiculed them. Party politics have rarely been the subject of situation comedy, although in the 1980s the BBC situation comedy series *Yes, Minister* and *Yes, Prime Minister*, which revolved around the manipulation of a cabinet minister and then prime minister by his senior civil servant, was praised by politicians, including Thatcher, for its observation of the relationship between cabinet ministers and civil servants. Thatcher awarded a knighthood to Antony Jay, one of its writers. While the main political character, Jim Hacker, was presented as a bungler out of his depth in high politics but who often emerged triumphant by accident rather than by design, the comedy was at its most mordant when directed at Sir Humphrey, the leading civil servant, and probably had more capacity to provoke animosity towards the civil service than towards politicians.

By the 1970s and 1980s leading politicians appeared occasionally on television entertainment programmes. Whereas Chancellor of the Exchequer Denis Healey appeared on *Jim'll Fix It*, Thatcher appeared in a *Yes, Minister* sketch and was the first prime minister to take part in a television chat show. Kinnock appeared in a pop video in 1984. Prominent parliamentary politicians have appeared on televised entertainment programmes, perhaps because they hoped that this would help them to seem in touch with the public and give them a more personable image. Appearing on entertainment programmes also shows how politicians had to conform to the perceptions that television had fostered of the qualities that the electorate sought in public figures.

Party politics have not often been the subject of soap operas. This is partly because of the requirement for television not to be seen as supporting any political party, and it may have been thought that making British party politics part of a storyline could make British-made programmes less attractive to overseas buyers. When characters in soaps have been elected or sought election to town councils, such as Leonard Swindley, Len Fairclough and Alf Roberts in *Coronation Street*, they have usually done so as independents, though the trade union and socialist sympathies of Bobby Grant were made clear in *Brookside*. Party politics has been the main theme for only a relatively small number of television plays and drama series. Where these have received critical acclaim, such as the series *Our Friends in the North*, broadcast by the BBC in 1996, their main political theme has generally been critical of Conservatism or sympathetic to the Labour Party or to the political left in general. The work of Dennis Potter and Alan Bleasdale, widely regarded as among the leading television playwrights in Britain, often exuded an antipathy towards Conservatism and especially Thatcherite Conservatism. In 2002 Mark Lawson, presenter of radio and television arts programmes, novelist and *Guardian* columnist, wrote that it had

> long been a failure of television drama that the scripts have been so consistently left wing. This is partly because most writers are oppositional by instinct, and the British governments of the last 40 years have all come from the right or centre. But there is also little doubt that the BBC drama department was – especially in the 1970s and 1980s – hostile to writers from the right unless they had the status of Tom Stoppard.[63]

The Falklands Play, written by Ian Curteis and commissioned by the BBC in 1986, celebrated Margaret Thatcher's conduct of the Falklands War in 1982 but was not broadcast until 2002. The BBC drama department argued that screening it while Thatcher was Prime Minister would have violated the BBC's requirement to observe a balance between parties.

While evading party politics, soaps and drama series have dealt with issues that have been the subject of political controversy. By presenting in a personalised form issues such as unemployment, drug addiction and the economic problems of single parents, drama series and soaps may have deepened public awareness of their political dimension, but it is never clear whether such programmes have followed or shaped public opinion. As changes in government policy have always been the product of a combination of arguments and pressure, it is impossible to measure the impact of a televised representation of an issue on the political process. *Cathy Come Home*, the BBC Wednesday Play broadcast in 1966, which highlighted the effects of homelessness on a young family, was thought to have stimulated the foundation of Shelter, the housing charity and pressure group, and to have given housing more political prominence. It can also be argued that many television dramas and series that personalise issues with a political dimension ignore broader political contexts. Hospital and crime programmes, for instance, rarely touch on how to fund the NHS or the causes of crime, matters that are clearly related to the political management of the economy.

Television as a Force for Political Conservatism

Chapter 1 showed that there has been much debate about the capacity of television to promote cultural and social change. Speculation about the impacts of television, of course, is part of a bigger debate about the influence of the mass media in general. Critics such as those of the Frankfurt School and Gramsci and Althusser saw the overall tendency of cultural institutions such as television as helping to uphold the established social and political order by persuading the great mass of the population of its legitimacy. The liberal tradition, on the other hand, has seen television and other forms of the media as essentially democratic and politically enabling by providing the masses with information that can stimulate political activism.

On balance, television appears to have done more to uphold than to change the political order in Britain. This may seem hardly surprising, given that it is governments that have established how television is organised and financed; but it also needs to be remembered that governments have generally accepted that television should be free from day-to-day control by government. In some respects parliamentary politicians have often seemed afraid of television. Television has tended to validate the existing political order. Station controllers, producers and broadcasters have almost all been committed to parliamentary government. Supporters of alternative systems of government have rarely been given air time. The style of reporting at parliamentary elections suggests that this is the natural way of choosing governments. When changes to the electoral system, such as the introduction of proportional representation, have been considered, arguments for and against them have been presented. The practice of interpreting political impartiality as giving more or less equal air time to the three major parliamentary parties can be seen as legitimising the existing form of party politics. When television interviewers have claimed that they are holding politicians to account, they have usually meant that they want to act as a brake on the behaviour of politicians. They imply that they are doing what parliamentary politicians are failing to do. They have criticised politicians, not the form of government.

Impressionistic evidence suggests that public esteem for parliamentary politicians has declined in the television age, though perhaps it would be more accurate to say that respect for politicians has not increased. If the public perceptions of politicians have changed, television may have contributed to this. Television's presentation of politics, along with that of radio and the press, has often dwelt on the failures of governments, especially in economic matters and in recent decades in education, the health service and crime. It may well be that the public's expectations of politicians have been too high, but television has perhaps added to a feeling that politicians have been unable to deliver what they promised. As many politicians have become skilled in not giving direct answers in television interviews, this may have led many to assume that politicians as a group are shifty and untrustworthy. The broadcasting convention of having representatives from opposing parties in studio discussions can easily degenerate into point-scoring, and many viewers may find this tiresome. Televised political satire may have reflected and stimulated disdain for politicians. Yet any distaste for politics has been accompanied by political apathy and fatalism and not by calls for the establishment of an alternative form of government. Indifference helps to maintain existing political structures because it stimulates no alternative. The low turnout of electors at the 2001 general election could indicate that political apathy is growing.

Television has been an additional source of political information but much of its political content has been more or less the same as that of radio and the press. The televising of the House of Commons did not start until 1989, and only very small numbers watch televised parliamentary debates. The limited extent of investigative journalism on television has meant that television has not had a prominent role in exposing malpractices by politicians. Because of the costs of making television programmes and the difficulty of finding a station to broadcast them, marginal groups have found it difficult to gain access to television and especially to terrestrial television. There has not been an alternative television service similar to the underground press. The video recorder has been seen as an instrument of political democracy in that it has allowed dissident groups to make their own television programmes, but distributing them is not easy and it is almost impossible for them to be given national television exposure. Even though cable and satellite television has increased the number of channels, none could be described as politically radical. The nearest to politically radical channels have perhaps been those concerned with sexual politics and particularly those advocating gay lifestyles. The ITC has the power to license any channel provided its content is not illegal, but the costs of establishing a channel have probably been prohibitively expensive for fringe political groups. The Internet rather than television has been the source of information about alternative politics in recent years.

In the television age, the monarchy has not been at the centre of politics, and television satirists have ridiculed royalty. The prestige of the monarchy in recent years may have been damaged by the television interviews in which Prince Charles and Princess Diana spoke about the collapse of their marriage. Yet television did much to maintain support for the monarchy. Until the 1970s television in Britain maintained a respectful distance between the royal family and the public, which probably helped to retain the mystique of monarchy. The televising of annual events, such as the state opening of Parliament and trooping the colour, and coverage of royal visits in newsreels may well have helped to boost acceptance of the institution of monarchy.

Few issues have been added to the political agenda by being covered on television. Probably no major piece of legislation has originated from television. Television, like the press and radio, tends to react to issues once they have entered the political domain. The power of television over the agenda of politics has been largely negative. Television can reveal the extent of popular opposition to an issue and so cause politicians to be more cautious in how they deal with it, but by their nature politicians have a very acute awareness of the public mood. It is often alleged that, by bringing the horrors of the conflict into American drawing rooms, television caused the Vietnam War to become less popular. It is hard to find instances of television having a similar effect in Britain.

Television has been primarily a medium of entertainment. The term 'infotainment' suggests that programmes can be entertaining and educational in the broadest sense, but many may have used television as escapist entertainment, a relief from social and economic problems. In these respects, television may have helped to sustain the established political and social order by being a distraction from economic and social grievances. The increase in the number of terrestrial channels and the rise of cable and satellite television have multiplied the opportunities to watch only escapist entertainment programmes. Educational programmes and documentaries, particularly those about the natural world, pollution, diet and health, can be seen as being related to the political aims of the green lobby, but they have not been accompanied by expanding electoral support for environmentalist parties.

In recent years increasing opportunities to watch only entertainment programmes and the inclusion of more human-interest items in news bulletins have been condemned as 'tabloid' television, which in effect disempowers the populace by concentrating on trivia and by discouraging its access to informed debate about more important issues. A case can be made, however, for seeing 'tabloid' television as a force for democracy. More entertaining news formats, like the tabloid press, may reach and engage those who do not bother with a more serious presentation of news. Daytime television chat shows, especially those with a large interaction between audiences and 'expert guests', provide opportunities for those whose voices have often been ignored by the media to be heard and can be regarded as an expression of political activism. But arguably this is too exalted an interpretation of tabloid television. Such debates are mediated events and participants may be manipulated by presenters. It is not clear how much choice audiences have in the selection of the subject matter of these studio debates. If such discussions prioritise emotion over reason, this is not likely to lead to a considered evaluation of political alternatives.[64]

Television technology has boosted the potential power of the state to coerce dissidents and the public at large. Closed-circuit television, linked to computerised forms of image recognition and data storage, has become installed in public open spaces, public buildings, commercial and industrial premises. The justification for the installation of such technology has usually been that it discourages crime and anti-social behaviour. While this is true, the technology can also be used as a means of patrolling public spaces and of identifying those involved in street protest, strikes and political demonstrations. Surveillance technology, as David Lyon has pointed out, raises questions about civil rights and 'the erosion of the democratic public sphere'.[65] Closed-circuit television and other forms of surveillance technology may not have been used to suppress political dissidents but there can be little doubt that they have expanded the ability of established authority to do this should it so wish.

Television does not present the world as it is. It presents a mediated version, one shaped by the preferences of those who control and work for television. Such people have often been critical of politicians but by and large they have wanted the behaviour of politicians, not the structure of politics, to change. The culture of television would seem to confirm the view that the media tend to discourage fundamental political change. Politicians may complain about television but its general tendency has been to maintain their area of activity.

Chapter 5

TELEVISION, RADIO AND THE PRESS

In 1952 Sir William Haley resigned as Director-General of the BBC to become editor of *The Times*. It now seems unthinkable that a Director-General of the BBC would make such a move. His successor, Sir Ian Jacobs, continued to regard radio as more important than television. Yet by the 1960s the scale of television viewing meant that it was rivalling the press and radio as a form of mass communication. Television never extinguished newspapers and radio as sources of mass communication but developed a symbiotic relationship with them. Yet, to survive as organs of mass communication, newspapers and radio had to adapt themselves to the presence of television.

It has long been supposed that organs of mass communication have a profound ideological impact on society. Down the ages censorship has reflected a belief that the media can stimulate social and political change. By providing individuals and groups with data about the world, it has been assumed that the media fashion attitudes and consequently behaviour. Many on the political left have seen the mass media as a form of social control which discouraged support for militant socialism and helped to uphold the established political and social order with a minimum of physical coercion. Liberal perspectives have regarded press freedom as expression of democracy and the variety of messages that emanate from the media as politically enabling and liberating. Any impact of the media on political attitudes, of course, is dependent on the meanings that are drawn from them and as Chapter 1 has shown, there has been much debate in the past three decades about how far different people derive the same meanings from media messages. Even if the media do shape attitudes and behaviour, it is virtually impossible to distinguish the impact of one medium from another or from that of other social and cultural influences.

Television and the Reading of Newspapers

There is still no agreed answer to the long-asked question of whether newspapers shape, reflect or ignore their readers' perceptions of the world. Few read all that is printed in a newspaper and not all readers may find the same sections of a newspaper equally credible, especially as readers do not consult newspapers for the same reasons. However, it is likely that the potential for one newspaper, or for the press as a whole, to influence opinion depends on the number of its readers. The greater the number of readers, the greater presumably is the potential to shape perceptions of the world, though, of course, this will be influenced by how and why people read newspapers.

Initially, the expansion of television was accompanied by a rise in the sale of newspapers. Between 1947 and 1957 the total circulation for each issue of national daily, Sunday and provincial newspapers rose from 67 million to nearly 75 million. After 1957 newspaper sales dropped. By 2003 total circulation had fallen to below 42 million but in the same year that of free newspapers was 40 million. Adding the circulations for purchased and free newspapers in that year gives a higher combined circulation than that for purchased newspapers in 1957, though how many copies of free newspapers are not read in the homes to which they are delivered is not known. Not all purchased newspapers have lost circulation to the same extent. Since 1957 national Sunday newspapers lost over half their circulation whereas that of national morning daily newspapers dropped by about a quarter.[1] In 1960 the *Daily Mirror* had the highest circulation of any daily newspaper. By 2003 its circulation was less than half that of 1960. The *Sun*, Britain's best-selling daily in 2003, had a circulation about double that of 1970 when it became a tabloid. *The Times* and the *Daily Mail* were the only daily newspapers that sold more copies in 2003 than in 1994. In 2003 the circulation of the *Daily Express* was less than a quarter of what it had been in 1960, whereas that of the *Daily Mail* had fallen by roughly 20 per cent. Between 1960 and 2003 the *Daily Telegraph* always had the largest circulation of the broadsheet daily newspapers, but its circulation fell while that of all other national daily broadsheets was higher in 2003 than in 1960.

The *News Chronicle* in 1960 became the first national daily newspaper established before the Second World War to close, and its collapse meant that there was no longer a popular newspaper associated with the Liberal Party. In 1960 and 1961 the national Sunday newspapers the *Sunday Graphic*, the

Empire News and the *Sunday Dispatch* closed.[2] The *Daily Herald*, which had consistently supported the Labour Party, closed in 1964 and the Conservative *Daily Sketch* in 1971. The London evening newspaper the *Star* closed in 1960 and London's other two evening newspapers, the *Evening News* and the *Evening Standard*, amalgamated in 1989. Between 1945 and 1994 ten provincial daily evening newspapers closed.[3] New national daily newspapers have been launched since television became a mass interest, but of these only the *Sun*, the *Star* and the *Independent* were still publishing in 2003.

Television viewing was an important though not the sole cause of the decline in newspaper circulation after 1957. Television competed with newspapers for the time of readers, though many can glance at a newspaper and watch television at the same time, and some may have stopped buying newspapers because television provided a more satisfying supply of what they had sought from newspapers. Loss of advertising revenue seems to have been a more potent cause of the closure of newspapers than falling circulation revenue. When the *News Chronicle* closed, its circulation was higher than that of *The Times*. When the *Daily Herald* was closed in 1964 it had 8 per cent of the national daily newspaper circulation but only 3.5 per cent of the advertising revenue.[4] Advertising revenue was vital if newspapers were to remain profitable. Sales provided a higher proportion of income for mass circulation newspapers than for the 'qualities' but, except for the period of newsprint rationing during and immediately after the Second World War, no national newspaper could have made a profit from sales alone.[5]

The peak of newspaper sales in 1957 coincided with the take-off of commercial television and its competition for advertising. Between 1956 and 1960 television's share of all advertising expenditure in the UK jumped from 6 per cent to 22 per cent. By 2000 television received 27 per cent of advertising expenditure. Between 1956 and 2000 national and provincial newspapers' share of total advertising expenditure dropped from 49 per cent to just under 30 per cent.[6] While this declining proportion of advertising expenditure made life harder for some newspapers, its importance as a cause of the closure of newspapers can be exaggerated. Because the total volume of advertising had grown, press income in real terms from advertising had not fallen. Between 1985 and 2000 the press's share of total advertising fell by around 8 per cent but, when adjusted for inflation, its real value rose by over 60 per cent.[7] Such statistics suggest that the failure to boost newspaper sales, which television may have made more difficult, and to live within their means may have been more significant reasons for the closure of newspapers. Local weekly newspapers may have lost much of their advertising revenue to free newspapers. It has been widely assumed that Rupert Murdoch's transfer of the production of his newspapers from Fleet Street to Wapping in the early 1980s undermined the power of newspaper trade unions whose restrictive practices had pushed up costs and delayed the introduction of new technology. James Curran and Jean Seaton, however, have argued that, while Murdoch's defeat of the unions led to mass redundancies among print workers, its effect on newspaper finance has been mythologised. Before the introduction of new technology, production wage costs amounted to only a fifth of newspaper costs.[8]

The fall in the circulations of purchased newspapers has been accompanied by an increase in the number of their pages. Between 1950 and 1968 the average number of pages per issue for national newspapers more than doubled, from just under ten to over twenty-three, the major reason being the lifting of restrictions on newsprint and paper.[9] Another surge in the size of newspapers occurred in the 1990s. By the end of the 1990s national broadsheets usually had three sections each day, while popular and tabloid newspapers had more pages per issue. In the 1980s the *Daily Mirror* usually contained between 28 and 32 pages, but in the first week of 2000 no issue had fewer than 40 pages and one had 64. On three days a week, it included magazine-style supplements, each of 40 pages. This expansion in newspaper size has hardly ever been attributed to television, though newspaper proprietors may have thought that bigger editions could help them withstand the competition from television. Rises in the real value of newspaper advertising for most of the 1990s may have encouraged the trend towards more pages.

In some respects, television stimulated the sales and reading of newspapers. By 1960 nearly all daily newspapers listed the day's television programmes. In 1985, when the BBC's programme magazine *Radio Times* and ITV's *TV Times* were each selling more than 3 million copies every week, opinion surveys by the BBC and Independent Television Publications Limited had shown that three-quarters of the respondents used newspapers for programme information, though it does not follow that this was the main reason why they bought newspapers.[10] By the 1990s almost all the national daily newspapers provided a supplement giving programme listings for the following week, a service also provided by local weekly newspapers. It seems unlikely that newspapers would have included such programme material had they not expected that it would boost, or at least help to maintain, their circulations. Advertisements for newspapers on television may have helped to sell copies, though their major purpose may have been to discourage readers from buying rival newspapers. In 1999 News International Newspapers in twenty-ninth position and Associated Newspapers in thirty-second position were among the fifty concerns in Britain spending most on television advertising. Chapter 2 discussed how newspaper coverage of television-related news has increased since the 1950s. While this may have been an easy and cheap way of filling newspapers, editors have probably also assumed that it would benefit circulation.

Television and Radio Listening

The extent of radio's possible impact on perceptions of the world also depends on the number of its listeners. In the 1950s television replaced radio as the major form of broadcast mass communication in the home. The number of licences that permitted the watching of television first exceeded those for receiving radio alone in 1958. By 1961 each person in the UK spent on average over thirteen hours watching television each week but only seven hours listening to radio. As most people find it difficult to listen to radio and watch television at the same time – in 2002 the Radio Advertising Bureau found that only 8 per cent of its respondents did so – it seems likely that television was the prime cause of this decline in radio listening. But television never obliterated radio listening. A sample survey undertaken by the BBC Research Department in April 1961 suggested that, between noon and 1 p.m. on Sundays, the hour when radio had its biggest audience, more than 40 per cent of adults in Britain were listening to radio, but Sunday was the only evening when more than one in ten of adults listened to radio.[11] This pattern was still broadly the same in 2002 when, according to the Radio Advertising Bureau, the numbers listening to radio peaked at breakfast time and fell below those watching television only in the early evening.[12] From the 1960s the average number of hours spent watching television and listening to radio both rose, though radio never caught up with television. The Radio Advertising Bureau claimed that in the autumn of 2002 an average of nearly thirty hours each week were spent watching television and nearly twenty-two hours listening to radio. The extensions to the hours of television broadcasting between the 1960s and the introduction of virtually round-the-clock television in the 1990s was accompanied by a rise in the extent of television viewing but also coincided with higher listening figures for radio. In some respects this rise in the average hours of radio listening since the 1960s is deceptive. Between 1970 and 1991 the proportion of the population who listened to radio at some time during the day fell from 52 per cent to 47 per cent, indicating that the average number of hours of radio listening per week had risen because a smaller number were listening for longer periods.[13] The popularity of small portable transistor radios in the 1960s and the fitting of radios into most cars in the 1980s and 1990s probably contributed to the rise in the number of hours spent listening to radio.

The Press and Ownership of Television

There has always been a strong newspaper presence among the owners of commercial television stations in Britain. Some newspaper groups no doubt realised that commercial television would compete for advertising revenue and that watching television might discourage the buying of newspapers, though initially the commercial success of ITV was far from certain. Only two newspaper groups, Associated Newspapers, publishers of the *Daily Mail*, and the Westminster Press, which owned the *Birmingham Mail*, were among the first ITV licence holders. The Kemsley Press, owners of the *Sunday Times*, had been members of the group that had been awarded a licence to broadcast in the Midlands and North at weekends, but withdrew before it started broadcasting. The ITA had tried without success to persuade the *Manchester Guardian*, the *News Chronicle* and Odhams Press (which published the *Daily Herald*) to join groups applying for licences.[14]

Table 5.1 indicates the extent of press shareholdings in ITV companies in 1961 and 1988. The shareholdings of newspaper-owning groups exceeded 20 per cent of the shares in seven companies in 1961 but in four in 1988. Most of the holdings were in the smaller ITV companies, though press concerns may have held large blocks of shares in companies such as banks and insurance businesses, which were important shareholders in many ITV companies. Press shareholdings at some companies had declined before 1988. The Associated Newspapers Group, one of the original shareholders of Associated-Rediffusion, sold its shares in 1956 when the television company had losses of £2.6 million.[15] In 1979 Rupert Murdoch's News International Group, the *Daily Telegraph* and the *Observer* held between them a third of the

Table 5.1 Percentages of shares in ITV companies held by press groups, 1960 and 1988

Press group	ITV company	Percentage of shares held in ITV company	
		1960	1988
Associated Newspapers	Southern	37.5	
BET	Thames		28.25
Belfast Newsletter	Ulster	8	
Berrows Newspapers	TWW	4	
Birmingham Post	ATV	5	
Bond Corporation	TV-am		14.9
Cumbrian Newspapers	Border	21.5	18.47
Daily News	Tyne-Tees	21	
East Anglian Daily Times	Anglia	4	
Eastern Counties Newspapers	Anglia		1.43
Mirror Group	ATV	16	
	Border		14.96
Liverpool Daily Post and *Echo*	TWW	14	
Guardian and *MEN*	Anglia	21	5.09
Norfolk News	Anglia	5	
News of the World	TWW	20	
George Outram	Border	12.5	
Pearson	Yorkshire		20.04
Pergamon	Central		19.92
D.C. Thomson	Southern	25	
	Central		19.59
Roy Thomson	Scottish	80	
Tweeddale Press	Border	5	2.48
Westminster Press	ATV	7	

Note: Shareholdings of less than 1% omitted. Newspaper ownership was not the major area of business for BET, Bond Corporation, Pergamon and Pearson.

Sources: *Report of the Committee on Broadcasting 1960: Volume 1, Appendix E: Memoranda Submitted to the Committee* (London: HMSO, 1962), Cmnd. 1819, p. 407; *British Television: A Controller's Profile* (London: Fulcrum, 1988).

voting shares in London Weekend Television. In 1988 they had no shares in the company. In 1979 *Yorkshire Post* Newspapers held 8 per cent of the voting shares in Yorkshire-Tyne Tees Television but in 1988 had shares in neither Yorkshire nor Tyne Tees. In 1979 Trafalgar House, owners of the *Express* newspapers, held 8 per cent of the voting shares in ATV, and BPM Holdings, which owned the *Birmingham Post* group, held 5 per cent of the voting shares; but in 1988 neither was listed as holding shares in Central, the ITV company into which ATV had been subsumed.[16]

Colin Seymour-Ure's analysis of voting shares at the ITV companies has shown that, up to 1994, ABC, Granada and Meridian were the only central network companies, that is, the bigger ITV companies that provided most of the networked programmes, in which the press had never held voting shares. Press interests had held more than half the voting shares at very few ITV companies. Roy Thomson, the newspaper magnate, held 80 per cent of the voting shares in Scottish Television at its formation in 1957, but the ITA insisted that this be cut to 55 per cent in 1964 and to 25 per cent in 1968. In 1955 British Electric Traction held 75 per cent of the voting shares in Associated-Rediffusion, 50 per cent from 1961, and then 28 per cent of Thames, which was created in 1968 when the ITA instructed Associated-Rediffusion and ABC to merge. In 1955 British Electric Traction controlled 34 radio rediffusion companies, railway and road transport concerns, laundries, hotels and warehousing, but its television income had helped it to move into local newspaper and magazine publishing by the early 1970s.[17] It was one of the few companies that used television revenues to diversify into newspapers. In 1961 ATV, in which press interests held 40 per cent of the voting shares, was the only one of the four network ITV companies in which newspapers held voting shares. Of the seven network companies in 1994, newspaper groups held 14 per cent of the voting shares in Yorkshire, 5 per cent in Carlton and 15 per cent in GMTV, but none in any of the other network companies. In 2000 the RTL Group, which included the Bertelsmann concern, the German-founded global publishing giant, and Pearson, whose interests included ownership of the *Financial Times*, owned nearly two-thirds of Channel 5.[18] The ICC Juniper database of shareholdings suggests that by 2003 press shareholdings in ITV companies were lower than at any previous time. The only holdings seemed to be the Cumbrian Newspapers press group, which held nearly 14 per cent of the Border shares, and D.C. Thomson, which held about 12 per cent in Carlton.

Some ITV companies may have collapsed but for injections of cash from newspaper groups. In 1956 ATV was saved from liquidation when Cecil King's *Mirror* Group bought from Associated Newspapers 26 per cent of the voting shares, but the ITA specified that it could not have more than three directors on the ATV board. LWT would probably have crumbled in 1970 had not the *News of the World*, owned by Rupert Murdoch, agreed to underwrite a new share issue.[19] In 1984 a financial restructuring of TV-am was made possible by an injection of £4 million by the Australian press and television tycoon Kerry Packer. Bruce Gyngell became the representative of Packer's company Consolidated on the TV-am board and in 1984 became the Managing Director of TV-am.[20]

There has been anxiety in Britain that the cross-ownership of newspaper and commercial television companies could threaten parliamentary democracy. The Pilkington Committee in 1962 mentioned fears that cross-ownership could lead to 'an excessive concentration of power to influence and persuade public opinion' with 'an increasingly one-sided presentation of affairs of public concern' and possibly 'a failure to present some of these affairs sufficiently or not at all'. The Committee did not argue that the press holdings in ITV companies had influenced the content of current affairs and news programmes and did not recommend a complete ban on press involvement but, as a safeguard against press influence becoming too great, suggested that no press group should be allowed to be the largest single shareholder in an ITV company. It recommended that the licence of Scottish Television, in which Roy Thomson, who owned 80 per cent of the voting shares and all of the non-voting shares and was also the proprietor of a chain of newspapers in Scotland and the rest of the UK, should not be renewed in 1964 unless he ceased to be the major shareholder.[21] In 1961 Thomson told the Shawcross Commission on the press that he did not interfere in the political stances of the editors of his newspapers and had allowed Scottish Television freedom in news broadcasts and in programme scheduling. Cecil King and Hugh Cudlipp of the *Mirror* Group, which held 28 per cent of the voting shares and 17 per cent of the non-voting shares in Associated Television, told the Shawcross Commission that the *Mirror* Group did not provide 'any services' for ATV other than occasional use of its library. In their view, having two directors on the ATV board was advantageous to the *Daily Mirror* because this helped the newspaper to understand television, and newspapers needed to know about television as they also had to know about the law, politics and medicine.[22] By holding shares in the ITV companies that owned Independent Television News, press groups had an interest, but only a minority interest, in the organisation that has provided the ITV national news service. In 1977 the Annan Committee recommended that no press group should hold more than 10 per cent of the voting shares in an ITV company or more than a quarter of the total shares, but this was not included in the 1980 Broadcasting Act.

The relative lack of public concern about newspaper shareholdings in independent television in the late 1960s and 1970s may have meant that fewer were worried that the newspaper presence in television might restrict political information and debate. Concern over Rupert Murdoch acquiring a major shareholding in London Weekend Television in 1970 focused not so much on his political opinions as on whether it was appropriate for a television company, which had been granted a licence because of its promises to provide intellectually stimulating programmes, to become dominated by the man whose control of the *News of the World* and the *Sun* was thought to have degraded the British press. The Annan Committee was more concerned over the political ramifications of newspaper involvement with local radio than with television.

Campaigns in the 1990s by British press groups for a relaxation of the laws on cross-media ownership were primarily commercial. The 1990 Broadcasting Act restricted newspapers and commercial radio station shareholdings in ITV companies but placed no limit on the number of shares that a newspaper group could hold in a satellite television company. Newspapers complained this arrangement gave an unfair commercial advantage to the Murdoch organisation, whose News International owned 50 per cent of BSkyB and whose newspapers accounted for around a third of the circulation of Britain's national newspapers. The ITC could fine a terrestrial commercial broadcaster up to £15 million for breaching its franchise contract, but the maximum fine it could impose on BSkyB was £50,000.[23] Owners of British newspapers also grumbled that limiting their shareholdings to 20 per cent of an ITV company disadvantaged them *vis-à-vis* European rivals. In 1993 the British Media Industry Group, representing Associated Newspapers, the *Guardian–MEN* and the *Telegraph* groups, maintained that the 1990 Act was preventing its diversification into other media areas that were 'a natural extension' of its current businesses.[24] Sir David English of Associated Newspapers argued that all newspaper groups 'must be involved in

TV and electronic media by the next century', while Murdoch MacLennan of the *Scottish Daily Record* claimed that all newspapers would have to be published electronically and 'cannot be restricted to the print ghetto'.[25] Newspaper groups may, of course, have been more concerned with increasing their shareholdings in television companies in order to have a bigger stake in what had been a profitable area of investment than in order to become electronic multi-media companies. Will Hutton, economics editor for the *Guardian*, pointed out that newspapers and television companies did not have very much in common and that newspapers were in the fortunate position of maintaining their share of the advertising market while technology was cutting their costs. He argued that the danger was not of newspapers becoming 'commercial lepers in a stagnant market; rather it is of being used as cash cows to support the ambitions of proprietors establishing global multi-media companies – and their role in the political, sporting, business and cultural life of the nation being diminished thereby'.[26]

The Broadcasting Act of 1996 allowed newspapers to buy terrestrial broadcasting companies which had less than 15 per cent of the national television audience but any company with more than 20 per cent of total newspaper circulation was not allowed to own a terrestrial television company.[27] In part this was intended to prevent Murdoch from adding a terrestrial television station to his business empire. The Communications Act of 2003 prohibited any concern that held more than 20 per cent of the national newspaper market from holding an ITV licence and from having more than a 20 per cent stake in an ITV company. It also prevented an ITV company from holding more than a 20 per cent interest in a newspaper concern that had more than 20 per cent of the national newspaper market. There were worries that these regulations would not prohibit Murdoch from taking control of Channel 5.

Press shareholdings have been stronger in satellite than in cable television. By 2002 almost all of the 3.6 million homes that were receiving cable television did so from either Telewest or NTL.[28] In 2002 no newspaper groups were listed as owning either of these companies. In 1994 Associated Newspapers established Channel One with the intention of providing a national network of local cable television stations, but in 1998 it closed its news-gathering and production services in London and Bristol, though it kept open Channel One in Liverpool, which was operated jointly with the *Mirror* Group. The operations in London and Bristol were estimated to have cost between £30 million and £40 million.[29] Also in 1994, the *Mirror* Group bought Wire TV, a company that made programmes for showing across the cable television network, and in 1995 launched L!ve TV which, it was hoped, would boost subscriptions to cable television by providing a continuous live television programme for all cable operators. In 1996 *Variety* reported considerable doubts whether Channel One and L!ve TV could ever be 'anything more than vanity channels for the newspaper publishers who finance them'.[30] L!ve TV attracted relatively few subscribers and in 1996 was accused of providing downmarket television when it broadcast topless darts. By 1997 one cable operator had gone to court in an attempt to ensure that it would not be obliged to carry L!ve TV.[31] In 1987 British Satellite Broadcasting, which had been awarded a franchise by the IBA to provide a satellite television service in Britain, had funds of £225.5 million. Pearson had provided £30 million of this sum, Anglia Television, in which newspapers held 9 per cent of the voting shares, provided £11.5 million and Trinity International Holdings, which published the *Liverpool Post* and the *Liverpool Echo*, £2 million. The Australian entrepreneur Alan Bond provided £50 million.[32] Rupert Murdoch's Sky Television was controlled by his media conglomerate News Corporation, which also owned *The Times*, *Sunday Times*, the *News of the World* and the *Sun*. Newspapers held two-thirds of the voting shares in BSkyB, formed by a merger between BSB and Sky in 1990. By buying Thames in 1993, the Pearson Group acquired its BSkyB shares but sold them in 1995.[33]

Some press groups have owned independent companies that make television programmes for sale to the terrestrial channels and also to cable and satellite television. In the early 1990s Broadcast Communications, a subsidiary of the *Guardian* Group, held the contract for the televising of the House of Commons and made *Business Daily*, Channel 4's breakfast service.[34] The *Daily Mail* Group Television Limited, a subsidiary of the *Daily Mail* and General Trust PLC, owned four television production companies. Trinity Mirror PLC, which controlled the *Mirror*, owned Mirrortel, whose subsidiaries included the City Television Network, L!ve TV, Birmingham Live, Wire TV and Channel One Liverpool. Pearson PLC owned seven production companies including the prestigious Grundy Productions and Thames Television Services. It also owned SelecTV and Clement/La Frenais Productions, which held extensive programme libraries. The EMAP Group owned the satellite Box Television channel and the cable channel Kiss TV, four newspaper groups and sixteen local radio stations.[35]

Newspapers and the Content of Television

There is very little evidence to show whether, and how far, newspaper shareholdings in ITV companies influenced the content or presentation of programmes. Sir Paul Fox has recalled that in the 1970s *Yorkshire Post Newspapers*, which held 8 per cent of the voting shares in Trident, the company that controlled the Yorkshire and Tyne-Tees ITV companies, never tried to influence the content of programmes.[36] It may be significant, however, that, of the two longest-running ITV current affairs programmes, *World in Action* (which ran from 1963 to 1998) was made by Granada, in which press groups had no voting shares, and *This Week* (which ran from 1956 to 1978 and then from 1986 to 1992) was made by Associated-Rediffusion and Thames, companies in which BET had voting shares but BET owned only local newspapers. Thames's programme *Death on the Rock* was savaged by national newspapers but none had voting shares in Thames. Newspapers with strong television interests have not campaigned for the legal prohibitions on television taking an editorial line to be relaxed. Newspapers were always quick to point out what they saw as political bias on the part of the BBC or ITV companies.

The search for profitable investments seems to have been a more powerful motive than political propaganda for newspapers becoming major shareholders in commercial television. Roy Thomson told the Shawcross Commission that he owned newspapers and had bought into Scottish Television in order to make money. Cecil King claimed that Associated Television's only effect on the *Mirror* Group was as 'a successful investment'. After the first two or three years of commercial television, newspapers made handsome profits from their investments in television. In less than five years, the *Mirror* Group's original investment in Associated Television of £410,0000 was worth £5.5 million.[37] By 1960 the average profits for the twelve press groups with shareholdings in ITV companies had been 14 per cent before tax and, for the three with the biggest investments, more than 20 per cent. Some BBC journalists suspected in the 1990s that the need for newspapers to boost the value of their investments in commercial television led sections of the press to be especially critical of the BBC.

The extensive coverage of television by the press in the 1980s and 1990s was no doubt driven by hopes that this would boost circulation and advertising revenue, though it may also have been intended to stimulate interest in television and so protect newspaper investments in television. In the late 1980s it was thought that advertising for Sky Television in the Murdoch press helped it sell more satellite receivers than BSB. Roy Thomson told the Shawcross Commission that advertisements for his newspapers were placed on Scottish Television when there were gaps in its advertising schedule, but his comments that this was 'normally paid for' and that 'if we had no association with Scottish Television there would be a decision to be made as to whether we wanted this particular form of advertising' led the Shawcross Commission to think that his newspapers were being given an advantage over their competitors.[38] In 1992 Greg Dyke, then the managing director of LWT, claimed that soccer's Premiership had been promised the support of the Murdoch press if BSkyB were awarded the contract to televise Premiership matches live. BSkyB did win this contract but a spokesperson for the Premiership dismissed Dyke's comments as 'total bollocks' and pointed out that the *Sunday Times*, owned by the Murdoch organisation, was 'gunning for' the Premier League. Dyke also asked how long would it be before 'the Murdoch organisation offers the support of its television stations to enable one of its newspapers to buy a contract it needs'.[39]

Television and the Organisation of Radio

By becoming the dominant form of broadcasting, television provided much of the context for the restructuring of radio that occurred in the late 1960s and early 1970s. In 1967 the BBC Home Service which had begun at the start of the Second World War, and the Light Service and the Third Programme which had been set up in 1946, were replaced by Radio 1, which broadcast current popular music and was intended to appeal to a mainly youth audience, Radio 2, which broadcast mainly light music though in effect popular music but with less emphasis on what was currently most popular, Radio 3, which carried mainly classical music, other 'high' art programmes and intellectual discussions, and Radio 4, which was concerned primarily with the spoken word. This ended the BBC practice that originated in the 1920s of mixing high and more popular culture in generic radio channels, reflecting Reith's belief that one of radio's prime functions was to raise the artistic tastes of the masses, although the Third Programme which had begun broadcasting in 1946 had concentrated on 'high' culture. The establishment of these four radio channels was the beginning of niche broadcasting, channels with output focused on one area of interest. In 1969 Gerald Mansell, who had chaired the BBC report *Broadcasting in the 70s*, argued that 'our four networks will provide for these four basic tastes' – the three groups of roughly the same number who each wanted what was offered by Radios 1, 2 and 4, and the smaller group whose interest in serious music was being met by Radio 3.[40] This introduction of specialist radio channels recognised that, as radio had lost its mass audience to television, there was little likelihood of it introducing large numbers to 'higher culture'. Terrestrial television channels in Britain, including BBC2 and Channel 4, which were intended to cater for minorities, have always carried mixed broadcasting. Niche television channels came only with cable and satellite networks.

Television was not the sole reason for this restructuring of radio. The immediate cause for the reorganisation of the BBC's radio services was that the existing stations no longer appeared to meet the requirements of listeners. BBC television and radio had largely ignored the massive interest, especially among the young, in popular music that had stemmed from the arrival of rock'n'roll in the mid-1950s and the 'swinging sixties' explosion of British popular music. The small number of popular music programmes on radio and television in the 1950s had helped Radio Luxembourg to maintain its cult following among the young and stimulated the establishment in the mid-1960s of commercialised 'pirate' radio stations, which broadcast primarily popular music to Britain from ships just outside British territorial waters.[41] As some 'pirate' radio transmissions interfered with wave bands used for shipping, the Labour government argued that it was bound to act against them, but Labour politicians had also complained about Conservative political broadcasts on pirate stations. Ted Short, Labour's Postmaster-General, condemned what he called 'all [the] anti-Labour political broadcasts as being contrary to the non-party political nature of radio in Britain'.[42] The distinguished radio critic Gillian Reynolds was told by Harold Wilson that he agreed to outlaw the pirate broadcasters rather than legalise them, which some wanted, because this would be the means of obliging the BBC to agree to carry broadcasts for the Open University.[43] The Marine and Broadcasting (Offences) Act of 1967 attempted to destroy the pirate radio stations by making it illegal to work for a pirate station, buy advertising time on one, sell records and equipment to them or ferry food and supplies to them. As this was eradicating a form of radio that many wished to hear – the £2.5 million spent on advertising on pirate radio stations revealed their popularity[44] – the government was more or less obliged to permit the BBC to introduce a service devoted to popular music. Within two weeks of Radios 1 and 2 starting in October 1967, BBC radio gained 2 million listeners.[45]

The establishment of Radios 1, 2, 3 and 4 coincided with an expansion of local radio stations, based on cities, towns and their immediate surroundings. The first, located in Leicester, Sheffield and Merseyside, began broadcasting in 1967. By 1970 the BBC was operating twenty such stations for the major conurbations in England. Their introduction was linked to a realisation that the regional programmes of radio and television were not providing a broadcasting service for areas more localised than regions. The Conservatives' Sound Broadcasting Act of 1972 ended the BBC monopoly of radio broadcasting in Britain. In 1967 the Local Radio Association had begun campaigning for commercialised local radio. The 1972 Act changed the Independent Television Authority into the Independent Broadcasting Authority and gave it responsibility for awarding and monitoring commercial local radio stations. In addition to its commitment to private enterprise, the Heath government may have preferred commercialised local radio to a further expansion of the BBC local services, which could have involved increasing the BBC licence fee or, as was canvassed at the time, financing local radio from the rates. Commercial television's capacity to sustain itself and probably a sense that the ITA had helped to raise the standard of ITV broadcasts after the criticisms of the Pilkington Report probably made it easier to break the BBC radio monopoly and introduce commercial local radio. By 1987 thirty-two local radio services were operated by the BBC and forty-nine by commercial broadcasters. By the mid-1990s the BBC had thirty-eight but the number of independents had soared to over 160, partly because the 1990 Broadcasting Act had made it easier to apply for commercial franchises and had relaxed restrictions on programme content. The 1990 Act replaced the IBA with the Radio Authority, a new supervisory body. It also permitted the creation of national commercial radio franchises, but this does not seem to have been influenced by television.

The Content of Newspapers and Television

If organs of mass communication have influenced perceptions of the world, this has been largely through the messages they transmit in their content about the world, and also by how they present these messages. Television and newspapers provide data about the world but, because they are different forms of media, their representation of the world is not identical. One obvious and major difference has always been that much of television's output is fictional drama in its varied forms. Stories written as fiction have formed only a tiny part of newspaper content. Documentaries, such as those on natural history and more recently political and social history, have been common on television but rarely feature in newspapers. The recent expansion of reality television is another television format with no direct newspaper equivalent. Yet much overlap can be found in the content of television and newspapers. Both report natural disasters and accidents. Both have covered sport extensively. Although broadsheet newspapers have much more detailed coverage of politics than the tabloid press, most newspapers have usually agreed about the major political news of the day and these assumptions are usually shared by television.

Some newspaper content was not often found on television. Television has provided regional news but only local cable and more recently restricted-licence broadcasters have had an equivalent to the town-based news of local newspapers and local radio. The detailed listings of horse race runners and riders that figure in daily national newspapers have not been duplicated by terrestrial television, nor has the detailed coverage of greyhound racing that has been carried by specialist horse and dog racing newspapers. Until the start of ITV's teletext service Oracle in 1973 and the BBC's Ceefax in 1974, television had no information about share prices similar to that of the daily press and still lacks the breadth of such information found in the *Financial Times*, though shifts in share values during the day are recorded by teletext. Small ads are a further example of press content not found on television, except on teletext services – and even these have not matched the range of small ads in newspapers.

Assessments of whether television caused changes in the content or presentation of newspapers can only be tentative. It is impossible to separate any effects of television from those of other cultural forces such as feminism, the expansion of higher education, the multi-ethnic nature of big cities and rising living standards, and probably these helped to shape television as well as newspapers. Different newspapers have very different content and styles of representing the world. It is often contended that, because television reports events sooner than newspapers, newspapers have provided more comment about news. In the 1990s newspapers were giving more space to columnists who commented on news than in the 1940s and early 1950s, but this could also be related to the bigger size of newspapers. Television's ability to provide news more quickly than newspapers is merely continuing a trend begun by radio. Since the 1970s the tabloid press may have increased its reporting about the sex lives of the rich and famous and provided scurrilous details about royalty because these forms of news were not usually found on television.

Another common contention, though again impossible to confirm, is that television has enhanced the role of the visual over the printed word in modern culture. If this is the case, it may explain why broadsheet newspapers carry more pictures than in the 1940s and 1950s. The assumption that a newspaper with many photographs was lowbrow seems to have disappeared, or at least has lost much of its force. Colour television may have encouraged newspapers to have more coloured photographs, though this could have been connected with technological developments in printing. Pictures in newspapers are clearly an attempt to capture attention and an invitation to read the accompanying story. While newspapers have continued to present stories without pictures, the available pictures may now determine how a story is presented by the press. In the 1990s the tabloid press was especially eager to have exclusive photographs of royalty and of events such as weddings of celebrities. Clearly, some of these stories would not have been reported had there been no appropriate pictures, but this may not be due to television. Some have argued that the rise of the remote control and zapping between television channels has reduced attention spans and that this has led newspapers to present news in a more arresting style to attract attention, and to use more bullet-point presentation. Proving that attention spans have declined because of television is almost impossible. In the 1930s and 1940s the *Daily Mirror* was presenting news in a snappier fashion, perhaps following the example of the American newspapers.

The overlap of much newspaper and television content suggests a shared culture between those who work in the two media. Many television journalists, especially those who worked in television during the three decades after the relaunch of television in 1946, had been newspaper journalists and may have brought newspaper assumptions to television. The press and television usually agreed about what constituted 'serious' stories. *Press Conference*, one of the BBC's first current affairs programmes, which started in 1952, consisted of a prominent politician being questioned by newspaper journalists. Breakfast time television's more relaxed approach to news, with its greater coverage of news about show business, and the Channel 5 presentation of the news may have been encouraged by a desire to capture the ethos of the popular press. Some of those who have worked in television described their aims through comparisons with newspapers, though possibly because often they had worked for newspapers. The former Labour MP, philosopher and broadcaster Bryan Magee has recalled that, when he was a reporter for the Associated-Rediffusion current affairs programme *This Week*, 'We said to ourselves that we were making *Guardian* content available to a *Mirror* readership.'[46] Peter Jay, the chairman and chief executive of TV-am who had also been a newspaper journalist, claimed that TV-am had been granted the national commercial television breakfast time franchise in part because the IBA was impressed with its ambition to offer the public a popular daily newspaper from 'the front pages to the back', combining a 'mission to explain' with an intention 'to be fun'.[47] L!ve TV, started as a national cable channel by the *Mirror* Group in 1995, was widely thought to have been an attempt to bring the style of tabloid journalism to television, though others have thought that it was influenced more by the late-night television youth show *The Tube*.

It is hard to find examples of television programmes that were broadcast as a result of pressure from newspapers. The recent vogue for programmes about selling and revamping homes may owe much to their relatively low production costs, but it could be related to press attention on the property market. In the early 1990s a channel controller told Jeremy Tunstall that all channel controllers, regulators and board members monitored the press each morning for news about television, because 'When you have a public board (such as the BBC, ITC and Channel 4 all do) you have the Great and the Good on those boards; they're hyper-sensitive to the agenda of the press, and to rows, manufactured rows, stoked up by the press.' Michael Grade has recalled that his only worry about the press while he worked for the BBC was that it could work up the governors and cause them to start worrying programme controllers.[48] Sir Paul Fox has recalled that when he was Director of Programmes for Yorkshire Television from 1973 to 1984 he never took off a programme because of adverse press criticism,[49] but press criticism could enhance and discourage public interest. Such comments do imply that press animosity could discourage viewing. Occasionally those connected with a programme may have tried to stimulate press antagonism in the hope that this would stimulate the interest of viewers. Tunstall has pointed out that those he calls 'channel barons' made speeches intended for press coverage in order to maintain the image and reputations of their channels. Television producers, he found, had a low opinion of press comment but were eager for positive newspaper coverage. Television station publicity departments would feed promotional material to newspapers, while producers, to obtain preview press coverage, would send video recordings of programmes to newspapers.[50] Sir Bill Cotton has said that when he was Head of Light Entertainment for the BBC he would not allow the press to see previews of his programmes. He believed that, if press critics viewed programmes at the same time as the public and then gained a sense of how the public was responding to them, they would be less likely to write hostile reviews.[51]

Evidence of programmes being scrapped because of press criticism is hard to find. Press criticisms of *At The Edge of the Union*, a BBC documentary which included an interview with Martin McGuinness, believed to be a leader of the IRA, seem to have played a part, along with government pressure, in persuading the BBC governors to take the unprecedented step of viewing the programme before its transmission and then deciding that it should not be broadcast. Press hostility, again fanned by the Thatcher government, to the Thames documentary *Death on the Rock*, may have been a factor in the decision of the IBA to hold an enquiry into the veracity of the programme. In 2002 Angus Deayton and John Leslie were dropped from television shows following press speculation about their sexual exploits. There seems to have been a symbiotic relationship between the popular press and popular television programmes, which stimulates viewing. News about soap operas in the popular press, for instance, both reflects and fosters their popularity. The unexpected popularity of some programmes suggests that favourable press coverage is not so much the cause of the popularity of a series but that, once its popularity is established, press interest can sustain and boost it. In 1962 *That Was The Week That Was* was not expected to attract a large audience, though once it did so, press reporting, by no means entirely supportive, seems to have drawn more viewers to the programme. More recently, a similar phenomenon occurred with *Big Brother* and *Pop Idol*.

Soon after becoming editor of the *Sunday Times* in 1983, Andrew Neil added a new section to the newspaper titled Screen, which merged cinema, television and video coverage and examined their business and cultural roles.[52] By the 1990s the daily broadsheet newspapers had weekly media supplements or extensive coverage on one day each week of matters such as the financing and organisation of television, programming plans, government broadcasting policy plus advertisements for media jobs. Chapter 2 has already given details of how television material in the tabloid press expanded between 1960 and 2000. Newspapers have paid more attention to television than television has paid to the press. *What the Papers Say*, a weekly review of the press and sometimes of how the press has treated one topic, has run since 1956, but its length has usually been restricted to fifteen minutes and in recent years it has not been screened in peak viewing hours. Always made by Granada, it is one of the few programmes to have been broadcast, though in different years, on ITV, Channel 4 and BBC2. Journalists have figured as characters in television drama – for a time Ken Barlow of *Coronation Street* was the editor of the free local newspaper, the *Weatherfield Reporter* – but few long-running drama series have been based on newspaper offices. The BBC soap opera *Compact*, which ran from 1962 to 1965, was centred on the office of a glossy magazine.

The Content of Radio and Television

The concept of public service broadcasting, though never easy to define, changed its meaning over time but it has always helped to shape notions of what can be broadcast on television. While the BBC had a monopoly of television broadcasting, assumptions about what subjects could be broadcast, the language of broadcasters, the prohibition on sexually explicit language and material were common to radio and television and were an extension of radio conventions to television. Television obviously had pictures, which radio lacked, but there are hardly any subjects that were treated by television that were not also the subjects of radio. Many television programme formats are adaptations from radio. Television drama can be regarded as an offshoot of radio drama, though it has also been influenced by the conventions of theatrical plays and cinematic film. Reality television is perhaps the only television genre that is not also a form of radio. Some sports that are difficult to describe in words alone, such as snooker, ice dancing and gymnastics, have been shown extensively on television, but have hardly ever been broadcast on radio. Ballet music has often been broadcast on radio but, because of their visual nature, ballet performances have not been the subject of radio. The massive increase in the ownership of video recorders and players since the early 1980s indicates that many want to record and watch recordings of television programmes and films but, even though the technology has been available for a longer period, the recording of radio programmes by listeners seems to have been less widespread. Audio recordings of radio comedies are sold but probably no shops trade exclusively in recordings of radio programmes or rent only recordings of radio programmes.

The subject matter of radio and television has often overlapped. News bulletins on radio and television have usually covered the same topics, though not always in the same order. Radio and television have broadcast important sports events at the same time. Occasionally classical music concerts and operas have been broadcast simultaneously on Radio 3 and BBC television. No major radio genres were abandoned because of television. Television station controllers such as Sir Bill Cotton have stressed that, while they tried to maximise their viewing numbers, they would avoid putting on their most popular programmes at the same time as the most popular programmes of other television stations. In their memoirs television schedulers do not mention that avoiding clashes with radio programmes figured prominently in the arrangement of television programming, though it has been claimed that Grace Archer's death in the radio soap *The Archers* in 1955 was timed to distract attention from ITV's launch on the same night.

Until the early 1980s, radio's broadcasting hours were longer and this enabled it to treat some subjects in more depth. The expansion of local radio led to the broadcasting of city- or town-based news bulletins that had no equivalent on television until cable television stations began broadcasting local news in the 1990s. From the Second World War, at least some Football League matches were broadcast live on radio but, except for a brief experiment in 1960, they were not broadcast live on television until 1983. House of Commons debates were broadcast on radio from 1978 but on television only from 1989. The rise of television seems to have encouraged radio to concentrate more on what television could not do or on broadcasting genres in which pictures were not necessary. The influence of television on radio broadcasting of the arts is discussed in Chapter 8.

Television has drawn programmes and performers from radio. In the 1940s and 1950s many of the big names of television had made their mark in radio, though given the novelty of television this was perhaps not surprising. By the early 1950s the BBC was recruiting and training as television producers people who had not worked in radio. They included, for example,

Sir David Attenborough and Sir Bill Cotton. Programmes and performers have moved from television to radio, though impressionistic evidence suggests that there has been more movement in the opposite direction. Situation comedies such as *Hancock's Half Hour* were transferred from radio to television in the 1950s, a trend that has continued to the present (the relationship between radio and television comedy is discussed further in Chapter 8). Drama series have been transferred from radio to television. *Rumpole of the Bailey*, for instance, began as *Dock Brief* on radio. The television current affairs discussion programme *Question Time*, first broadcast in 1979, was based on *Any Questions*, which has run on radio since 1948. Despite several attempts, television has not been able to sustain a daily women's magazine programme similar to radio's *Woman's Hour*, which has been broadcast since 1946. Radio had soaps such as *Mrs Dale's Diary* and *The Archers* before television, but the rise of television soaps may have owed more to the example of soaps on American television. Tony Warren, the originator of *Coronation Street*, did not expect initially that it would run for more than a few weeks, and seems never to have claimed that his original intention was to imitate radio soaps.

The influence, if any, of television on radio's style of presentation and forms of representing the world is no clearer than its impacts on the press. Establishing whether the use of language for different radio programme genres has changed since the rise of television would be a massive exercise in textual analysis. Impressionistic evidence suggests that since the 1950s the language of radio has become less formal and more conversational but, if this is the case, it could be due to more discussion programmes, or programmes that are not limited to a script and may have little connection with television. The less formal presentation of news bulletins by BBC radio and television seems to have been influenced by the more relaxed approach of ITN in the mid-1950s. One of the most striking changes in radio presentation since the Second World War has been the talk of disc jockeys on popular music programmes, a style that was developed by 'pirate' radio stations and was probably influenced by American radio. Television had relatively little influence on this other than by contributing to the context that led to the expansion of pop music channels. Radio cricket commentaries may have become more literary and more self-referential to emphasise their distinctiveness from television commentaries. The restructuring of the BBC in the 1990s by the Director-General John Birt introduced bimediality into departments such as news, current affairs, comedy and light entertainment, which were expected to service television and radio.

This resulted in series being assigned to the medium where it was thought that they were best suited, which can be interpreted as emphasising how radio differed from television.

Television and the Influence of the Mass Media

Generalisations about whether, and how far, television has affected the structure of the mass media and their impact on public attitudes have to be guarded. We shall probably never know for certain how, if at all, television affects the way people perceive the world and of how they use the media. Different groups may well draw different messages from the media. Newspapers, radio and television have all evolved since the BBC television service restarted in 1946. Within each medium, the various organs of communication have differed greatly. Changes in education, rising living standards, new forms of employment and the women's movement have shaped responses to the media and stimulated changes in them, though their extent cannot be measured.

Television was a new form of mass communication, and the foregoing discussion has shown how radio and newspapers had to adjust to the presence of television; but they also helped to shape television. Some newspapers have closed because of television, and since the 1950s more time has been spent watching television than listening to radio. But television never obliterated the press and radio. Newspapers and radio have continued to provide most people with data about the world. They are still major forms of mass communication. They have been complemented, not supplanted, by television. Television has extended the range of mass communications but it is easy to exaggerate the extent of this. Except for the rise of cable and satellite television over the last fifteen or so years, the number of television channels was restricted and offered far less choice than the press. Overseas radio stations could be listened to, and before the 1990s radio broadcast for more hours than television. It is often contended that the increased number of cable and satellite television channels has not brought greater variety to television but merely more channels showing more of the same. Much of the content of television is not so very different from that of the press or radio. What is covered by television has usually also been covered by the press and radio, and some forms of information about the world that are found in the newspapers have been largely absent from television. Television and radio in

Britain have never been allowed the political partisanship of the press, though the political reporting of both forms of broadcasting has concentrated on established political practice and has largely ignored those outside the mainstream. Television has never been especially strong in investigative journalism and has not exposed the lives of the rich and famous on a scale similar to that of the tabloid press. The novelty of television's contribution to the mass media may lie in how it presents data about the world. It creates a sense of immediacy, gives an impression that it is showing events as they unfold and allows us to imagine that we know intimately those we see on the screen. All the time, of course, television, like the press and radio, is not providing reality but a mediated, edited version of reality. As Marshall McLuhan suggested, the medium may well be the message.

Chapter 6

TELEVISION, GENDER AND SEX

The Television Industry, Women and Male Power

Men have dominated the television industry in Britain, though the presence of women in it has been stronger than in many other areas of British life and by the early twenty-first century was stronger than ever. Since the start of television the influence of women in television broadcasting organisations has grown in spurts rather than at a steady rate. The expansion of television in the 1950s created more senior jobs for men than for women. The proportion of women in senior grades at the BBC was more or less the same in 1930, 1970 and 1980. In 2002 women made up 46 per cent of the national labour force whereas half of the 25,000 employed in broadcast television were women. Fifty-four per cent of the BBC's broadcast television employees were women but only 45 per cent in commercial television.[1]

By 2000 women were not equally represented in all areas of television. In 1990 Jane Arthurs had found that their jobs were 'systematically less well-paid . . . lower status and less likely to lead to promotion than jobs that are predominantly done by men'.[2] In 2002 over 90 per cent of all hair and make-up artists and over 80 per cent of those with jobs in costume and wardrobe for film and television in Britain were women, whereas only around 10 per cent of those working with lighting, broadcast engineering, cameras and sound were women. A sample survey of UK prime-time television drama and comedy revealed that in 2001–2 only 8 per cent of the directors were women and only 25 per cent of the scriptwriters. A quarter of all women's jobs in 2002 in film and television were in general management, sales and marketing, professional support, secretarial/administration and premises operation, types of office work traditionally associated with women.[3] In 1992 men in television were paid on average £10,000 per year more than women and were twice as likely to be promoted. Ten years later women's earnings across television kept pace with men's until they were in their late thirties.

Women in their forties and fifties were earning less than men and less than their younger female colleagues.[4]

Women have formed only a minority of those who have regulated television. When BBC television restarted in 1946 one of the seven BBC governors was a woman. In 1970 there was still only one woman governor but by 2002 four of the twelve governors were women. No woman has been chairman of the BBC governors. Lady Plowden was the vice-chairman of the IBA from 1970 to 1975 and then chairman from 1975 to 1980. The other six chairmen of the ITA/IBA were men. Twenty-two of the 103 members of the ITA/IBA between 1954 and its dissolution in 1990 were women. Patricia Hodgson in 2000 was the first woman to become Chief Executive of the ITC. The ten original members of the ITC in 1991 included three women but in 1998 only two were women. Elspeth Howe was appointed chairman of the Broadcasting Standards Council in 1993 and of the Broadcasting Standards Commission that replaced it in 1997. In 1997 more than half the members of the Broadcasting Complaints Commission were women.

Women began occupying more of the senior positions in television in the late 1990s. No woman has been Director-General of the BBC. In 1980 all members of the BBC's Board of Management were men. In 1986 no woman was in the *BBC Handbook* list of the nine most senior television positions. Only two women in the mid-1980s, one of whom was the note-taker, attended the weekly BBC programme review meeting, a meeting of crucial importance for programming.[5] By 2003, four of the fifteen members of the BBC's Executive Committee were women. In 1999 Jane Root became the first woman controller of a BBC television channel when she was appointed Controller of BBC2. In 2000 Lorraine Heggessey became the Controller of BBC1. Alison Sharman became Controller of Daytime Television in 2002 and in 2003 Glenwyn Benson was appointed Controller of Factual Television, so that four of the six television controllers were women. In 2002 Jana Bennett became the Director of BBC Television. This increased presence of women at the highest level of BBC television was partly the result of a deliberate policy, which in turn can be related to a realisation in society at large, stemming from the rise of the women's movement, that women ought to occupy more positions of power and influence. In 1979 43 per cent of those accepted onto the BBC's graduate-training schemes had been women. Support for sexual equality was built into the 1990 Broadcasting Act. Jeremy Tunstall has pointed out that 'during the 1980s equal opportunities and the need to have more women in senior positions became part of British TV orthodoxy'.[6] Following Spot the Difference, a conference organised in 1991 by the BBC on the future of women in television, John Birt, the Director-General-designate, introduced a six-point plan for achieving sexual equality in BBC television by 2000. Between July 1992 and the end of 1993, the proportion of women employed in the level just below that of the Board of Management had risen from 15 per cent to over 30 per cent and in the middle management band from 20 per cent to just below 50 per cent.[7] By 2000 36 per cent of those just below the Board of Management were women.

ITV remained much more under male control. In 1992 a survey of the top 500 UK companies revealed that the BBC was ahead of most British companies and ahead of Channel 4 and several of the larger ITV companies in recruiting, monitoring, targeting and allowing flexible work patterns to promote equal opportunities.[8] No woman has been Director-General of the ITA/IBA. Women have formed only a tiny proportion of the directors of ITV companies. The Pilkington Committee reported in 1962 that the 149 directors of the ITV companies included only five women. In 1974 only eight of the 179 directors of ITV companies and only three of their 142 executive officers named in the IBA annual report of that year were women. Between 1982 and 1992 the proportion of women who were senior programming executives with the five biggest ITV companies rose from 7 per cent to 10 per cent, but by 2002 exceeded 20 per cent. By 2002 amalgamations between ITV companies had reduced the number of directors but only three women were listed as directors by the *Kompass* business directories. In 2002 Brenda Smith was Managing Director of Granada TV and Menna Richards the Managing Director for the Wales division of HTV. When GMTV began broadcasting in 1993 its staff consisted of eighty women and fifty-four men, but the only woman member of its ten-person board was sacked soon after it went on air.

At the start of Channel 4 three of the thirteen directors were women and also two key executives, the heads of presentation and marketing. Two of the three senior commissioning editors were women but only two of the thirteen commissioning editors.[9] Vanni Treves became chairman of Channel 4 in 1998. Dawn Airey was its Director of Programmes from 1996 to 2000. Almost half of the Channel 4 senior executives, and six of the nine commissioning editors, listed in the 2002 *Guardian Media Guide* were women. Commissioning editors had a crucial role in determining what programmes

The BBC televising the 1939 Boat Race. Sports events were among the earliest television outside broadcasts. *(BBC Photograph Library)*

Mary Whitehouse handing a petition with 366,355 signatures to James Dance, the Conservative MP for Bromsgrove, in 1965. The petition called on the BBC to produce programmes that would 'build character . . . instead of destroying it'. *(PA Photos)*

Members of the cast of the BBC satire show *That Was The Week That Was* in 1963. From left to right Willie Rushton, Lance Percival, Millicent Martin, David Frost and David Kernan. *(PA Photos)*

Robin Day. In interviews with politicians he was said to put 'his blunt, loaded questions with the air of a prosecuting counsel at a murder trial'. *(London Weekend Television/REX FEATURES)*

Television has been used to shape the public's perceptions of politicians. Margaret Thatcher at the Rovers Return with the cast of *Coronation Street*. (*REX FEATURES*)

Right: The *Spitting Image* puppet head of Margaret Thatcher. (*Toby Melville/PA Photos*)

Spike Milligan playing an Irish Pakistani in London Weekend Television's *Curry and Chips* in 1969. *(London Weekend Television/REX FEATURES)*

The cast of *The Fosters* (left to right, standing, Norman Beaton, Lenny Henry; sitting, Sharon Rosita, Isabelle Lucas, Lawrie Mark) in 1976. *The Fosters* was the first British-made situation comedy to have an all-black cast. It was a British adaptation of an American sitcom. *(London Weekend Television/REX FEATURES)*

Moira Stewart, who in 1981 was the first black woman to be a national news-reader on BBC Television. *(Ken McKay/REX FEATURES)*

The playwright Harold Pinter being interviewed on the *South Bank Show* in 1977. Melvyn Bragg said that this interview gave 'a terrific sense of the man . . . in a more complete way than you might get in print'. *(London Weekend Television/REX FEATURES)*

Carla Lane, one of the first women to be a successful television comedy writer. Her acclaimed sitcoms include *The Liver Birds*, *Butterflies* and *Bread*. *(Peter Brooker/REX FEATURES)*

Lynda La Plante, the television drama writer whose work has included the highly praised *Widows*, *Prime Suspect* and *Trial and Retribution*. *(Ilpo Musto/REX FEATURES)*

Jane Root, who became the BBC's first woman television channel controller when she was appointed Controller of BBC 2 in 1999. *(Emma Boam/REX FEATURES)*

Lorraine Heggessey, who became Controller of BBC 1 in 2000. *(Johnny Green/PA Photos)*

From left to right, Charlie Hunnan, Craig Kelly, Antony Cotton and Denise Black, members of the cast of Channel 4's *Queer as Folk 2* in 2000. *(Matthew Fearn/PA Photos)*

Beth Jordache, played by Anna Friel, and Margaret Clemence, played by Nicola Stephenson, in the first lesbian kissing scene to be shown in a British soap. This was on *Brookside* in 1993. *(By kind permission of Phil Redmond, the creator of* Brookside*)*

were shown. From 2000 to 2002 Airey was Chief Executive for Channel 5 and then became Managing Director of Sky Networks. From 1996 until 2001, Elisabeth Murdoch, the daughter of Rupert Murdoch, was the managing director of BSkyB. In the early 1990s women had a slightly stronger presence at the higher levels of the bigger independent production companies than at ITV companies. Tunstall found that over a quarter of the 'principal names' at thirty-five of the bigger independent companies were women.[10]

The number of women engaged in producing programmes is far from clear, partly because the BBC and ITV companies had differing grades of producer and because statistics about employment in the independent sector lump together those working for the cinema and television. A survey in 2003 showed that television producers could be executive producers, series producers, senior producers, producers, development executives or promotions/trailers producers, while jobs in production could be subdivided into production, production management, archive research, script writing and directing. The number of women producers seems to have grown. In 1969 15 per cent of the BBC's television producers were women, though this figure did not include production assistants or assistant producers.[11] In 2002 over 40 per cent of those in the various levels of producers across television were women.[12] Comparing the number of women producers for random samples of fifty programmes or series made in the 1960s and 1990s listed in Jeff Evans's *The Penguin TV Companion*, an invaluable aid for research into television history, suggests that, while more women had become producers, they remained outnumbered by men. In the 1960s there had been seven women producers but thirty-five in the 1990s. The number of men had risen from 99 to 112. This sample is, of course, far from scientific and Evans did not usually name assistant producers or researchers. In 1970 the *BBC Handbook* named sixty-three television managers, including the heads of thirty departments that made different categories of programmes or provided services needed to make programmes. Only the Assistant Controller for Television Developments, the Head of Children's Television Programmes and the Head of Make-up were women. By 1991 almost a third of those employed by the BBC in the four grades that included executive editors and editors of major programmes, producers, assistant producers and researchers were women, but, as these grades also included many who worked in technical areas where women were not usually employed, the percentage of women producing programmes could have been higher. Gender ghettoisation has occurred in the production of some television genres. In the late 1960s most women producers were employed making programmes primarily for women and children, and in early 1992 fewer than one in five of those holding senior positions in light entertainment, sport and news and current affairs were women.[13]

Men hardly ever said that they had deliberately tried to exclude women from working in television, though some women complained that men had resented women working in some areas of television. Jenny Russell, a Channel 4 news producer, recalled that, when she worked for the BBC, 'at news meetings women who speak out and make a name for themselves and challenge are penalised by being ignored, demoted, or not sent out on jobs'. A camerawoman had to show that she was good at the job before her male colleagues accepted her. Prominent women broadcasters in the early 1990s complained about a masculine culture in television and how this had restricted their careers. Janet Street-Porter was reported to have said that the BBC resembled a 'Masonic league full of ritualistic men in grey suits' and that prime-time television on Saturday nights 'still transmits programming hosted by unattractive, sexist, middle-aged men. One could argue that this represents the type of people who run television as a whole.'[14]

It is likely that the cultural assumptions of men, and probably of many women, led them to assume that certain areas of work would be dominated by men, but such assumptions have changed over time. Political and Economic Planning, for instance, found in the 1960s that it had been assumed that filming trips abroad were unsuitable for women, but this was no longer the case in the 1990s. The domination of engineering by men and women's reluctance to train as engineers do much to explain the low number of women involved with the technology of television. In the late 1980s Angela Coyle and Reena Bhavnani found that working methods in television, with long and often unpredictable hours, suited the pattern of men's lives. After-hours socialising and bullshitting one's way into promotion also advantaged men, while women were judged as women first and professionals second and had to prove themselves in ways that men did not.[15] No doubt these cultural practices were even stronger in earlier decades. In his *A Survey of Television*, published in 1967, Stuart Hood, Controller of Programmes for BBC television from 1962 to 1964 and certainly not a male chauvinist, invariably used the pronoun 'he' when describing the work of television producers, directors and administrators, which suggests that, when the 'new feminism' was starting to attract more media attention, it was assumed in television that controlling and making television programmes were largely a male preserve. In 1975, Sarah Boston, who had made five documentaries for BBC television, claimed that producers who felt 'partisan about being a worker, a woman, black, or about the evils of the system we live under' were 'politely requested to either suppress . . . their feelings or go out of the door'.[16] Jane Arthurs in 1991 thought that many women in television loved their work so much that it was a 'kind of vocation' and their dedication allowed 'the industry to exploit and undervalue them'.[17]

The women holding the six most senior positions at the BBC in 1986 told Marmaduke Hussey that 60 per cent of the reason so few women occupied senior positions at the BBC was the governors and 40 per cent of women themselves. Jane Drabble, editor of the religious documentary programme *Everyman*, pointed out that many women did not wish to be involved with 'all the managerial jealousies, discords and the competition ladder'.[18] Liz Forgan, who was the Director of Programmes for Channel 4 before becoming Managing Director of BBC Network Radio in 1993, also said in the early 1990s that women were happier working in 'a non-hierarchical environment'. The intensity of the work and the long hours involved in producing programmes raised difficulties for women with young children, though Drabble considered that having young children and a career was a challenge but a manageable one. In the early 1990s the television director Sharon Miller, on the other hand, felt that women had to choose between their careers and personal lives. She said, 'I neglected my private life while my professional life benefited hugely. You are permanently under attack in this business, your confidence, your energy and your vitality, and it's difficult for any partner to understand the complexity of what you're going through.'[19] In 1993 Elizabeth Clough, one of the two executive producers in the BBC documentary department, and Phillippa Giles, who had a first-class degree but started working for the BBC as a secretary before becoming a producer, each thought there was 'a glass ceiling' beyond which women producers found it hard to rise. Clough said that some producers put their lives on hold while making a programme and mistakenly assumed that women who were not prepared to do this were not keen on their jobs. For Clough, women were 'keen on one's work and something else as well'. In her experience the BBC treated best women with no children or those who had had children at an early age. Belinda Giles, a producer who had left the BBC after having children, explained that a television station 'cannot go on air with a blank screen because you want to go to your child's school concert'. Having children meant that she could not go to the BBC Club in the evenings where 'a lot of networking is done'.[20] The problem of balancing a career and the demands of a family was not, of course, unique to television.

Women have been talented writers of television drama. In 1965 Nell Dunn's Wednesday Play *Up the Junction*, which dealt with the lives and sexual encounters of working-class women in Battersea, was regarded as ground-breaking, but arguably no woman television drama writer has matched the national reputations of Jack Rosenthal, Alan Plater, Alan Bleasdale, Troy Kennedy Martin, Dennis Potter, Alan Bennett or Ted Willis. Julia Hallam has argued that the work of Lynda La Plante, author of *Prime Suspect* (1991, 1992 and 1993) and *Trial and Retribution* (1997), and that of other women writers, has suffered critical neglect for reasons 'primarily institutional, generated by facts within the broadcasting industry as well as in the critical echelons of academia that situate female writers on the margins of the "quality" drama tradition in spite of their considerable success in creating innovative interventions in popular series formats'.[21] The BBC drama series *The Wednesday Play*, which ran from 1964 to 1970, and its successor *Play for Today*, which lasted until 1984, are often regarded as peaks of television drama. Each production was a single play. Irene Shubik produced thirty-one between 1967 and 1971, but none of them was written by a woman and only one was directed by a woman.[22] Women have often been employed in the teams of jobbing writers who write scripts for soaps.

Women on the Television Screen

Women have been prominent on the screen, but even here the male presence has been stronger, though this has varied between programme genres. Cumberbatch, Maguire and Woods found that in 1994 70 per cent of all appearances on UK television were by men. On sport programmes male appearances outnumbered those by females by eleven to one and on national news programmes by four to one, though there was nearly a fifty-fifty split on children's programmes. In 1987 Thoveron had found that a little over half of all the actors in advertisements on British television were women.[23]

The employment of women as newsreaders and reporters for national news bulletins indicates how opportunities for women in television have expanded, though on a limited scale. Stuart Hood wrote in 1967 that 'it seems unlikely that the BBC or ITN will take a step forward – by employing a woman to read the news. For one short period the BBC did employ a woman announcer who was at once intelligent and good looking; but the weight of masculine prejudice among her colleagues was too powerful and the experiment had to be discontinued.'[24] At its start ITN had employed Barbara Mandell and Lynn Reid Banks for a short time as newsreaders. Sir Bill Cotton has recalled that when Angela Rippon started to read the BBC national news in 1974 many at the BBC thought that women lacked the gravitas to deal with serious items, yet within a very short time women newsreaders were accepted as natural by broadcasters and the public. In the late 1960s a former editor of BBC Television News told Political and Economic Planning that he had introduced a woman reporter over 'the dead bodies of my entire staff . . . in spite of the fact that she is intelligent, good-looking, the right age, and very good, it was a failure because the men wouldn't give her the service they gave other men. She came and said to me, "It's not working", and of course it wasn't, because the men were just not co-operating.'[25] In 1993 Alexandra Henderson, the editor of *Question Time* who was the daughter of an ambassador and an Oxford graduate, said that when she worked as a reporter at ITN the newsroom was 'full of very tough, beerswilling Australians who didn't like me, particularly since they thought I was posh . . . Because they wanted to do me down, they used to give me stories about the Royals and ships being launched.' She did add that, when she was working on *Question Time*, the BBC encouraged her to include more women panellists.[26] In recent years, most news bulletins have been broadcast with two newsreaders, a man with greying hair and a younger, physically attractive woman. The man introduces the more 'serious' items and an impression is created that the man is the senior partner of the team. A BBC journalist has explained that focus groups in America and Britain have suggested that viewers place more trust in programmes with two newsreaders and in which the older man deals with 'more important' matters.

The enormous number of situation comedies on television makes generalisations about women in them hazardous. Comedy series that received great critical acclaim and achieved massive audiences were usually written by men. In 1966 Frank Muir, who had written comedy scripts for radio and television and was to be Head of Entertainment for London Weekend Television, said that in Britain 'all our comedy is written by about twenty-four gentlemen. No ladies',[27] and, although women did break into comedy writing in the 1970s, arguably only Carla Lane and Victoria Wood have been regarded as among the ablest comedy writers. Probably a majority of the highly acclaimed sitcoms have given equal weight to men and women characters, though such classics as *Hancock's Half Hour*, *The Army Game*, *It Ain't Half Hot Mum*, *Porridge*, *The Young Ones* and the later series of *Blackadder* were set in a masculine environment with women playing only supporting roles. Male characters dominated the early series of *Only Fools and Horses*, but the making of longer episodes for Christmas and a series of fifty-minute episodes in 1989 saw the inclusion of the wives of Delboy and Rodney. This gave the writer John Sullivan more opportunities to develop character; but it could be argued that this reflected the widening horizons of women in society at large. *The Rag Trade*, which the BBC first screened in 1961, was possibly the first sitcom with a predominantly female cast, although its main subject was the conflict between women making clothes and their male boss. Nine series of *The Liver Birds* were broadcast between 1969 and 1979. These were concerned with two young women sharing a flat in Liverpool and, although a recurrent theme was their encounters with young men, the two women were very much the central characters. *Birds of a Feather*, which had seven series on BBC1 between 1989 and 1997, centred on how two sisters coped while their husbands were in prison and on their relationship with a nouveau riche female neighbour. It was long believed that women were not successful as producers of comedy, although this assumption was dented by Susan Belbin's production of *One Foot in the Grave* in the 1990s. *Absolutely Fabulous*, first shown in 1992, restricted men to little more than walk-on parts and was written by women. Regarded as a major advance in female comedy, its director and usual producer were men.

The extent to which female characters and their concerns have dominated television drama has varied among the different categories of drama. Strong women characters have always been a staple of television soaps and many scenes in soaps have taken place in the home, a location usually regarded as a centre of feminine expertise. Until the 1980s women rarely had significant roles in crime dramas, although *Cagney and Lacey*, the first police drama with women as the main leads to attract large audiences, was imported from America and first shown in Britain in 1982. It can be argued that the male emphasis in police dramas reflects the dominant role of men in police forces and the fact that more reported crimes are committed by men. Drama series with a predominantly female cast have been rare but seem to have increased in the 1980s and 1990s. *Tenko*, a series about British women held prisoner by the Japanese in Malaya during the Second World War, was screened by the BBC from 1981 to 1984. *Prisoner: Cell Block H*, set in an Australian women's prison, had a cult following when it was shown by ITV between 1979 and 1987. In recent years *Bad Girls* has been set in a women's prison.

Opinions among women producers have been divided over whether women writers and producers create different kinds of programme. Several women producers told Jeremy Tunstall in the early 1990s that they could usually recognise whether a man or a woman had produced a programme, though often this was because male and female producers dealt with different subjects rather than having different production styles. Women producers tended to choose social subjects and men subjects concerned with business or politics,[28] though this could also have reflected the assumptions of those who employed producers. Juliet Blake, an independent comedy producer, said in the early 1990s that 'If you look at comedy programmes in which funny women are not portrayed as silly, simpering pea-brains, you will find that women have been at the helm of production.' Verity Lambert, who had produced television programmes since 1963 and had set up her independent production company Cinema Verity in 1985, did not believe that she could tell whether a drama had been made by men or women. Antonia Bird, who had produced *Casualty* and *Inspector Morse*, took the opposite view. She claimed that *The Men's Room*, whose production staff were nearly all women and which had attracted complaints about its sex scenes, would have been very different had men made it.[29] It is likely that, as more women became directors and handled a wider range of subjects, any differences in the types of programmes made by women and men would be harder to notice.

Television Audiences and Gender

Chapter 2 has shown that women watch more television than men, though not vastly more, and that for both sexes watching television has been a source of pleasure. Occupational patterns do much to explain why more women than men have watched television. BARB data show that the proportion of housewives that watched television was often higher than the proportion of the total female population that watched television. Daytime programmes with more men than women viewers were rare on weekdays, probably because more men were out at work. A sample of ten programmes analysed by the IBA for the London area in 1975 showed, not surprisingly, that the gap between the number of women and men viewers was usually highest in the afternoons.[30] More women than men watched breakfast-time television, perhaps because more men were then journeying to work. Most evening programmes were viewed by more women than men, perhaps because more men spent leisure time outside the home. Explaining the viewing habits of women would be easier if more data had been released to the public about the age, social class, ethnic identity and geographical location of women who watched particular programmes.

Channel controllers and schedulers may well have targeted programmes at women, though very few have admitted to doing so. Lew Grade was unusually frank when he told a House of Commons Select Committee in 1972 that he wanted to introduce a daytime magazine programme aimed at women.[31] In 1967 Stuart Hood pointed out that originally, following the practice of radio, BBC television had 'long persevered in a belief that there was a valid category known as "women's programmes"'. He claimed that these had not succeeded because they were screened at times when the total audience was small, and so not representative of women, and because they tried to find a woman's dimension to subjects of general interest. He argued that men read the best women's journalism and that women resented being treated as 'beings with different interests and a limited view of life and its problems'. Hood thought that there was little protest when such television programmes were scrapped.[32] It has been said that BSkyB has paid so much to broadcast live sport because this was a form of television that was thought to attract young adult male viewers.

Television has carried programmes related to what have been considered the interests of women, but few programmes have included the word 'women' in their titles, and none has enjoyed a longevity similar to radio's *Woman's Hour*. At present one cable/satellite channel is called *Men and Motors*, but there is none with women in the title. Controllers of terrestrial channels may have thought that designating a programme as appealing to women could discourage men from watching it. Yet the content of many programmes seems to have been decided in the expectation that it would appeal more to one sex than the other. So many daytime television programmes may have been concerned with relationships and marital problems because more women are able to watch daytime television. Although many men watch soaps, these have often been considered essentially programmes for women, and in the 1990s the 'soapification' of drama series such as *The Bill* may have been in part an attempt to boost their appeal to women.

Watching television may have been popular among women because this harmonised with the cultural connotations of femininity. For many women television emphasised what it meant to be a woman and reinforced existing notions of womanhood. Although many pubs have had television sets since the 1960s, and they were soon to become common in hotel bedrooms, watching television has always been primarily home-based, and has buttressed rather than challenged the ideologies of domesticity with which many women wish to be associated. As more women worked outside the home, they may have assuaged guilt about not being full-time housewives by pursuing a home-based leisure activity which could be combined with performing other domestic tasks, but watching television could have reduced the tedium of some household tasks. Before the acquisition of second sets in the 1970s, watching television was often a family activity and could be interpreted as reinforcing family bonds. The Audience Tracking Survey of the 1990s found that disagreements between couples about what to watch could be 'fraught', but more than three-quarters of couples stated that they made joint decisions about what to watch.[33] While many television programmes, and particularly soaps and drama series, have centred on marital breakdowns and changing relationships, these have often implied that the nuclear family is the ideal to which all couples should aspire. At the same time, for women whose relationships have collapsed, the portrayal of broken relationships on television may have been a form of reassurance. It has been argued that soaps have attracted such high numbers of women viewers because they tended to be centred on the home, an area of feminine expertise, while the multiple storylines and the avoidance of narrative closure reflected the world of women, in which the demands of domesticity were never-ending. Soaps have often included strong female characters, though their strength has often not extended beyond the domestic sphere.[34]

Television and Gender Identities

In very general terms it can be said that television in the 1990s depicted women pursuing a wider range of activities than in the 1950s. In this respect television reflected changes in society at large, though it is difficult to be sure of how far television has been ahead of changes in society or merely kept abreast of them. In the 1940s and 1950s women were rarely shown on television in positions of authority, although adaptations of classical drama included women who were strong characters. Women announced programmes but did not often introduce them. In the 1950s and 1960s women rarely chaired studio discussion of politics or interviewed leading politicians. Although more men's sport was broadcast, television sport programmes featured female performers, especially when they were performing well for Britain in international competitions. Women did not usually provide the commentary on broadcasts of women's sport before the 1990s, though they gave expert summaries on women's tennis in the 1970s. Even in the 1990s women commentating on men's sport was unusual, but men were commentators on women's sport.

Gradual changes can be traced in television representations of housewives. From the start of ITV television commercials have reflected the assumption that running a home and child rearing are primarily responsibilities of women, though in the 1980s and 1990s more advertisements depicted men showing an interest in cooking and being involved with childcare. Impressionistic evidence suggests that in the 1950s and 1960s many advertisements concentrated on women who were full-time housewives; but after this more advertisements tried to show how their products could help women balance the demands of running a home and pursuing a career. Certainly by the 1980s many advertisements seemed to be aimed at women who were in control of their lives and had careers outside the home. In the 1960s plays written for television such as *Cathy Come Home*, *Up the Junction* and *Poor Cow* and *Edna, The Inebriate Woman*, first screened in 1971, offered realistic portrayals of the hardships of working-class women, whereas the fictional *The Avengers*, first broadcast in 1961, was one of the earliest drama series that showed women having physical and mental strengths equal to those of men.

There are no definitive answers to the question of how far television has encouraged women to broaden their social horizons and enter cultural spheres previously dominated by men. Women now have more economic and social power than when television restarted in 1946. Indeed, the higher numbers of women with senior positions in television is one indicator of this increase in women's power. In part this increasing emancipation of women is a product of the new feminism that began to grow in Britain in the 1960s. Although the major advocates of women's liberation since the 1960s have appeared on television, only occasionally has television provided them with a platform for propagating their views. When feminists have been shown on television, this has often been in discussion programmes on which those with opposing views have been given equal air time.

Whether television has promoted the emancipation of women also depends on whether television has influenced the way men perceive themselves. Television, of course, is only one of many cultural forces that have determined notions of masculinity among men; and men have not agreed about what constitutes male identity. Television has presented many conflicting images of men. To a degree television has reflected notions that nature has given the two sexes distinctive capacities and that these justify the separate roles of men and women, which in turn often leads to assumptions that positions of political and economic power are the natural province of men. Although television shows how the social roles of women have expanded, much television has emphasised the exercise of authority as a male trait. Even at present in current affairs programmes senior interviewers and journalists are more likely to be men; and those areas that women dominate, such as family welfare, have traditionally been regarded as areas of women's expertise. As already noted, in teams of male and female newsreaders men introduce the more serious items. The concentration of soaps on the domestic milieu may have strengthened the assumption that it is natural for the world outside the home to be dominated by men. Sport has been crucial in shaping notions of masculinity and in recent decades this has been done largely through television. Far more male sport has been broadcast by television and so has probably helped to consolidate, or at least done very little to discourage, beliefs among many men that male interests should take precedence over those of women.

As a visual medium television has always been concerned with physical appearance and has registered notions of physical attraction. If concern with physical appearance is regarded as a female characteristic, television has done little to challenge this and may well have increased social pressures on women to conform to prevailing conceptions of an acceptable physical appearance. At the same time, television may have made men more anxious about the physical image they present to others. It is sometimes argued that in post-war Britain men became feminised, though this very broad generalisation depends on how femininity is defined. James Obelkevich has suggested the use of deodorants, the marketing of perfumes for men – sales of men's toiletries grew from £390 million to £550 million between 1991 and 1997 – and the increased interest in clothes fashion were instances of men adopting what had been considered feminine interests.[35] One can argue that market forces have driven these changes and that television advertisements were crucial to their acceptance by men. There has also been talk of the 'new men', that is, men who felt that they should be more considerate and more involved with child rearing and that domestic chores should be shared by the sexes. Some men have spoken of wanting to be more in touch with the 'feminine' side of their natures, but how many men take such a view and whether they have been influenced by television is not clear. The actor John Thaw played a police detective in two highly popular television crime series – Jack Regan in *The Sweeney* between 1975 and 1978 and *Inspector Morse* between 1987 and 2000. The character of Regan resorted to violence more often, and had a more aggressively macho persona, than Morse, which could indicate that male viewers in the 1990s found it had become easier to identify with a less aggressively assertive, less brash expression of masculinity.

The 1990s, on the other hand, also saw the growth of what was called 'lads' TV', programmes screened late at night that celebrated rowdy behaviour, heavy drinking and casual sex. Some might say that this reflected traditional male behaviour. At the same time, such programmes also involved the rise of what were called 'ladettes', young women who were pursuing a lifestyle similar to that of the lads. Some may have regarded such behaviour by women as an expression of women's emancipation because it represented women enjoying a style of life that had previously been monopolised by men. Lads could also be seen as the antithesis of the new men – which illustrates the difficulty of deciding what forms of masculinity have been presented by television as the most acceptable social roles for men.

Television and the Presentation of Sexuality

Feminists have often argued that regarding women primarily as sex objects not only demeans women but also supports the social power of men by undervaluing the abilities of women. As a visual medium television, sometimes inadvertently, has drawn attention to physical appearance. It has been unusual to see on television those of either sex who do not conform to prevailing notions of female and male beauty. Scraps of evidence suggest that physical appearance is important in deciding whether women appear on television. In 2002 Kate

Adie, who had been employed as a BBC television news correspondent on such dangerous assignments as Libya, Tiananmen Square, the Gulf War and Kosovo, complained that only women with 'cute faces and cute bottoms with nothing else in between' were being appointed as news correspondents, although Lindsey Hilsum, diplomatic correspondent for Channel 4 News, recalled meeting 'more brainless but beautiful young male reporters on the road'.[36] When the historian Bettany Hughes became one of the first women historians to present a television history series in 2002, Maggie Brown of the *Guardian* commented that there was 'no point ignoring the obvious. Hughes . . . is handsome, and a natural communicator.' 'Nigella Lawson hits ancient Greece', the comment of a male television history presenter, shows that some assumed that Hughes had been given the series because of her looks.[37] It is impossible to establish how many people may have been refused work in television because they were not considered sufficiently attractive to the other sex.

In the 1940s and 1950s BBC television's presentation of sexuality was still prudish and influenced by its Reithian tradition of puritan restraint. Initially, ITV was equally reserved in its presentation of sexuality. In 1960, after consulting the ITA, Associated-Rediffusion decided not to screen the play *On Easy Terms* in which a salesman tried to seduce a housewife. This led Philip Purser, a television critic for the *News Chronicle*, to write that the ITA deplored anything 'politically or diplomatically tricky, violence, and, above all, sex'.[38] In the 1960s, and particularly the late 1960s, the portrayal of sex on television became more liberal, though only a little more liberal when viewed from the perspective of today. In 1966 the ITA, for instance, decreed that a scene from David Jacobs's *Words and Music* would have to be cut because a dancer's skirt was too short for a programme being broadcast at 7 p.m.[39] The date of the first female nude scene in a television drama broadcast in Britain is uncertain but was probably in the late 1960s. *Up the Junction*, Nell Dunn's BBC Wednesday Play broadcast in 1965, was concerned with the sexual promiscuity of young working-class women in London and was considered innovative and daring but it contained no nude scenes. In 1971 Dennis Potter's *Casanova*, a six-part television play, included nude scenes and realistic simulations of the sex act. As complaints about this did not mention that it was the first television drama to include nude scenes, nude scenes had probably been screened in some dramas before then.

During the 1970s and 1980s the depiction on television of sexual behaviour became less restrained, though some material shown today was not permitted even in the 1980s. In 1973 the decision of the IBA to allow a documentary about the American artist Andy Warhol, which included four-letter words and a scene in which a naked woman used her nipples as a paint brush, created much controversy when Ross McWhirter, a member of the National Viewers' and Listeners' Association, failed to persuade the courts that the IBA had not observed its statutory obligation to prevent the broadcasting of material offensive to public feeling, decency and good taste. The Border and Anglia ITV companies were reluctant to screen it and Sir Hartley Shawcross, the chairman of Thames TV and a former Labour Attorney-General, expressed his personal distaste for the programme.[40] In the late 1970s the BBC abandoned making Ian McEwan's play *Solid Geometry* because the central prop was a nine-inch penis preserved in formaldehyde. Channel 4 showed another production of this in 2002. In 1999 John Willis, who had been Director of Programmes for Channel 4, recalled that in the 1980s already clothed nipples were covered with plasters in cold studios to avoid stimulating viewers.[41] In 1983 the IBA would not allow Channel 4 to broadcast Bertolucci's *Last Tango in Paris*, which was thought to have artistic merit but contained many scenes of sexual intercourse between a naked man and woman, but this was shown on BBC4 in June 2003.[42]

Research for the Broadcasting Standards Council shows that depictions of sexual activity and nudity increased on terrestrial television in the 1990s. In one week in 1992 the four terrestrial channels screened 277 programmes and 524 commercials. These contained fifty-seven scenes of sexual activity. In more than half the sexual activity consisted of kissing, but a quarter depicted the coital act. All the sexual activity was heterosexual.[43] A different sample of terrestrial programmes in the later 1990s found that the proportion of scenes involving kissing and the coital act remained around the same between 1997 and 1999, although the total number of sex scenes increased by around 15 per cent. Incidents of nudity rose from 63 in 1993 to 165 in 1999. In 1999 nearly 40 per cent of programmes in the sample included talk about sex, almost twice the percentage in 1993.[44] Another survey for the Broadcasting Standards Commission showed that between 1993 and 1996 the proportion of scenes involving sex shown in soaps, all shown before 9 p.m. and which attracted very large audiences, had risen from 8 per cent to 23 per cent.[45]

In the 1990s and early twenty-first century, terrestrial channels have broadcast documentaries about sexual behaviour and workers in the sex industry as well as programmes such as *Sex Tips for Girls* that concentrate on improving one's sex life. Some would probably describe programmes such as *Ibiza Uncovered* about young adults on holiday as little more than soft porn or voyeuristic television. The American-made comedy *Sex and the City* was more openly concerned with sex than comedies in previous decades. In the late 1990s Dawn Airey was reported to be trying to build an audience for Channel 5 by showing 'football, fucking and films'. In 2000 Channel 4 was the first terrestrial broadcaster to screen a film of actual sexual intercourse rather than a simulation.[46] Some terrestrial broadcasters wanted to limit the depiction of sex. In 1992 Will Wyatt, the Managing Director of BBC Television, reminded Alan Yentob, Controller of BBC1, and Jonathan Powell that the level of sexual frankness of three recent dramas had been 'at the outside limit of what we can transmit' and did not want it to be taken for granted in other programmes. He felt that showing a naked breast in *Spender*, a popular police series, had been neither right nor necessary.[47] In 1996 Bruce Gyngell, the Chief Executive of Yorkshire TV and the former head of TV-am, refused to transmit *The Good Sex Guide* and *God's Gift*, described as a 'raunchy dating show', because he considered that such broadcasting 'demeans those who take part and saddest of all, demeans the audience'. Gyngell thought that ITV 'had now reached the stage where so-called entertainment, once found only in the seedy cellars and basements of Soho clip joints, is paraded on mainstream television as if it were respectable'.[48]

Satellite and cable channels that screened pornographic material were launched in the 1990s. In 1992 the Adult Channel was the first to start broadcasting. At its start it had 6,000 subscribers but soon claimed to be receiving 8,000 subscription applications per day. By 1998 five of the 170 channels licensed by the ITC were described in the *ITC Factfile* as providing adult viewing. All were subscription channels. The content of such channels was soft porn. Paul Dunthorne, channel controller for the Fantasy Channel said in 1999 that 'No mainstream channel would schedule what we are allowed to – and quite rightly so.' When the Adult Channel began broadcasting, the sociologist and broadcaster Laurie Taylor described its content as a 'typically British view of sex. Knickers pulled off, double entendres and pneumatic women. You expect Frankie Howerd or Barbara Windsor to enter at any moment.' The film-maker Michael Winner found it 'inestimably tedious and silly' with 'nothing other than the most dopily faked attempts at sexual intercourse'.[49] Rita Lewis, who ran the Playboy Channel that started broadcasting in 1995, said that it would show 'nothing . . . that is deviant or weird or degrading' but would be therapeutic and enliven the sex lives of viewers.[50] While distinguishing between hard and soft pornography is a matter of taste, governments and the ITC have moved against what they regarded as hard-core pornographic channels. In 1993 the Red Hot Dutch channel was outlawed and in 1995 Virginia Bottomley, the National Heritage Secretary, made it a criminal offence to supply smart cards and decoders for TV Erotica, a Scandinavian pornography channel.[51]

The increasing sexual content of television was part of a wider shift in public attitudes. Greater openness about sexual behaviour was not restricted to television but was found in all art forms. Cinema film was often more frank in its portrayal of sex than television. As a result of the *Lady Chatterley's Lover* trial in 1960 detailed descriptions of the full range of sexuality became common if not de rigueur for novelists. Ending the Lord Chancellor's power to censor theatre plays in 1968 led to sex being presented with more frankness on the stage. In some respects television's depiction of sex may have illustrated a less puritanical attitude to sex in society at large. The marketing of the contraceptive pill in 1962 and the legalisation of abortion in 1967 have been seen as encouraging more relaxed attitudes to sexuality, which also reflected the sexual freedom associated with the rise of the so-called permissive society in the 1960s. In 1984 a MORI poll found that over 80 per cent of women aged between eighteen and twenty-four were in favour of pre-marital intercourse.[52] Popular newspapers were more open about sexual matters in the 1990s than they had been in the 1950s, though in the 1950s much of the content of the *News of the World* had consisted of reports of court cases with a sexual dimension. Stories about the sexual lives of celebrities were part of the staple fare of the tabloid press by the 1990s.

From the 1960s many who worked in television wanted a less puritanical approach to sex. Being allowed to use sexual material was regarded as a necessary form of artistic licence and beneficial for society at large. Arthur fforde, Chairman of the BBC Board of Governors from 1957 to 1964, believed that those in authority at the BBC had a duty to assure 'those creative members of the BBC staff, who must take the daily, hourly, and even instantaneous decisions . . . that measure of freedom, independence and élan without which the arts do not flourish'[53] – which could be taken to mean that restrictions on programme content should be kept to a minimum. In 1964 Charles Hill, chairman of the ITA, after emphasising that the ITA had a remit from Parliament to prevent the broadcasting of what offended 'good taste and decency', said that 'a dramatist should not be debarred from dealing with the uglier side of life' but added that 'we don't want too much of the sordid and the off-beat' and asked 'Just where *do* you draw the line?'[54] In 1971, Lord Aylestone, Hill's successor as chairman of the ITA, argued that television could not allow itself 'to be used simply to reflect the embalmed taste of the nineteen-thirties, never involving itself in the ecstasies and the agonies of the seventies about sex . . . what it must try to do is to try to keep in step with what people want to say'.[55] Director-General of the BBC Hugh Greene said in a speech that his successor Charles Curran helped to draft

> I believe that broadcasters have a duty to take into account, to be ahead of public opinion, rather than always wait upon it . . . great broadcasting organisations, with their immense powers of patronage for writers and artists, should not neglect to cultivate young writers who may, by many, be considered 'too advanced' or 'shocking'. . . . Relevance is the key – relevance to the audience, and to the tide of opinion in society. Outrage is wrong. Shock may be good. Provocation can be healthy and indeed socially imperative.[56]

Often those who worked in television had little time for those who objected to a less puritanical depiction of sex. For some programme makers, broadcasting sexual material of a nature that had previously not been shown was considered a form of prestige. Writing in *The Times* in 1973, Greene, looking back over his time as Director-General of the BBC, admitted that some 'plays, selected for television reflected a changed attitude towards sexual morality and were thought, perhaps correctly upon occasion, to imply a contempt for earlier standards'.[57] In 1977 the Annan Committee reported that 'Too often producers, scriptwriters and comedians deliberately exploit sex in order to win praise from their professional colleagues for being daring and anti-authoritarian. What passes for exploration is in fact exploitation.'[58] In 1999 Julian Petley, an academic, suspected that sex was 'seeping into areas which many find inappropriate . . . because programme-makers constantly test the limits of the permissible in an overly-nannyish system'.[59]

Many in broadcasting were contemptuous of those who complained about the sexual frankness of television. Hugh Greene accused those who protested at what they saw as 'unnecessary dirt, gratuitous sex, excessive violence' of threatening 'a dangerous form of censorship – censorship which works by causing artists and writers not to take risks, not to undertake those adventures of the spirit which must be at the heart of every truly new creative work'.[60] Tony Benn in 1971 told a House of Commons Select Committee that, while he did not agree with the views of Mary Whitehouse, the most prominent member of the Viewers' and Listeners' Association, the BBC's response to her had seemed 'grossly offensive'.[61] In the House of Lords Lord Annan said that it was common for the 'intelligentsia and the broadcasters' to sneer at Mary Whitehouse. The television writer Lord Willis retorted that Whitehouse and her followers were 'reactionary in the extreme. They are the floggers, the bring-back-the-censorship people. They are the worst kind of people . . . My opinion is that she is a very dangerous woman.'[62]

In the 1990s some television channel controllers admitted to screening late-night sex programmes to boost viewing figures. In 1998 Tom Leonard, a *Daily Telegraph* media journalist, wrote that the 'obsession with "frank and revealing" programmes about sex has led to accusations that terrestrial channels saw it as a rating-grabbing solution to competition from satellite, cable and digital TV'.[63] In 2000 Channel 4 was alleged to have shown more nudity in *Big Brother* to prevent viewers becoming bored.[64] Dawn Airey claimed that Channel 5 received 17 per cent of the national television audience, nearly three times its average proportion of the national audience, when it screened *Sex and Shopping*, a programme which the Broadcasting Standards Commission condemned as 'tacky'.[65] Michael Svennig's research showed that some of Channel 5's late-night adult programmes such as *Compromising Situations* and *Hotline* added about a quarter of a million viewers to audiences of 1 million.[66] Paul Dunthorne of the Fantasy Channel complained in 1999 that much late-night viewing on Channels 4 and 5 was 'unadulterated porn. It's often not put in context and it's not erotica – it's actually porn, and it's free-to-air.' When the Bravo satellite channel which was available free to subscribers to BSkyB began screening *Erotic Confessions* nightly at 11.30 p.m., Catherine Mackin, its head of programming, was reported to have said that 'It goes without saying that erotica answers a very obvious demand. You know it will work in your schedule so you put it on – simple as that. It's not exactly a cynical exercise in engineering ratings – it works, so you show it.'[67] In 1999 Andrea Millwood Hargrave who had investigated in detail the attitudes to sex on television for the Broadcasting

Standards Commission found that nearly three-quarters of her sample of viewers thought that sex was shown 'purely because the broadcasters want to increase programme ratings'.[68]

The low cost of sex programmes, especially when the fragmentation of audiences was increasing competition for advertising, may have encouraged their showing. In 1999 erotica consumed 2 per cent of Channel 5's air time but accounted for only 1 per cent of its programme budget. *Broadcast* calculated in 1999 that an 'adult' programme cost between £500 and £1,250 but could rise to over £3,000 for a big premium. The Fantasy Channel was thought to be spending between £3,000 and £12,000 per hour for its broadcasts. Many erotic programmes were acquired from overseas and dialogue had to be dubbed. Dubbing a film with a lot of dialogue could cost £2,500.[69] In 1997 Channel 4's sports programmes, the cheapest genre of programmes shown on BBC1, BBC2, ITV and Channel 4, cost on average £30,000 per hour.[70]

Television and Gay and Lesbian Identities

The proportion of the population who are homosexual or bisexual is not known for certain. Modern thinking suggests that, rather than being sharply distinct, homosexuality and heterosexuality should be regarded as opposite poles of a continuum and that most people's sexual natures are somewhere between these poles. Educated guesses estimate that between 5 per cent and 10 per cent of the population are predominantly homosexual, though higher figures have been suggested. If 5 per cent of the population is homosexual, then they have been under-represented in television dramas and comedies. The criminal status of male homosexual relations until 1967 discouraged unambiguous portrayals of gays on television before that date. *Are You Being Served?*, a report by the Lesbian and Gay Broadcasting Project, found that gays and lesbians appeared in only nine of the 268 hours, or 3.38 per cent, of all television broadcast on terrestrial television over one week in 1986.[71] Research for the Broadcasting Standards Commission found that BBC2 was the terrestrial channel with the highest proportion of homosexual and bisexual people who spoke on it in 2000, but this figure was only 1.1 per cent, whereas that for BBC1, the channel with the lowest number, was 0.2 per cent. These statistics included those who could be implied to be homosexual or bisexual as well as those who were openly so, but how many may have concealed their sexual identities was not known. Fiction, light entertainment and factual programmes accounted for nearly two-thirds of all programmes in which homosexual or bisexual people appeared.[72] David Wyatt's listing of the explicitly gay, lesbian, bisexual and transgendered who have appeared in at least three episodes of English-language comedy series, dramas and soaps shows that the presence of homosexuals in these programme genres has grown since 1960. Series made in Britain in the 1960s included only one homosexual character. There were twelve between 1971 and 1980 but eighty-five between 1991 and 2000, though this included twelve in *Queer as Folk*. Wyatt's list omitted programmes with homosexual characters made overseas but broadcast in Britain.[73]

Programmes aimed primarily at gay and lesbian viewers increased in the 1980s and 1990s but formed only a tiny fraction of all television programming. In 1979 John Birt, Controller for Features and Current Affairs at London Weekend Television, created the London Minorities Unit to prepare programmes for London's ethnic minority and gay population. Under its auspices Michael Attwell produced in 1980 *Gay Life*, which surveyed aspects of the gay scene in London and was probably the first series about gays to be broadcast on terrestrial television in Britain.[74] It was not shown nationally. Channel 4, with its remit to cater for minorities, led to more programmes featuring the interests of gays and lesbians. In 1989 it broadcast *Out on Tuesday*. Channel 4 screened *Camp Christmas* in 1994 and in 1995 its *Dyke TV* was the first terrestrial television series screened nationally about lesbian life and issues in the UK, although in 1993 a lesbian relationship had been a *Brookside* storyline. *Brookside* was reputed to have included the first lesbian kiss on British television in 1993, though John Mortimer's *Voyage Round My Father*, made by Thames in 1982, had included a lesbian kissing scene. In 1999 Channel 4 screened an eight-part mini-series *Queer as Folk* about the lives of eight young gay men in Manchester, which concentrated on them as individual characters rather than on gay issues. The Broadcasting Standards Commission censured Channel 4 for including an explicit scene in *Queer as Folk* of a schoolboy having sex with an adult man. The Commission also ruled that scenes involving under-age sex and three men having sex together 'exceeded acceptable boundaries'.[75] The BBC screened *That Gay Show* on its satellite channel BBC Choice in 2001, but before this it had screened gay programmes made by other production houses, such as Planet 24's *Gaytime*

TV.[76] *Rhona*, broadcast on BBC2 in 2000, was probably the first lesbian television comedy screened by a terrestrial television channel in Britain. Channel 4 in 1994 broadcast the first terrestrial television commercial in Britain aimed at gays, although gays had figured in an advertisement in 1982.[77] Cable and satellite television have had few channels targeted at gay and lesbian viewers. In 1994 Gay TV, a hardcore gay pornographic satellite channel, began broadcasting to Britain and by 1998 the ITC had licensed the Rainbow Television Network, which was to broadcast light entertainment for a gay audience, but these seem to have been on air for only a short time.[78] In 2003 subscribers to BSkyB could access TDC2, a satellite dating channel for gays, lesbians and bisexuals.

It is not certain who was the first person to admit on television to being homosexual. In 1973 a man who was to become a Labour councillor in Hackney mentioned that he was gay on Thames television.[79] In the 1990s some of those from the world of television were open about being homosexual or bisexual. Graham Norton, Julian Clary and Paul O'Grady have built their careers through an ostentatious celebration of gayness. At the same time other broadcasting figures such as the historian David Starkey and the comedian Stephen Fry have made no secret of being homosexual but have not exploited this in their television work. Greater openness about their homosexuality may indicate that society has become more tolerant of sexual diversity, though this is almost impossible to measure, and instances of homophobia are still easy to find. Will Wyatt has recalled that Graeme MacDonald, Controller of BBC2 from 1983 to 1987, was proud of being the first openly gay to be a channel controller but worried that the tabloid press might make a story of his homosexuality.[80] In 2003 two males kissing on *Casualty* outraged the *Sun* and the *Daily Mail*, Britain's highest-circulation newspapers.[81] Michael Grade, who had worked in television as a scheduler and channel controller from 1973 until 1997, cannot recall anyone's career being impeded because of homosexuality, though Lord Hartwell, the chairman of the *Telegraph* Newspaper Group, resigned as a director of London Weekend Television when it set up its London Minorities Unit.[82] There have been few public complaints that homosexuals have colonised certain areas of television and restricted career opportunities for heterosexuals.

Representations on television of male homosexuals have changed over the past thirty years. Stereotyped homosexuals, and particularly the highly camp or effeminate male, were often stock characters of television comedy. Among the more notorious were Mr Humphries, played by John Inman in *Are You Being Served?* and Bombardier 'Gloria' Beaumont, played by Melvyn Hayes in *It Ain't Half Hot Mum*, comedy series that had huge popularity in the 1970s, and Guy Siner's Lieutenant Gruber in *'Allo 'Allo*, which the BBC broadcast from 1984 to 1992. The character Tom Farrell played by James Dreyfus in *Gimme, Gimme, Gimme*, first broadcast in 1999, shows that the camp gay male has not disappeared from situation comedy on terrestrial television in Britain. Stereotypical butch lesbians have also appeared in sitcoms, but none has quite achieved the star following of the Humphries and Beaumont characters. Openly gay but not camp characters, such as the gay chef in *Fawlty Towers*, were less common.

The Naked Civil Servant, a ninety-minute dramatisation of the highly effeminate male homosexual Quentin Crisp, screened in 1975 by Thames, was possibly the first sympathetic television presentation of a gay character that received widespread artistic acclaim. The principal characters of crime series have rarely been homosexual. In the 1990s the British-made series *Taggart* and *Burnside*, both shown on ITV, included gay detectives but they did not have the chief role. Within the past two decades, soap operas have included gays and lesbians and presented them as individuals rather than stereotypes. This can be linked to a conviction among those who work in soaps that their popularity and credibility depends on having some likeness to 'real' life, and including homosexual characters may have reflected a growing familiarity with homosexuality among the general population. It is also possible that the constant need for new storylines led soaps to include gay characters. *Brookside* in 1985 was the first British soap to have an openly gay character. The following year a gay character was introduced to *EastEnders* but *Coronation Street*, Britain's longest-running soap, did not have an openly non-heterosexual character until a transsexual was introduced in 1998. In 1995 a hairdresser had been introduced to *Coronation Street* who was meant to appear gay. A spokesperson for Granada said that the 'sexuality of this character is implicit rather than explicit although he is very flamboyant and colourful'.[83] Eleven homosexual characters appeared in *Emmerdale* in the 1990s. In 1991 Christine Geraghty pointed out, however, that, with *Brookside* and *EastEnders*, homosexuality tended to be treated as a 'problem issue', with homosexual characters being used almost didactically to explain their position. Homosexual experience tended to be represented as 'homogeneous and univocal'. Geraghty found that gay relationships were not presented with the full-blooded drama of heterosexual passion and she speculated whether a gay relationship in *EastEnders* had been ended with one of the characters becoming straight because 'the issue had got too much for a programme with a huge family audience'.[84]

Gays, lesbians and bisexuals criticised their representation on television. In the early 1980s, during an LWT series about male and female homosexuals, a group of lesbians picketed the LWT Tower with placards proclaiming 'LESBIANS ARE PEOPLE TOO'. They demanded separate programmes from those for gay men. Sado-masochistic lesbians wanted their own programmes, distinct from those for other lesbians. Black lesbians 'objected to the obvious prejudice and absurdity of lumping them together with gay men (either black or white), or white lesbians (either sadistic or masochistic)'. Others wanted to be called 'dykes' instead of 'lesbians'.[85] In 1980 Roger Baker pointed out that what he called the 'Gay Image Brigade', gays who tried to form relationships that replicated the heterosexual, mythical ideal of 'middle-class respectability, monogamy and falling in love, of upward mobility, and presenting a normal appearance to the world', did not like television plays because they gave 'a bad image of gays'. The 'Gay Image Brigade' wanted to hide such images and persisted in 'refusing to recognise the diversity of the gay experience'.[86] The gay press often complained that gay relationships were treated less frankly than heterosexual relationships. Homosexual kisses and scenes of homosexual lovers in bed, but not those between heterosexuals, were cut from the omnibus editions of soaps because children could be viewing. *Capital Gay* asked in 1988 why no gays had appeared on *Blind Date*.[87] In the same year Jonathan Sanders argued that gay men on television were 'almost totally de-sexualised. They rarely even touch each other, and any kiss is just a peck on the cheek or forehead (usually delivered when the peckee is ill or upset).'[88]

Homosexuals could also be highly critical of programmes targeted at them. Megan Radclyffe of *Gay Times* wrote that *Dyke TV* was 'based on a metropolitan world of under 25's who wear lipstick and will rave to the grave. I can only hope that (in future) there'll be even more acceleration towards normal dykes, rural dykes, proper dykes (old, dead, new whatever).'[89] In 1999 Radclyffe had written of the third series of *Gaytime TV*:

I really did think it couldn't possibly get any worse. Yet another title sequence and another new set – full of brightly coloured globes, hexagons, bottles and steel borders – and an unequivocal club ambience. A new trendy, fit audience swarmed all over the place . . . Obviously well-trained by the floor manager, they whooped like baboons, but always a second or two too late . . . alas and alack, the whole affair for me was summed up for me by the titles of *Gaytime*'s weekly soap, *Scene in Brum* (the heady and oh-so-electrifying tale of the expansion of Angel's Café Bar in that very same megalopolis) where the manager was holding up a plank of wood . . . I must go, I feel quite sick now.[90]

Kristian Digby, the main presenter and director of *That Gay Show*, had a different but no less hostile view of *Gaytime TV*, which he condemned as the 'religious programming of gay television. It was so politically correct! . . . God forbid you would leave a section of the gay community out.' Digby maintained that *That Gay Show* would be 'certainly a departure from soft furnishings . . . we are doing something quite different and very *edgy*. This is far more cutting edge.' Yet, to Rupert Smith of *Gay Times*, Digby's promise of appealing to gay young men with fashion and lifestyle sounded 'like it's going to be a bit fluffy'.[91]

Homophobia and Television

In some respects Britain has become less intolerant of homosexuality in the age of television. In England and Wales sexual relations between consenting males were decriminalised in 1967, but this was extended to Scotland only in 1980 and to Northern Ireland in 1982. The age of consent for male homosexual sex was lowered to eighteen in 1993, but in 1999 the House of Lords refused to equalise the age of consent for heterosexual and homosexual sex. In 1977 Maureen Colquhoun became the first MP to reveal in public that she was a lesbian and in 1984 Chris Smith was the first MP to declare in public that he was gay. In 1997 Smith was the first openly gay politician to become a Cabinet minister. Yet there has been considerable evidence of hostility towards homosexuals. When Maureen Colquhoun was facing moves to deselect her as a Labour parliamentary candidate, she was disappointed by the lack of support from the national leadership of the Labour Party. In 1982 homosexual smears against Peter Tatchell were important in his loss of the previously safe Labour seat of Bermondsey, though Tatchell himself maintained that opposition within the Labour Party to his left-wing community politics and the standing of a 'Real Labour' candidate were more important causes of his defeat.[92] The spread of AIDS in the 1980s and resentment over initiatives such as the Greater London Council's spending £750,000 to establish the London Lesbian and Gay Centre provoked waves of homophobia in the press. In 1989 the police recorded over 2,000 offences of 'indecency between males', a figure close to that of the mid-1950s, when sexual relations between males were illegal. At least twenty-three men in 1989 were jailed for having sex with males aged between sixteen and twenty-one.[93] Section 28 of the 1988 Local Government Act, which prohibited local authorities from promoting homosexuality and banned state schools from teaching homosexuality as an alternative form of family relationship, was still in force at the start of 2003.

Television played little part in the campaigns to decriminalise male homosexual relationships. The recommendations of the Wolfenden Committee in 1957 that sexual relations between male homosexuals aged over twenty-one should no longer be a criminal offence were reported on news bulletins, but the League for Homosexual Law Reform was given few opportunities to advocate a change in the law on television. In the ten years between the Wolfenden Report and the legalisation of adult male homosexual relationships, no television programme or series provoked massive public interest in the legal status of homosexuality similar to that taken in homelessness following *Cathy Come Home*. Representatives of the Committee for Homosexual Equality, formed in 1969 to campaign for gay sex to have the same legal status as heterosexual sex, and the Scottish Minorities Group, also formed in 1969, which called for the decriminalisation of sex between men in Scotland, spoke on television current affairs programmes but so too did their opponents. Stephen Jeffery-Poulter's *Peers, Queers and Commons*, a study of the campaigns for homosexual law reform since the 1950s, scarcely mentions television.[94]

Whether television led to greater acceptance of homosexuality is unclear. After monitoring all radio and television programmes for one week in 1986, the Lesbian and Gay Broadcasting Project concluded that 'it is clear that the broadcasting media are reinforcing prejudice and perpetuating ignorance'.[95] Yet television rarely adopted a stridently hostile tone similar to that of much of the popular press. In 1993 the BBC Producer Guidelines specified that lesbians and gays were entitled to be portrayed accurately and not as stereotypes.[96] Television did not follow the tabloid press in calling AIDS the 'gay plague'. Comedy series continued to present stereotypes of highly camp gays, but in the 1980s and 1990s the greater number of lesbian and gay characters in television dramas may have raised public awareness of the varieties of homosexuality. Two-thirds of an opinion survey by Channel 4 in 1987 did not want gays to have their own programmes,[97] but opinion samples for the Broadcasting Standards Commission showed that between 1992 and 1998 those who thought it acceptable to show homosexual relationships on television because they were part of life rose from 46 per cent to 58 per cent.[98] In 2001 Rupert Smith wrote in *Gay Times* that nothing had so 'disarmed the endemic homophobia of the British media as much as *Big Brother* and *Pop Idol*' and that such programmes were 'the nearest we'll ever get to a referendum on homosexuality'. He believed that reality television had become 'a conduit through which gay people can present themselves to the world, get famous and knock out a few prejudices along the way . . . Being gay is no longer something to hide; it's a very canny way of standing out from the crowd . . . Nowadays it's safe to assume that anyone attractive and witty on a reality TV show could be gay.'[99]

Programmes with homosexual content may have been intended to promote greater tolerance of homosexuality, but they could provoke outrage and may have stimulated homophobia, though there is no method of proving this. In 1983 the tabloid press attacked Channel 4 for showing *One in Five*, an exploration of gay lifestyles. The Conservative MP John Carlisle described it as 'TV for minorities indeed . . . A large section of the public is already thoroughly disgusted by the low standards on Channel 4 . . . The channel is an offence to public taste and decency, and should be drummed off the air forthwith.'[100] The comments of the *Daily Mail* columnist Paul Johnson in the 1990s showed that for some, gay and lesbian sex was perverted and ought never to have been screened. He wrote

Lesbians, homosexuals and sex perverts, necrophiliacs, fanatical anti-papists, students of scatology and animal cruelty, people who like watching other people being grossly humiliated and abused and who want to see the man whose penis was cut off by an angry wife – these minorities, if that is the word for them, are well catered for by Channel 4.[101]

Television and Changing Sexual Behaviour

Statistics about sexual activity are notoriously unreliable, but probably few would disagree that sexual behaviour in Britain has been transformed since the 1940s and 1950s. Impressionistic evidence suggests that premarital sex and having sex with a wider range of partners have become more acceptable, though many still disapprove of such behaviour. Many have accused television of encouraging sexual licence. The continuing insistence of governments and regulatory bodies that sexually explicit scenes and strong language cannot be shown before 9 p.m. suggests that politicians believe that a large proportion of the public is convinced that television can influence the behaviour of at least the young. The National Viewers' and Listeners' Association was convinced that television could change sexual attitudes. In 1965 the Clean UP TV campaign, the precursor of the NVLA, accused the BBC of employing those 'whose ideas and advice pander to the lowest in human nature and accompany this with a stream of suggestive and erotic plays which present promiscuity, infidelity and drinking as normal and inevitable'.[102] By the 1990s Christian morality figured less often in condemnations of the television presentation of sex.

Opposition to the presentation of sex on television has been part of campaigns against pornography in general. Feminists such as Andrea Dworkin argued that pornography degraded women and reduced them to commercial objects, but not all women took this view. Some argued that, where women decided for themselves to take part in what others considered pornographic, this was an expression of female emancipation, of women choosing how their bodies could be used. When women were consumers of pornography, they were entering a cultural sphere previously dominated by men. The noted feminist Erica Jong, whose writings had pioneered sexual freedom for women, was often branded a traitor by other feminists for supporting pornography. Yet Jong also pointed out that it was wrong for women to imagine that because of equal pay legislation and because of 'women talking dirty on *Sex and the City*', the television comedy show that celebrated sexual promiscuity for women, 'we don't need to fight any more'.[103]

The degree of public opposition to sex on television has never been clear. Many thousands have signed petitions protesting about sex on television but, as the supporters have rarely prepared counter-petitions, this cannot be taken to be a scientific measure of public attitudes. The fact that Winston Churchill's private member's bill, which would have listed sex acts that could not be shown on television, was not passed in 1985, despite the support of Margaret Thatcher, suggests that most MPs did not believe that there was massive public demand for such legislation. Had viewers refused to watch programmes with sexual content, it is unlikely that the numbers of such programmes would have grown. Between November 1996 and the end of January 1997, the Broadcasting Standards Council received far more complaints about bad language than about sex in television and radio programmes, but the total number of complaints about violence, sex, language and issues of taste and decency were less than a hundred – although, of course, some who felt strongly about a programme may not have complained to the Council.[104] In a survey carried out by the Broadcasting Standards Commission in 1999, just over a third of respondents said that there was too much sex on television but even more thought that there was too much sex in newspapers. Over three-quarters thought that sexual activity could be depicted on television when they felt that it was genuinely part of a storyline. Only 12 per cent of those surveyed were more concerned about sex than about violence or bad language on television.[105]

Academic researchers are far from agreeing that television has affected sexual mores. As with almost all attitudes and behaviour, it is virtually impossible to separate the impacts of television from those of other agencies. Age, gender, occupation, peer groups, religious beliefs, education and family background probably mean that different individuals respond to televised depictions of sex in different ways. Barrie Gunter has pointed out that little research has been conducted into the possible effects of the presentation of sex by different programme genres.[106] The context of how a sexual act is presented may well influence how it is perceived and appraised. Long-term exposure to televised sex may gradually weaken resistance to some sex acts, but measuring changes in attitudes covering decades is fraught with practical difficulties. There has been much concern about whether television may have encouraged rape and other forms of sexual violence but, by highlighting the effects of sexual violence on its victims, television may provoke revulsion at such behaviour and so discourage it. The inability of researchers to produce unequivocal proof that television influences sexual behaviour does not mean that it has had no impact on sexual attitudes and behaviour. Its most profound effect may have been to make the public more knowledgeable about sexual matters by revealing the varieties of sexual activity.

Chapter 7

TELEVISION, RACE AND ETHNICITY

Since the Second World War Britain has become a multi-ethnic society. Small communities of those who were not white had lived in Britain for generations, but the beginning of African-Caribbean migration to Britain in 1948 and from southern Asia in the 1950s and 1960s caused the numbers of those who were not white to expand, particularly in England. Between 1991 and 2001 those who described themselves as not white increased from less than 6 per cent of the total population of England to 8.6 per cent. In 2001, 1.3 million were black, 2.1 million of Indian, Pakistani or Bangladeshi descent and over 800,000 had other Asian origins. Around half of England's ethnic minority population lived in the London area, with other concentrations in the big provincial cities, the towns of the Midlands, and what had been the textile towns of Lancashire and Yorkshire.

In the nineteenth and early twentieth centuries, race was thought to be a scientific register of innate variations between human populations that originated in different parts of the globe. Physical characteristics, such as facial features and the shape of the head, but especially skin coloration, were taken as the signifiers of race, and different races were believed to have different intellectual capacities. In recent years the status of race as a scientific concept has been questioned. The intellectual capacities within all populations are so varied that physical characteristics do not indicate that one population has higher mental abilities than another. Use of the term 'ethnicity' reflects a realisation that the differing lifestyles of differing populations are the product of culture rather than inherited qualities, though the words 'ethnicity' and 'ethnic' are sometimes used as politically correct euphemisms for 'race' and 'racial'. Everyday conversation, on the other hand, shows that there is still a deep-seated belief among many who are white that humanity can be divided into distinct races on the basis of skin colour and that races with the lighter complexions have greater mental ability and are more 'civilised'.[1]

The expansion of Britain's ethnic minority population has not been free of conflict. Those who are not white have complained of racial prejudice and social deprivation. Their incomes, employment prospects and housing have been inferior to those of most whites. Racial disturbances occurred in Notting Hill in 1958, Brixton, Southall and Liverpool in 1981, Broadwater Farm in 1985, Bradford in 1995 and Oldham and Burnley in 2001. Since the 1960s the control of immigration has been a subject of political controversy. Yet one can also show that the ethnic minorities have made a massive contribution to the economy and public services in Britain, especially in London, and that they have enriched Britain's cultural diversity. The rise of a multi-ethnic Britain has coincided with the expansion of television, and television's relationship with the various ethnic minorities in Britain is one register for the extent of racial harmony and conflict in Britain.

The vocabulary for describing ethnic groups in Britain can be confusing. 'Black' can refer to all of those who are not white, but it also has a more restricted reference to those who have some ancestral roots in Africa south of the Sahara. Whites often describe those of mixed parentage as black. 'Asian' is often used to mean only those with ancestral origins in India, Pakistan and Bangladesh. Where the phrase 'non-white' is used in the following pages to describe those who are not white, it is not meant to imply that whiteness is the skin colour against which all other complexions should be judged. 'Black' will refer to those of black-African ancestry, including those who came to Britain from the Caribbean.

Television as a White Institution

Little data have been released to the general public about the extent of watching television among ethnic minorities, but it is widely assumed that the programmes that are most popular with white viewers are also highly popular with black and Asian viewers. In the mid-1970s, when only television broadcast from stations in Britain could be received, over half of Asians in Leicester watched television for more than two hours per day on average. Even those with little understanding of English watched television every day.[2] This may indicate that those from the ethnic minorities had not found television to be more racist than what they encountered in other areas of life. Had those from the ethnic minorities thought that television was objectionably racist, it seems unlikely that they would have watched it so

much. In the 1980s and 1990s English-language newspapers aimed at the
ethnic minorities, such as the *Voice*, *Caribbean Times* and *Asian Times*,
highlighted instances of racial prejudice in Britain but mentioned this in
television only rarely – which suggests that such prejudice in television was
not considered very important. An opinion survey carried out by the *Sun* in
1988 found that nearly two-thirds of those from the ethnic minorities
thought that television programmes and advertisements did little to help
them, though a quarter did not object to television's image of them.[3] In the
mid-1990s a study of more than 350 ethnic minority television viewers
carried out for the BBC found that they did not feel that they were 'valued as
a specific viewing public' or that 'their viewing needs were being met'.[4]

The control and regulation of television have always been largely a white
male monopoly, though the presence of those who are not white among those
who control and regulate television has grown over the past quarter of a
century. In 1969 Learie Constantine, an African-Caribbean born in Trinidad
who had achieved international fame as a test-match cricketer between the
wars, was the first black governor of the BBC. In 2003 the twelve governors
of the BBC included one of Asian and one of African-Caribbean descent. Only
two members of the ITA/IBA were not white and the first of these was
appointed in 1989, only months before the IBA was abolished. Pranlal Sheth,
who had become a member of the IBA in 1990, was among the original
members of the ITC. In 2002 all members of the BBC Executive Board were
white. All BBC's television channel controllers have been white. No head of
an ITV company has been non-white and all but a handful of directors of
ITV companies have been white. The chief executives of Channels 4 and 5
and of BSkyB have been white. A report published by the Broadcasting
Standards Commission in 2002 found that only a fifth of a sample of those
from the ethnic minorities who worked in television felt that the number of
ethnic minority staff with decision-making roles in television had increased
over the previous five years.[5] The white presence among those who control
television is probably no stronger than in other large organisations in Britain.

Statistics about the ethnic backgrounds of those who have produced,
directed, written and provided the technical support for television
programmes, and of how far these may have changed over time, are scarce.
The Black Media Workers' Association claimed in 1983 that only thirty-five
black people other than those working on programmes made especially for
the ethnic minorities were employed in production grades.[6] In 1986, the

Ehrlich Report, the BBC's first attempt to monitor the ethnicity of its workforce, found that black workers were massively under-represented, except among the catering and cleaning staff.[7] Another report discovered in 1989 that only 6 per cent of the BBC's 28,000 labour force were not of European descent and these were employed overwhelmingly in catering, cleaning and clerical work.[8] *Time Out* reported in 1988 that when a new, black script editor reported for work, the whites assumed that he had come to mend the photocopier. 'When black people are appointed to influential positions,' it continued, 'they turn up to find their white colleagues with their Freudian slips showing. The subtext is that a black face is appropriate as a Xerox machine mender or a carpet layer or a cleaner – white people can handle that psychologically. But when they turn out to be script editors it buggers up the categories.'[9] After interviewing twenty ethnic minority producers in the mid-1990s, Simon Cottle concluded that 'the major difficulties and stumbling blocks confronting producers of ethnic minority programmes are thought to relate less to racism and more to the established working traditions, the social composition of the BBC, its institutional hierarchy and programme production conservatism'. A senior producer also told Cottle that the BBC was 'an institution insensitive to *both* black audiences and programme makers'.[10] When he became Director-General of the BBC in 2000, Greg Dyke declared that senior production was 'hideously white', and Peter Bazalgette, head of the independent production company Endemol, had found that senior production staff in television news were 'predominantly white'.[11] By the end of the 1990s over 5 per cent of Carlton's employees, and 6 per cent of those of London Weekend Television, belonged to the ethnic minorities.[12] At the start of 2003, 8.6 per cent of those employed on long-term contracts by the BBC were black or Asian, a higher proportion that the non-white proportion of the total UK population, but no details were issued about the levels of their jobs. The BBC hoped that by the end of 2003, 10 per cent of its employees would be black or Asian. Channel 4's target for the end of 2003 was 11 per cent. Endemol was trying to attract more trainees from ethnic minorities by advertising in ethnic newspapers and on radio stations.

In the early 1990s Nadine Marsh-Edwards said that, regarding funding and commissioning, 'Everybody's very quick to give you an equal opportunities form to fill in for your company but then when you walk through their door you don't see any black people. There's a lot of talk about equal opportunities but I don't personally see that much being done by the institutions.' She had found that it had become recognised that stories about black people could interest general audiences, but having 'black people . . . in control of making those stories is still not happening often enough'. Programmes were commissioned from black-led independent production companies in the 1980s and early 1990s, such as the Black Audio Film Collective, Sankofa, Retake and Ceddo, but Thérèse Daniels pointed out that they had rarely been given major commissions and their business positions were precarious.[13] In 1999 some ethnic minority producers complained of being asked to make programmes only about those with the same ethnic backgrounds.[14]

All television organisations have claimed to pursue equal opportunity employment policies. The very low numbers from the ethnic minorities among the regulators of television and senior broadcasting executives before the 1980s and 1990s can be attributed to assumptions in broadcasting about the education and experience that those positions required, and few from the ethnic minorities had acquired these. Yet assumptions about what constituted appropriate education and experience can be seen very much as reflections of white preconceptions. It can also be argued that, if so few from the ethnic minorities were unqualified for such positions, this was the result of how they had been disadvantaged by society at large. An article in *Time Out* in 1988 talked about 'far too many bleeding-heart liberals in broadcasting' and of sincere efforts to have more black people on both sides of the camera, but that 'all this conscious (not to say self-conscious) egalitarianism prevents a real examination of the problem'. Giving blacks an equal chance was seen as 'an ideological duty, a commitment to egalitarianism which is laudable. Laudable but wrong . . . a misplaced sense of charity.' It concluded that only quotas would result in having 'more black faces in the places where they count'.[15] In Peter Bazalgette's view, the rise of independent production companies and the associated casualisation of production had made it more difficult for those who were not white to be employed. Because of the low pay, those entering production had to be subsidised by their parents and consequently the typical entrant was 'white and middle-class'. Those whose parents worked in television found it easier to be taken on and these 'Notting Hillbillies relying on tribal loyalties' added to the obstacles facing those from the ethnic minorities.[16] Interviews carried out by the Joint Research Programme of the Broadcasting Standards Commission and the ITC in the early twenty-first century showed that many from the ethnic minorities saw radio and television as 'a White industry' and this discouraged them from applying to work in broadcasting.[17]

Ethnic Minorities on the Television Screen

The overwhelming majority of those who have appeared on television have been white, but there has always been a non-white presence and this has increased over time. The presence of those who are not white has not expanded at a uniform rate and has varied between programme genres, with some groups having a far stronger presence than others in some programmes. In 1990 Elaine Sihera counted what she regarded as negative and positive images of black people on television broadcast between 6 p.m. and 11 p.m. over thirty weeks. She found that 8 per cent of the BBC's output and 6 per cent of that of ITV and Channel 4 featured black people, percentages that were higher than the non-white proportion of the total population. However, she calculated that only 3.5 per cent of the BBC's output and 4.5 per cent of that of ITV portrayed black people positively. She found no black serious commentators in programmes about education, politics or finance.[18] Statistical surveys of the ethnic minority presence on terrestrial television have also been made each year since 1995. In that year 7 per cent of those who appeared in programmes broadcast between 5.30 p.m. and midnight were not white. By 2001 over 8 per cent of those with speaking parts on television were from the ethnic minorities, a figure roughly equal to the minority ethnic proportion of the total population. In 2001 very nearly half of all programmes included ethnic minority speakers. Those described as black made three times as many appearances as Asians. About two-thirds of all non-white appearances were by males. Programmes made in America had higher proportions of ethnic minority participants than those made in Britain. Three-quarters of the appearances in which ethnic minority participants had speaking parts were in news, factual programmes and fiction, but very many would have had non-speaking roles in sports broadcasts. Only 8 per cent of all ethnic minority participants were classed as making major contributions to programmes.[19]

For earlier decades, evidence about the ethnic minority presence on television is less detailed. Black performers appeared often in variety programmes which were a staple of peak-time weekend television viewing from the 1930s to the 1970s. Buck and Bubbles, black American song and dance artists, appeared on the first day of BBC television in 1936, though the pianist Winifred Atwell in 1956 was probably the first black performer to be given her own series.[20] Sport is another area in which appearances by blacks have been strong. Two of the three cricket test matches against the West Indies in 1939 were televised, as were athletics competitions with black competitors, but the first black women athletes to be televised may have been those taking part in the 1948 Olympics. In recent years televised football, rugby, cricket and athletics events have invariably included ethnic minority competitors, but almost all commentators have been white. All television sports commentators who achieved cult status, such as Eddie Waring, Peter O'Sullevan, Harry Carpenter, Murray Walker and Dan Maskell have been white, but in the 1990s it became more common for ethnic minority sports players to be used as expert summarisers in sports with high numbers of ethnic players.

Black actors appeared in the early days of television. Robert Adams in 1937 was probably the first black actor to take part in a televised drama and in 1947 became the first black actor in a television production of Shakespeare.[21] In 1938 *The Emperor Jones*, a television adaptation of a stage play, was the first televised drama to deal with the lives of black people. In 1956 *A Man from the Sun*, written by the white author John Elliott and dealing with the experience of African-Caribbean immigrants in Britain, was the first play written for television about an ethnic minority in Britain. Jim Pines's survey of black actors on television argues that the 1960s began 'promisingly, in the sense that black actors started to appear in a wider variety of programmes including soaps, serials and one-off television plays', but he also mentions that at this time there was a 'recurrent failure to develop black characterisation in interesting and imaginative ways'. In 1964 Pat Williams wrote that 'the coloured actor still appears more often as an idea than a person'. The West Indian actor Barri Jonson told her that 'We're really "black" actors here in England, rather than just *actors*. In plays we're either goody-goodies or dope-pedlars and pimps.' Few black actors were able to earn a living from television alone. The Entertainment Division of Associated-Rediffusion, headed by Elkan Allan, was the only section of an ITV company with a policy of deliberately including ethnic minority people.[22] In the late 1960s and 1970s opportunities for black actors in quality drama seemed to be diminishing. It was not uncommon for white actors to black up. Even in 1980 the BBC cast the white Anthony Hopkins as Othello on the grounds that no black actors had the appropriate experience, though in 1955 Gordon Heath, a black American, had played Othello for a BBC production.[23] In the 1950s and 1960s Equity's ruling that membership cards could be granted only to those who had been employed for forty weeks in the West End worked against ethnic minority actors, and Equity established its Coloured Artists Committee only in 1974.[24] The 1970s did provide opportunities for black actors in television comedy, and in 1978 and 1979 BBC2 showed two series of *Empire Road*, the first television series to be written, directed and acted by black actors in Britain.

In the 1980s and particularly the 1990s it was more common for ethnic minority actors to be cast in drama series such as *Casualty*, *Holby City* or *London's Burning*, which dealt with organisations of everyday life. While it can be argued that this represented an advance in that black or Asian actors were playing parts that could have been played by whites, some black actors saw this as little more than tokenism and stereotyping, using black actors to give certain scenes an air of verisimilitude. Usually they were not the lead characters. Treva Etienne pointed out that few roles showed ethnic minorities in a positive light such as 'the fact that we have lawyers and doctors, and that we have been very instrumental in supporting this country economically'.[25] There were also complaints that attempts to give gritty reality to crime series resulted too often in negative images by casting ethnic minority actors as criminals such as muggers, drug dealers, pimps and prostitutes. In 1994 the writer Yasmin Alibhai-Brown wrote that black television producers 'now produce scandalous and even racist programmes, which acquire authenticity because they are made by insiders' and recorded 'only depravity and failure'.[26] Farruhk Dhondy, on the other hand, who had been a television writer and from 1984 to 1997 was Channel 4's Commissioning Editor for Multicultural Programmes, talked about a 'nascent bureaucratic black middle-class that lives off a grievance industry' and of 'a kind of political mafiaism' that prevented black writers from producing their best work by insisting that they wrote only what would help race relations or '"represent" somebody'.[27] In the 1990s drama series such as Channel 4's *Turning World*, *Peacock Spring*, *Little Napoleon* and *The Final Passage* and the BBC's *This Life* and *Holding On*, which were about black life in Britain or in which black actors had more than token parts, received critical acclaim. Yet very few ethnic minority actors appeared in highly popular drama series such as *Inspector Morse*, *Peak Practice* or *Heartbeat*, or in the highly prestigious adaptations of classic novels. One can argue that the popularity of these series showed that many whites were attracted by the image of a society with no ethnic minorities and often set in the countryside.

Before the mid-1980s few ethnic minority actors had parts in soaps. Gloria Simpson in *Emergency-Ward 10* in 1959 was probably the first black actor to have a speaking part in a soap. Joan Hooley, playing a house doctor – which must have been one of the first times that a black actor portrayed a professional person – took part in more than fifty episodes of *Emergency-Ward 10* in 1964. When her character became engaged to a white character, there was much press speculation about the first black–white kissing scene of British television, and this had to take place in a garden rather than a bedroom.[28] In 1970 Cleo Sylvestre appeared in *Crossroads*, which she left to avoid becoming typecast. Other black characters were also introduced to *Crossroads*. From its start in 1985 *EastEnders* had black and Asian families and has included black actors playing prestigious roles such as doctors and health visitors. The presence of ethnic minority actors in *EastEnders* may have owed something to the desire of its producers and writers to give this soap an air of gritty reality. Tony Holland, script editor for *EastEnders*, had promised that 'we are not going to duck any social issues. Our stories will deal with all the contemporary problems of London's East End.' *EastEnders* has dealt with racist issues such as a white man beating his black partner and the opposition of a black family to one of its members developing a relationship with a white. Sarita Malik, on the other hand, has argued that soaps, including *EastEnders*, have tended to play down the ethnicity of Asian characters and particularly language, dress and domestic life.[29] The Asian actor Shreela Ghosh complained that in *EastEnders* she kept 'playing scenes week in, week out which have no substance'. Until Gary MacDonald began to play the criminally inclined Darren Roberts in *EastEnders*, all the ethnic minority characters had been 'good'.[30]

Ethnic minority actors had small parts in *Coronation Street* in the 1960s. Thomas Baptiste played a black transport worker in 1963 and Cleo Sylvestre appeared in 1966, but black characters were largely absent until the 1990s. Stephen Bourne argued in 1998 that *Coronation Street* had 'failed more than any other' soap to involve black characters. In 1978 the black actor Angela Bruce played the part of Janice Stubbs, who was responsible for the break-up of the marriage of the white characters Ray and Deirdre Langton. Bill Podmore, the producer, needed much persuasion before agreeing that Bruce could have this role. He feared that this could have provoked racial prejudice and caused viewers to switch off. Initially he thought that a white actor could have played the part. Bruce hoped that she would be followed by other black actors in *Coronation Street*, but said in 1987 that 'they have since closed up and black people do not really feature'.[31] This may have been because socio-political issues were not emphasised in *Coronation Street*, which before the late 1990s tended to recreate a north-of-England working-class world that drew on idealised notions of what the north had been. In 1978 Margaret Walters wrote in *New Society* that the arrival of Bruce's character in *Coronation Street* was 'an intruder whose brief presence in the serial precipitates the break-up of a happy home. A non-white character is bound to disturb the cosy sense of kinship which soap opera celebrates, bound to intrude too much reality into its enclosed, backward-looking, whiter than white world.'[32] In 1981 H.V. Kershaw, a *Coronation Street* scriptwriter, wrote that by having ethnic minority characters 'we would again be forced to put unhelpful comments into the mouths of fictional men and women who command a wide following among the serial's millions of viewers, with potentially dangerous effect'. It would be 'quite wrong . . . for an entertainment programme to run such risks' or 'accept such responsibility'.[33]

Some from the ethnic minorities saw the increasing number of non-white characters in soaps as little more than tokenism. In 1988 Shreela Ghosh, who played the Asian character Naima in *EastEnders*, said ethnic minority characters on the soap were 'a political football for the show. A trump card over all the soaps – a few black faces.' In her view, the writing out of the Carpenters, the black family, from *EastEnders* by sending one to Bangladesh and another to Trinidad raised the question of whether 'there's no place for us in society? If you can't fit in, you go back home. It's a strong message.' She added that in one scene 'I came into the launderette and Pauline's supposed to be showing me how to use a washing machine. I haven't just stepped off a boat.'[34] Sarita Malik has speculated whether the lack of emphasis on the details of ethnicity in the black characters in soaps indicates 'a broader and prevailing fear of alienating the majority mainstream audience because of "ethnic distinctiveness" or "too much difference" (so that often the only "Black" aspect of the characters is that they look Black)'.[35]

The growing ethnic minority presence in Britain and a growing sensitivity to complaints that television was not catering for their interests help to explain why soaps with casts of predominantly, or including a sizeable number of, ethnic actors have been introduced over the past quarter of a century. The BBC2 drama series *Empire Road*, written by Michael Abbensetts who was born in Guyana, is usually regarded as the first ethnic minority soap opera made by British television. The major characters were Asian and African-Caribbean, though the producer, Peter Ansorge, was white. It was set in Birmingham and broadcast in 1978. Relationships between Asians and African-Caribbeans were one of its major themes. Granada's *Albion Market*, first broadcast in 1986, included market stallholders of white, Vietnamese, Ugandan Asian, African-Caribbean and Jewish origins. Soaps with a strong ethnic presence in the 1990s included *Family Pride, Brothers and Sisters, Tiger Bay* and *London Bridge*. No soap with a strong ethnic minority element attracted large audiences or lasted for more than two or three years, which suggests that they had little appeal to white viewers though they tended to be screened outside peak-viewing hours or were in competition with popular programmes on other channels. The two series of *Empire Road* consisted of only fifteen episodes, but a hundred episodes of *Albion Market* were made.

Black actors began to make more than occasional appearances in the most popular British-made television comedies in the 1970s. From 1954 to 1957 the BBC screened the American comedy series *Amos 'n' Andy*, which starred two black actors, but much of its humour depended on caricatures of blacks. In 1969 Kenny Lynch had a major role in *Curry and Chips*, an LWT sitcom written by Johnny Speight, the author of *Till Death Us Do Part*, but its stars were Spike Milligan and Eric Sykes. Rudolph Walker in 1972 was the first black actor with a leading role in a British sitcom when he starred in *Love Thy Neighbour*. The black comedian Charlie Williams achieved national celebrity when he appeared in *The Comedians*, a show for stand-up comics first screened in 1972. The black actor Don Warrington appeared regularly in the cult Yorkshire TV sitcom *Rising Damp*, of which four series were screened between 1974 and 1978. The black American comedian Bill Cosby, whose *The Cosby Show* was first shown on British television in 1984, was the first black comedy star to have a situation comedy that was immensely popular in Britain. No black British comedy star seems to have achieved a similar status. In the 1980s and 1990s Lenny Henry was probably the best-known black comedian in Britain, but most of his television work has been stand-up and comedy sketches. *Desmond's*, created by the black writer Trix Worrell, had a black cast and was broadcast by Channel 4 from 1989 to 1994, and is often regarded as the first black British sitcom to have acquired widespread critical acclaim and a following among white viewers, although *The Fosters*, which had two series between 1976 and 1977, is usually thought to be the first British sitcom with black actors in all the main roles. *Desmond's* was awarded the Best Sitcom prize at the 1993 British Comedy Awards. *Tandoori Nights*, broadcast in 1985, was probably the first situation comedy made in Britain with writers and performers of Asian descent. A comedy series with Asian writers and actors did not gain a cult following among white viewers until 1998, when the sketch show *Goodness Gracious Me* was broadcast. Eighty-five per cent of the viewers of its first series were white.[36] Evaluations of humour are subjective, but probably no one knows so much about television comedy in Britain as Mark Lewisohn, author of the monumentally detailed *Radio Times Guide to TV Comedy*, published in 1998. In his list of the top twenty British-made sitcoms – and probably few would quibble with most of his selections – only *Rising Damp* gave more than occasional parts to actors who were not white.

News reporting and the presentation of news bulletins were very much a white preserve until the 1980s. In 1976 only a scriptwriter and one on-screen reporter out of ITN's editorial staff of eighty were not white. The news and current affairs staff at London Weekend Television and Thames and Granada's *World In Action* team were all white. The BBC claimed that it was not its policy to record the ethnic origins of its staff, but *Time Out* established that in 1976 only two out of the 300 NUJ members employed in news and current affairs by the BBC were black.[37] In 1977 Trevor McDonald, an African-Caribbean who had joined ITN as a reporter in 1973, began reading the ITN news and in 1981 Moira Stewart of the BBC became Britain's first black woman newsreader.[38] By 1983 the BBC had three black women news presenters. Despite these initiatives the Council for Racial Equality reported in 1983 that its research had shown that over 80 per cent of Asians and 90 per cent of blacks wanted to see more presenters who were not white.[39] By the end of the twentieth century the ethnic minority presence among television newsreaders and journalists was much stronger. On most days it had become unusual for a news and current affairs programme not to have ethnic minority presenters or journalists. George Alagiah, the BBC newsreader of Sri Lankan origin, argued in 2000/1

A black person reading the news, or reporting, breaks the stereotypes of people thinking that all black people are muggers; many of them are educated, eloquent, analytical people. Black reports can change the news agenda . . . we recently covered Islamic Awareness Week; because we had reports from ethnic minorities, we asked if Islam should have the same rights as the Church of England. If we'd only had white reporters, we might not have asked those questions.

He believes black reporters acted as role models for other black people. He added that 'behind the screen, where the decisions are made, we've still some way to go'.[40] Jon Snow, the white television journalist and news presenter, pointed out in 2003 that, when non-whites joined television newsrooms, they were often encouraged to become on-screen reporters, with the result that senior news production remained a predominantly white area of employment.[41]

A variety of factors had contributed to this enhanced ethnic minority presence in news and current affairs. In 1976 Alex Lyon, a Labour MP, argued that the absence of black newsreaders on BBC television was 'reflecting and to some extent encouraging racial feeling'.[42] The Annan Committee emphasised that television ought to do more for minorities. The Campaign Against Racism in the Media in the late 1970s and the Black Media Workers' Association in the early 1980s pressed for greater opportunities in mainstream television for those from the ethnic minorities. In 1972 the BBC had set up its Community Programmes Unit, whose *Open Door* series allowed community groups to make programmes about their concerns. Its *It Ain't Half Racist, Mum*, made by the Campaign Against Racism in the Media, featured the black academic Stuart Hall and provided examples of racism in television. In 1979 LWT set up its London Minorities Unit. From its start in 1982, Channel 4 had a Commissioning Editor for Multicultural Programmes who commissioned current affairs programmes. Yasmin Alibhai-Brown has suggested that the employment of ethnic minority television journalists had been encouraged by the riots of 1981, which took British television by surprise and demonstrated that white reporters could not penetrate ethnic minority communities.[43] These moves also stimulated the expansion of ethnic minority news and documentary analysis series such as *Skin, Black on Black* and later *Bandung File*, which had ethnic minority producers, journalists and presenters, though some complained that such series amounted to 'ghettoisation', isolating black presenters and journalists in a television backwater. Yet some found such programmes an entry into mainstream television. Samir Shah, who produced *Eastern Eye* for Channel 4, became the deputy editor of news and current affairs programmes for the BBC in 1987, and from 1994 to 1998 was head of political programmes for the BBC. After producing Channel 4's *Black on Black*, Trevor Phillips became presenter and editor of LWT's *The London Programme* in 1987 and a year later editor of regional programmes.

Has Television Encouraged Racism?

Answers to this question depend, of course, on how racism is defined. What one person sees as racism others may regard as equitable treatment. Probably no whites who made television programmes in Britain since the Second World War have regarded themselves as racists or would have admitted to this in public. Yet some of the programmes that they broadcast were considered racist by those who were not white. In general, white broadcasters have subscribed to a liberal-humanist view of race relations. They have wanted to reduce ethnic prejudices and to promote ethnic understanding. In 1968 Charles Hill, Chairman of the BBC's Board of Governors, emphasised his support for the claims of the Director-General Hugh Greene, with whom he often disagreed, that the BBC could not be impartial over racialism and that the man 'who speaks in favour of racial intolerance cannot have the same rights as the man who condemns it'.[44] One element of the liberal-humanist perspective, however, was that freedom of speech had to be maintained and that, in order to promote understanding of the political world, views which some considered racist had to be broadcast. In 1977 the Director-General Ian Trethowan discussed the complexities of reporting racial matters. 'It was easy', he pointed out 'to say that we are against racialism – that is a definable evil' and that 'very few people in this country are racialists in the full, malign sense of seeking actively to stir hatred.' He went on to mention the 'fear and suspicion' between blacks and whites and the worries of many people about race. Some whites were concerned about 'the impact of immigrants on their communities' while many black people were worried about 'the special problems which they face'. He argued that the BBC had to report racial problems and that putting on air those alarmed about immigration and racial problems was not the same as giving air time to racists. By not reporting such issues the BBC could lose its credibility and surrender 'the channels of information to the rumour-mongers and the mischief makers'. Its responsibility was to 'report not just the signs of tension, but what is being done positively to ease it. More, we need to explore fresh ways of improving the situation. We need to "ventilate" the problem.'[45]

In the late 1960s many from the ethnic minorities saw Enoch Powell's views on immigration and repatriation as racist but, given the degree of attention that leading parliamentary politicians devoted to Powell, the liberal tradition of broadcasting led television to give extensive coverage to Powell and his supporters. The even-handedness of the liberal approach was also found in debates over immigration controls and over relations with apartheid South Africa and with Rhodesia following Ian Smith's unilateral declaration of independence, which again led to accusations that television was legitimising, though also criticising, racism. Open access television sometimes allowed air time to those whose views were considered racist. In the 1970s an *Open Door* slot allowed an anti-immigration group to broadcast its views. Sarita Malik has pointed out that the law, by entitling political parties fielding a given number of candidates at parliamentary elections to party political broadcasts, had allowed the British National Party to use television to publicise its views in the late 1990s and early twenty-first century.

It is not difficult to produce examples of television documentaries that have uncovered instances of racism in Britain, though they have formed only a small proportion of all factual programming. In 1955 *Has Britain a Colour Bar?* investigated the experiences of immigrants. Those who were not white spoke about racism in *Racial Discrimination*, an edition of *This Week* broadcast in 1967. Sarita Malik has argued that, while documentaries from the 1950s and 1960s highlighted instances of racial prejudice, their emphasis was often on how blacks were forming a problem for whites, and tended to portray blacks and whites in conflict.[46] In 1979 Thames produced a four-part series *Our People*, in which those from the ethnic minorities spoke about discrimination in housing and employment, immigration legislation and racist attacks. Investigative journalism programmes showed in 1988 that some white landlords in Bristol let accommodation to whites after refusing it to blacks.[47] In the 1980s and 1990s magazine programmes made by black producers and with black participants such as *Ebony*, *Asian Magazine*, *Network East*, *Black on Black* and *Eastern Eye* also discussed the everyday experience of racism among the ethnic minorities, though it is doubtful whether many whites watched them. Television newsreels covered in detail the violence at Southall, Toxteth, Broadwater Farm, Bradford, Burnley and Oldham; but the way in which these disturbances took television journalists by surprise suggests that they had been ignoring everyday racial intolerance.

In general terms it can be argued that the discourses of television news and current affairs programmes have tended to present those who are not white as racial groups while whites are not depicted in such a manner. Sarita Malik maintains that television discourses have represented those who are not white as a racialised Other and that issues such as riots, street crime and unemployment, and also racial political correctness and racial rights, are depicted as the result of blackness. In her analysis, these 'are seen to be directly *caused* by the presence of "Blackness" – not by historical context, structural inequality or racist attitudes, but by Others' ethnic specificity'.[48] Malik's content analysis shows this to have been particularly the case in the reporting of the Brixton riots in 1995. There was very little explanation of how and why a protest had turned into a riot or of the need for a protest which followed the death of a black man in police custody. Whites were depicted as the victims and the heroes of the riot. Particular emphasis was given to the views of the Home Secretary Michael Howard and Sir Paul Condon, head of the Metropolitan Police. In Malik's view, television's '"bystander" approach, which comes to the fore in "truth" discourses such as news, means that it rarely leads the debate or disagrees too strongly with the "official" agencies (the police, the immigration services, the law). The total effect is a prevailing sense of cooperation, consensus and agreement between television and other institutions.'[49]

On occasions whites accused television of exaggerating racial harmony and of disregarding white concerns about ethnic relations. In 1969 the BBC programme *Friendly Relations* was criticised for trying to show that whites and Asians were integrated in Southall. The programme makers were alleged to have persuaded whites to make purchases in Asian shops to demonstrate ethnic cooperation. The secretary of the Southall Residents' Association, to which a thousand white families but only two Asian families belonged, complained that it was 'ridiculous and misleading for the BBC to make out that this is a well-integrated area. It is not. The two communities, Indian and white, do not integrate well . . . to distort the situation gives a completely untrue picture of the area to the country as a whole.'[50] In 1979 Dudley Smith, the Conservative MP for Warwick, condemned *Our People*, the six-part Thames Television series about immigration, for implying to black viewers that Parliament and officialdom discriminated against them. He thought that the programme's underlying theme was that the majority of Britain's white population was 'anti-black' and much of its information 'misleading and some downright inaccurate'.[51] Garry Waller, the prospective Conservative parliamentary candidate for Brighouse and Spenborough, said that the programme's terminology might well have been taken from 'a textbook on Marxism' and that its objective was to 'arouse resentment among the ethnic minorities by emphasising and exaggerating their disadvantaged position'.[52] In 1989 the Conservative MP Harry Greenway described Channel 4's *Time and Judgement*, which included a dance routine in which a white policeman attacked a black man and Rastafarians claimed that British society offered them no hope, as 'deeply insulting', 'very offensive' and sounding to him like 'black propaganda'. Ivor Stanbrook, another Conservative MP, called it 'an insult to the nation to depict us as racist'.[53]

One can argue that cultural forms that provide positive role models of those who are not white can combat racism by boosting non-whites' sense of self-worth and by weakening assumptions among whites of their innate superiority. Television recorded achievements of those who are not white. Admiration for Nelson Mandela and his status as one of the great moral icons of the contemporary world were encouraged by television coverage of his release from prison. Some ethnic television performers have become national celebrities through their television appearances. Perhaps Cy Grant in the 1950s was the first of these. In the 1990s some moved from one area of television to another, such as the boxers Frank Bruno and Chris Eubank and the footballer Ian Wright, which perhaps indicates that television was becoming more multicultural. Television has recorded in detail black sporting achievements and does much to explain why Muhammed Ali is a greater celebrity than any other black world champion boxer. Without television, followers of football in Britain would have known little of why Pele has so often been regarded as the best footballer of all time. Many whites have been cheered by the sporting success for Britain of black athletes in the Olympics. Yet analysts of sport have argued that televised sporting success has been a mixed blessing for the ethnic minorities. Assumptions about blacks being genetically suited to sporting events led to their potential in other areas being neglected in schools and so became a form of social disadvantage. Television, and particularly sports programmes, has tended to ignore why so few from the ethnic minorities have become senior sports administrators. Televised sport can also reinforce white beliefs about the inferiority of those who are not white. The poor performances of the Indian teams on their tours of England in 1952 and 1959 led to accusations that they lacked the physical courage to face fast bowling. Pakistani teams in the 1980s and 1990s were dismissed as habitual cheats.

Television's ignoring of some areas of black achievement can be described as racial discrimination. Black actors have complained that television has provided few opportunities for them to display the range of their abilities. Almost all talking films made by the British cinema and by Hollywood, as well as those made in Australia and New Zealand, have been shown on British television, while very few Indian films – apart from those that have achieved international critical acclaim such as those of Sanjit Ray – have been shown on television in Britain, although Bollywood productions are shown on cable and satellite channels aimed primarily at Asian viewers. Blacks have made a vast contribution to popular music. Jazz was very much the creation of American blacks. Rock'n'roll is usually regarded as based on black American rhythm and blues music. Jazz has never had a strong presence on British television, though at some time all the big names of jazz have appeared on television. Although there have been popular music series from the mid-1950s on terrestrial television, they have provided only a tiny fraction of all television programming but have almost always featured black performers. In more recent years, terrestrial television in Britain has rarely featured predominantly black forms of popular music such as gangsta rap, though part of the appeal of such music to the young is that it lies outside mainstream popular culture of which television is so very much a part. Indian and Chinese music have been even more ignored by television. British television has shown regular cookery programmes since the 1950s, and their numbers rocketed in the 1990s, but although the eating of Chinese and South Asian food by whites has been a feature of post-war British popular culture, there have been relatively few cookery programmes concerned with Chinese or South Asian cuisine. Ken Hom and Madhur Jaffrey are probably the only specialists in such cooking to have become nationally known television cooks. Through presenting programmes on British cuisine, the black chef Ainsley Harriott has become very much a television personality in recent years, but is not usually associated with ethnic minority cuisine.

The representation of ethnic minorities by television in Britain has been racist in the sense that it has presented too simplistic a view of them, that it showed them as homogeneous wholes that overlooked their distinctive identities, cultures and needs. In 1984, when Britain's Chinese population was thought to be around 150,000, it was claimed in *Broadcast* that their representation on television was 'practically non existent'. Anthony Shang, who had just helped to set up Chinese Broadcasting, an independent production company established to make programmes about Chinese communities in Britain, thought that their stereotyped image on television was 'of gangsters in the underworld, or of the real idiot-looking Chinese waiter with greasy hair and ludicrous accent saying flied lice – this certainly doesn't give young kids the confidence that they are here to stay and have equal rights'.[54] In the early twenty-first century British Chinese were still complaining of being overlooked by terrestrial television. In the late 1970s and early 1980s, the LWT programme *Skin* dealt with issues concerning Asians and black people in Britain. Samir Shah, one of its reporters, thought that *Skin* brought black and Asian people together 'through the fact that they were non-white, which is a very negative definition of these groups' and that having to find issues that involved both groups resulted in many programmes about discrimination and conflict with whites. He thought that 'the Asian community had a much greater experience than that of discrimination or hassles with the immigration authorities . . . What they really wanted was a programme that reflected a wider range of activities.'[55] The launch of *Black on Black* and *Eastern Eye* by Channel 4 in 1982 recognised the differing interests of black and Asian viewers, but for the rest of the 1980s and 1990s terrestrial television had few series that catered for different groups of British Asians such as those of Indian, Pakistani or Bangladeshi descent, and so perhaps encouraged simplistic and stereotypical views of them. The writer Mike Phillips, who came to Britain from Guyana, argued that television has underplayed the mixed racial heritage of those from the Caribbean. He has pointed out that many from that area have some white ancestry but that television, and other cultural pressures, has 'invoked an ideological notion which is linked to Africa . . . we talk continually about the Caribbean as African, it is actually a mongrelised area, both genetically and culturally. Show me one black person who is, as it were, of pure African descent, and I'll eat the bugger!'[56]

The establishment of multicultural production units by terrestrial broadcasters and programmes about ethnic minorities made by ethnic minorities may have suggested that television was recognising the interests of those who were not white. Such programmes, however, were sometimes condemned as 'ghettoisation' television and accused of presenting ethnic minorities as appendages to British society rather than essential components of it. In the early 1990s Mike Phillips thought that, while ethnic minority programmes tried to present 'black people as real people', they tended to show those who were not white as 'more and more "ethnic", as "Third World", as "alien" to the concerns of the people of this country. So if you actually want to get a sense of what your life is like as a black person, you are left high and dry.' An alternative perspective was provided by Trevor Phillips, who argued that abandoning programmes made primarily for those who are not white would be saying that 'we think our experience is second-rate, not worth preserving, not worth having in its clear and separate form'.[57]

Multicultural production units became something of a backwater in terrestrial television. In 1992 one mainstream commissioner admitted that the existence of multicultural production units made him less likely to schedule ethnic programmes. Sarita Malik has claimed that in the late 1990s the most acclaimed BBC programmes that dealt with the experiences of the ethnic minorities were not made by multicultural units. News and Current Affairs made *Black Britain* and the Community Programmes Unit the Windrush season in 1998. Malik claimed that the BBC had a 'piecemeal, ambivalent response to its licence-fee-paying Black audiences' which was reflected in frequent changes in the structure of multicultural production and an uncertainty of direction. An African-Caribbean Programming Unit was established in 1989. In 1992 this was merged with the Asian Programmes Unit to form the Multicultural Programming Unit. In 1995 this was again subdivided when the African-Caribbean Unit was sent to Manchester. Such restructurings suggest uncertainty of direction. Black talent tended to move to other departments. When Malik worked for the Asian Programmes Unit in 1999, she concluded that there was

> deepseated inferential racism within the corporation, a lack of considered critical reflection about programme aims and strategies, internal bidding for commissions and funds that called for a market mindset that seemed antithetical to the worthy issues we found ourselves covering, a general fear of challenging the governing forces of scheduling, budgets, programme-direction and management, an overwhelming culture of silence, defensiveness, careerism and acquiescence, and a hierarchical departmental structure which did not encourage too many ideas and opinions below producer level.

By the late 1990s the BBC's Asian programmes looked 'dated'.[58] The growing number of satellite channels aimed at ethnic minorities may also have persuaded terrestrial broadcasters that commissioning multicultural programmes was less of a priority.

Fiercer competition for audiences and the harsher financial climate of the 1990s strengthened the tendency for multicultural units to present ethnic minorities as outside mainstream British society. Multicultural programmes were rarely screened at peak time. The European Media Forum claimed that between 1988 and 1995 ethnic minority broadcasting per year on Channel 4 fell from 163 to 64 hours.[59] The insistence of the ITC in 1999 that Channel 4 screen three hours of multicultural programmes each week with at least one hour at peak time seems to be further evidence of how ethnic minority programmes were being marginalised. Because of the high costs of producing drama, multicultural programmes in the 1990s tended to be studio discussions or dealt with news and current affairs. Consequently many programmes were concerned with discrimination and, while it can be argued that they exposed instances of racism, they also emphasised that those who were not white were a problem for society in general and had difficulties which set them apart from the rest of society. The need to boost viewing figures by appealing to white as well as ethnic minority viewers resulted in the broadcasting of programmes in the 1990s that concentrated on sordid aspects of ethnic minority life such as wife-beating, drug trafficking, violent crime and prostitution. Some who were not white complained that such programmes undervalued the positive achievements of black people and reinforced the stereotypical views of blacks and Asians held by many whites.[60]

Racism and Television Comedy

Light entertainment and particularly comedy have been areas of television in which programmes have been condemned as racist. From 1958 to 1978 the *Black and White Minstrel Show* was one of the BBC's main variety programmes, usually broadcast at a peak time on Saturday evenings. It won the Golden Rose of Montreux, a highly prestigious international award, in 1961. White song and dance artists who blacked up were a vital part of the show. In 1968 its title was changed to the *Minstrel Show* and complaints about its racial offensiveness contributed to its scrapping in 1978. How often stand-up comedians made racist jokes is unclear; but in 1972 the Granada series *The Comedians*, which consisted of stand-up comedians, broadcast a joke told by George Roper about an Asian waiter which was reported to the Race Relations Board.[61] As recently as 1985 Michael Grade, the Controller of BBC1, had to tell comedians to cut out racist and sexist jokes.[62]

Situation comedy provoked accusations of racism. It has already been mentioned that the BBC broadcast the American situation comedy *Amos 'n' Andy* from 1954 to 1957. From today's perspective these show this was offensively racist, but it was defended on the grounds that it was one of the earliest programmes to provide American blacks with opportunities to appear on television, and many of the minor black characters were depicted as hard-working and running their own businesses. Screening *Amos 'n' Andy* did not provoke massive complaints from whites in Britain in the 1950s. Using humour to subvert racism was a key theme of several sitcoms in the late 1960s and 1970s, the period when Powellism was a dominant theme of national politics. Between 1966 and 1975 the BBC screened seven series of *Till Death Us Do Part*. Its writer, Johnny Speight, had hoped to weaken racism through comedy by making the main character, Alf Garnett, a foul-mouthed working-class white racist bigot with a strong loyalty to crown and country, and those who shared his views, appear ridiculous. Garnett frequently used racist terms such as 'coons, kikes, nig-nogs'. Speight also wrote the series *Curry and Chips*, made by London Weekend Television and broadcast in 1969. This too tried to ridicule racists and starred Spike Milligan playing a Pakistani Irishman. The black actor Kenny Lynch played a black who detested Pakistanis. Milligan and John Bird also played Pakistanis in the BBC's *The Melting Pot*, of which only the first episode was shown in 1975. Eight series of Thames TV's *Love Thy Neighbour* were screened between 1972 and 1976. These revolved around conflicts and the trading of racist insults between a white couple and their black West Indian neighbours.

Defenders of such programmes usually argued that ridiculing racists undermined racism, but not all agreed. Some whites may have enjoyed such programmes because they provided opportunities to laugh at those who were not white. Johnny Speight recalled that some of those who congratulated him on *Till Death Us Do Part* did not realise that he was satirising them. In 1969, its first year of operation, the Community Relations Commission complained that Alf Garnett had given the impression that people in Britain accepted 'blatantly hostile language' in public speeches about race. In 1982 the Commission reported that *Till Death Us Do Part* had presented ethnic minorities as a threat to British society.[63] A BBC Audience Research Report in 1973 on *Till Death Us Do Part* concluded that most people saw Garnett as 'a harmless buffoon', while 'identifying with Alf legitimises some people's illiberal views', but it concluded that the programme did not seem to have any effect on those who did not already hold racially prejudiced views.[64] Shortly before the first programme of *The Melting Pot* was broadcast, when it was expected to be a series of seven episodes, Spike Milligan told the *Sun* that he was convinced that there would never be racial tolerance in Britain and that he was expecting a 'racial explosion'. He described the programme as having references to 'niggers, wops and wogs. That's what gets the laughs today. *I'm hating every minute of it. I'm contemptuous of myself.*' When he made remarks like 'nignogs' or 'wogs' to test people's reactions, he had found that 'Generally, their eyes light up. They say: "*You're dead right. We don't want them here. Clear them out.*"'[65] The BBC's decision to end the series after only one episode suggests that ethnic minorities would have found *The Melting Pot* objectionable.

One can argue that since the 1980s television comedy has probably done more to combat than to reinforce racial prejudice. In the first five series of *It Ain't Half Hot Mum* between 1974 and 1977 the white actor Michael Bates played Rangi Ram, an Indian servant. Part of the humour centred on Rangi Ram describing himself as British. Having a white actor playing an Indian came to be condemned as racist and in recent years *It Ain't Half Hot Mum* has not been re-shown on the BBC terrestrial channels, though it is broadcast on satellite comedy channels. The comment of Jimmy Perry, one of its writers, that 'BBC executives who had never been to India . . . thought it was racist' seems to confirm that television controllers have become more aware of ethnic minorities' sensitivities.[66] Hardly any comedies in the 1980s or 1990s tried to draw laughs from ridiculing white racists making racist comments about other ethnic groups, although in the recent past Ali G, the much-acclaimed creation of the British Jewish comedian Sacha Baron-Cohen, has parodied British-born African-Caribbeans. The American *Cosby Show* was broadcast in Britain from 1985 to 1994 and *Desmond's* had six series on Channel 4 between 1989 and 1994. These series portrayed their black characters as rounded individuals instead of ethnic minority stereotyped buffoons, and allowed ethnic actors to demonstrate the range of their skills. *Goodness Gracious Me*, first shown in 1998, and *The Kumars at Number 42*, first broadcast in 2001, showed how British Asians could make comedy out of their generational conflicts and aspirations and out of their relations with white society. These series indicated that British Asians were sufficiently confident to laugh about their Asianness in a style which appealed to whites as well as Asians, but was unlikely to be regarded as appealing inadvertently to white racist assumptions. In 2002 the BBC broadcast *All About Me*, made by the independent production company Celador, starring the white Jasper Carrott and the British Asian Meera Syal as a married couple with children of different colours from their first marriages. This presented mixed marriages as a normal aspect of life and made little attempt to use ethnic differences as a source of humour.

Television, Assimilationism and Ethnic Identities

In the 1960s the liberal-humanist philosophy of those who controlled television led to the introduction of Asian language programmes designed to help immigrants cope with life in Britain. In 1965 the BBC began broadcasting *Hi Ghar Samajhiye*, a programme for Asians learning English. *Nai Zindage Naya Jeevan*, a magazine programme of topical items and discussion of ethnic minority issues, was broadcast from 1965 until 1982 in Hindi and Urdu and was then restyled as *Asian Magazine*. In 1975, though broadcast at 9 a.m., it had an average audience of 1 million when the total number of Hindi and Urdu speakers in Britain was thought to be only one and a quarter million, which may have indicated a strong demand for Asian language programmes.[67] It can be argued that programmes intended to help immigrants adapt to living in Britain were assimilationist and, though planned to promote racial understanding and harmony, were in effect racist. Their underlying tendency was to encourage immigrants to conform to white British cultural norms, which involved abandoning or adjusting their traditional values.

Paul Gilroy has written about the black diaspora on both sides of the Atlantic Ocean, and how this has contributed to a culture of African-Caribbeans in Britain which fuses African, Caribbean and British values and traditions.[68] A similar argument has also been made about those of Asian descent living in Britain. In 2001 Bhiku Parekh, a professor at the University of Hull, claimed that second- and third-generation British Asians had 'created their own unique brand of British Asian culture based on their experience in the UK'.[69] It is difficult to be sure of how far television may have contributed to this rise in Britain of what have been called 'hybrid cultures'. If one accepts that television does shape senses of identity, a contention that many dispute, then it would seem that the rise of cable and satellite television in the 1990s has helped Asians in particular to retain their distinctive values. The *Guardian Media Guide* for 2002 listed thirty-seven satellite channels and cable operators aimed at Asian viewers, including three for Chinese viewers. Two others carried Caribbean material and one African. In 2000 *Eastern Eye*, an English-language newspaper targeted at Asians in Britain, carried the weekly television programmes for six Asian satellite channels. Some satellite channels broadcast in Asian languages such as Tamil, Urdu or Punjabi, but it could be said that channels such as the Asian Music Channel that broadcast in English are an expression of hybrid culture, though their content could also have reflected Asians' awareness of how they differed from white British society.

Television has uncovered instances of racism in Britain and television controllers have always tried to ensure that television has not been used to propagate racist views, although, as has been shown above, reporting the opinions of racists in news and current affairs programmes could be interpreted as giving air time to racists. During the last twenty or so years, the increasing number of appearances on television of those from the ethnic minorities has reflected to a degree the multi-ethnic nature of contemporary Britain, though the control of television has tended to be a white cultural space. Channel controllers and programme makers have shown greater sensitivity to the concerns of minorities, and some programmes screened in the 1950s, 1960s and 1970s are considered too racially offensive to be shown today. No doubt programmes are still being made that reflect an unconscious racism on the part of whites. Arguably television has done at least as much as the popular press to combat racism. Even in the early twenty-first century it can be maintained that much television presents white as the norm, that those who are not white are often represented as the problematic Other. The new world of television, with the fragmentation of audiences and the multiplicity of channels, may make it harder for television to promote ethnic harmony. Greater choice between channels may result in greater ghettoisation of audiences and so provide less capacity to promote respect for other cultural traditions.

Chapter 8

TELEVISION AND THE ARTS

Defining art has never been easy. In everyday discourse 'the arts' include opera, ballet, classical music, painting, sculpture, architecture, drama, novels, poetry and essays, but within all of these fields deciding whether, and where, a dividing line should be drawn between 'high' and 'low' art is problematic. The composer Michael Tippett declared that 'All the mass-based entertainment in the world cannot add up to a half-pennyworth of great art.'[1] There has probably been more than a trace of snobbery in conceptions of what constitutes art and often a suspicion that what is popular cannot be 'real' art and must always be inferior to it. It has even been argued that those who deride mass culture had to invent the notion of mass culture in order to demonstrate their superiority.[2] Yet what is dismissed as popular or trash in one period can be accepted as high art in another. The cinema is widely thought of as a 'serious' art form, but the early films of Chaplin, now esteemed as classics of cinematic art, were not regarded as high art by cultural pundits when they were made. In the last two decades the rise of postmodernism has strengthened the belief that there is no objective or absolute standard for defining what constitutes a work of art or its quality. Postmodernists have argued that the assumptions which influence what is thought to be high art are culturally conditioned and vary over time and place. For postmodernists, judgements of aesthetic merit are matters of taste and very much influenced by the personal preferences of those who are accepted as the arbiters of artistic merit.

It must be stressed that not all agree that judgements of what constitutes great art can only be subjective and relative. Richard Hoggart, for instance, is one of the most trenchant opponents of the postmodernist contention that artistic judgements are expressions of taste and that there can be no objective hierarchies of artistic merit. In his view, equating a Bob Dylan lyric with *Paradise Lost* shows that 'any length will be gone to avoid ever having to say: "But this *is* a better work than that."' Hoggart's test of what constitutes great art is its impact on the mind, 'that your mind is informed by the knowledge that things wider and deeper than you have guessed, as well as reflections of your own mundanity, exist in the world and that you have been made privy to them'. Yet even Hoggart has pointed out that not all readers will respond to the same work of literature, or of some other art form, in the same manner. Whether literature influences the reader depends on the disposition of the reader to be influenced by it. As Hoggart has written, 'the most one can say, is not that art certainly does influence us, whether for good or ill; but that it may, according to its own internal power and inclination, *stand available* to influence us if we so will'.[3] Some may think that this is very close to saying that judgements of artistic worth are based on the experience of the reader and that different readers draw different meanings from the same work of art.

Television as an Art Form

A strong case can be made for regarding television as an art form or, rather, as a medium with several forms of artistic expression. Television plays, drama series and comedies require the aesthetic skills of writers, producers, directors, actors, set designers, costumiers and camera crews, and call for the same level of creative talent as their equivalents in the theatre or cinema. Refashioning works prepared originally for other media, such as adapting a stage play for television, demands great creativity. But television has rarely received the critical attention devoted to other art forms. The volume of the *Cambridge Guide to Arts in Britain* that covers the period since the Second World War, published in 1988 and edited by so eminent an art critic and historian as Boris Ford, has chapters on music, ballet, the visual arts, new towns, the Third Programme, literature and drama, film, architecture, housing at Roehampton and industrial design, but no chapter on television.[4] In Britain there has been a long tradition, stretching at least as far back as Ruskin and Morris in the nineteenth century and reinvigorated in the first half of the twentieth century by D.H. Lawrence and the literary critic F.R. Leavis, that commercialism and art were antithetical, that a prime purpose of art was to undermine commercial values and that financial success was inimical to artistic integrity. The introduction of commercial television when television was beginning to attract a mass audience perhaps encouraged many to imagine that television had little artistic merit. The 'firm belief' of John Cruft, a Music Director for the Arts Council, was that 'the downfall of culture in this country comes from the introduction of commercial television, which has debased it ever since'. Andrew Sinclair in his history of the Arts Council wrote that television was 'the dominant influence in spreading cultures' but that it 'spoke of a product rather than of art or excellence . . . The medium was the Mercury of the arts, but the sweetmeats it carried were turned into slurry.'[5]

Since the expansion of television in the 1950s, all newspapers have published criticisms of television programmes, but with broadsheet newspapers they have not had the status of theatre, painting, or book reviews. No television critic has approached the general fame or status of, say, Harold Hobson, Kenneth Tynan, Sheridan Morley or Michael Billington as theatre critics, or Dilys Powell as a film critic. Impressionistic evidence suggests that Bernard Levin and Clive James became national celebrities through appearing on television rather than through writing television reviews for newspapers. Few collections of television criticism have been published. British actors with international reputations for their stage or film work have rarely acted on television. Alan Bennett and Dennis Potter are probably the only dramatists who received great critical acclaim for their work and who continued to work for television despite having success in writing for the cinema. Comedy scriptwriters such as Galton and Simpson, on the other hand, were widely praised for the quality of their writing but concentrated on television after working in films. Editors of television programmes have a key role in determining the structure and pace of a television programme and, although their names are included in the credits to programmes, no editors have become well known to the general public. No television cameramen in Britain have become household names, though this is also true for cameramen who have worked in the cinema. Composers and choreographers with national or international reputations have been invited to produce work for screening on television, but usually this has been only a tiny part of their total output.

Possibly television was not accepted as a major art form in its own right because much of its content has often been made originally for other media. Television has appropriated formats developed by other art forms. Television drama can be described as an extension of stage, radio and film dramas. Soap operas and thirty-minute situation comedies were pioneered by radio, though they were extended by television in ways that radio could not have achieved. Some may consider that original creations by television have included natural history programmes (though it could be claimed they are a refinement of educational cinema films), studio chat shows in which audiences interact with invited guests (though this format is also found on radio), and reality television such as *Big Brother*, in which viewers observe edited versions of a group of individuals interacting over several weeks. Quiz programmes for cash prizes were an important genre of ITV almost from its start and have appeared at peak time on BBC1, though not with large cash prizes. This programme format was inherited from Radio Luxembourg but it has been extended to new forms by television. Most, however, would probably not regard these natural history programmes, reality television or quizzes as art forms. It is also likely that few would think of sports presentations and news or current affairs programmes as art forms, even though they involve creative commentary and camera work, which is also true of natural history programmes.

Television itself has contributed to the notion that it is not a 'high' art form. Much television has been self-referential. Announcements of major changes to popular programmes have often been items on news bulletins. Guests on chat shows are often television celebrities. In recent years programmes have been made to explain how popular programmes were made. *How Not To Get Into the Big Brother House*, for instance, focused on how contestants for *Big Brother* were chosen. But criticism of television has very rarely been the subject of television, perhaps because of worries that adverse comment could cause viewing figures to fall. Only occasionally have the BBC, ITV or Channel 4 reviewed each other's programmes, perhaps as a result of fears that this would be free advertising for their competitors. Programme schedulers may have suspected that viewers would not be interested in television criticism, especially of programmes they may not have watched. The BBC weekly magazine the *Listener* carried printed criticism that took television seriously; but because of disappointing sales it closed in 1991. Television criticism was only part of the *Listener*'s content but its closure could have indicated that there was no great demand for highly intellectual criticism of television.

The Extent of Arts Broadcasting

Since its establishment in 1971 the Open University has broadcast art history and criticism, but usually only between midnight and 6 a.m. on weekdays and, not surprisingly, has attracted few viewers other than Open University

students. The problems of defining art make it difficult to calculate the extent
of arts programming on terrestrial television since the 1950s. One problem is
what constitutes an arts broadcast. Those who consider ballroom dancing an
art form would classify *Come Dancing* as an art programme but probably many
do not share this view. Are all forms of television drama and cinema films
shown on television arts broadcasts? Annual reports of the BBC, ITA/IBA and
ITV companies have not defined arts programmes in the same fashion – the
ITA/IBA often lumped arts programmes and documentaries together – and
this complicates attempts to trace fluctuations in the numbers of arts
broadcasts over time and between broadcasters. Glancing through
broadcasting schedules suggests that, if all drama and cinema films – staples
of television broadcasting – are excluded, 'high' arts programmes have formed
only a tiny fraction of all terrestrial television output. One's impression is that
since the 1950s the hours of 'high art' broadcasts have increased but, as
broadcasting hours have grown, they have formed a smaller proportion of all
broadcasting. Terrestrial television has never had an equivalent to radio's
Third Programme or Radio 3, although the cable Performance and the
satellite Artsworld channels are dedicated to the 'high' arts. Artsworld began
broadcasting in December 2000 but almost closed in July 2002, presumably
because it had failed to attract sufficient subscribers. The start in 2002 of the
satellite channel BBC4, which carried a high art programme on most nights,
may well have undermined the commercial prospects of Artsworld.[6] In 2002
the Classic FM digital television channel was started but it has tended to
broadcast more light music than its radio equivalent.

Arts programmes other than drama and film can be divided into those
which broadcast an artistic performance, such as a concert or an opera, and
documentaries which examine the work of an artist or group of artists,
though often these two forms of programme overlap.[7] Other art programme
formats have been competitions between enthusiasts for an art form, such as
Planet 24's *Water Colour Challenge* which Channel 4 has broadcast since
1998 for recreational painters, and *Come Dancing*, the ballroom dancing
competition which the BBC broadcast from 1950 to 1995. Ice dancing has
usually been billed as televised sport, but can also be regarded as a form of
artistic expression. Talent competitions for pop music and traditional variety-
style acts have been a staple of light entertainment since the 1950s. One of
the longest-running versions of this format was *Opportunity Knocks*, which
ITV screened from 1956 to 1978 and which was revived by the BBC as *Bob*

Says 'Opportunity Knocks' from 1987 to 1990. The immensely popular *Pop Idol* was one of the latest versions of this format. Such talent shows, however, are usually regarded as belonging to popular entertainment rather than 'the arts'. Relatively few series have concentrated on how to develop artistic skills, though children's programmes have given tips on painting and handicrafts. If ice-dancing programmes are accepted as art broadcasts, they have had the largest audiences of all art programmes. Twenty-four million people in Britain watched Torvill and Dean competing at the 1994 Winter Olympics.

It was often contended in the 1990s that terrestrial television's coverage of the arts was declining because of the more competitive broadcasting climate. In 1999 John Wyver, who had produced and commissioned arts programmes, complained that BBC2 and Channel 4, the channels which had 'traditionally nurtured individual arts documentaries', had 'quite suddenly lost almost all interest in them. BBC2 has been made over to look like a leisure-oriented cable service, and Channel 4 wants finally to grow up to become a focused "young-at-heart" brand.'[8] In 2003 the freelance arts producer David Herman lamented that in television 'there was no one who is prepared to champion obscure, the esoteric, the forgotten, the surprising'.[9] David Liddiment, who had been the managing director of Granada UK Broadcasting in 1996–7 and director of programmes for the ITV network from 1997 to 2002, thought that such programmes were 'on the margins of viability for any mainstream channel'. He explained that, as arts programmes were costly and did not attract many viewers, they were 'a lot of effort for little return' for the commercial terrestrial channels, while for the BBC the issue was 'if you run a minority channel and a highbrow digital channel as well, why would you want arts bunging up your main service?'[10] In 1998 and 2002 the terrestrial channels broadcast around one hundred hours of arts programmes in the peak evening hours, but in 2002 over eighty of these hours were provided by BBC2 and Channel 4. Between 1998 and 2002 ITV broadcast no arts programme in peak hours but its *South Bank Show* was screened late on Sunday evenings. Channel 5 had broadcast no peak-time arts programmes in 1998 but had eleven in 2002, and had shown that arts programmes could attract respectable audiences. Jane Root, Controller of BBC2, who had described arts television as dead in 1999, admitted in 2003 that 'We failed to appreciate that there is a bigger potential audience for the arts.'[11]

British-made arts magazine programmes have received great praise despite forming only a tiny fraction of the total output of television. *Monitor*, which the BBC broadcast from 1958 to 1965, covered the work of artists in a variety of fields and the films that it commissioned, from Ken Russell on Elgar and Debussy and John Schlesinger on Britten, were widely acclaimed. London Weekend Television's *Aquarius*, which was broadcast fortnightly from 1970 until 1977, adopted a similar arts magazine format. *The South Bank Show* replaced *Aquarius* and has run since 1978. It has included detailed interviews and profiles of artists and films about their work, and, ranging across the range of popular culture, it has been dedicated to the notion that there is no distinction between 'high' and 'low' art. The BBC has broadcast *Arena* since 1977 and like *The South Bank Show* considered popular culture as well as the 'high' arts. Often, however, these programmes were screened late in the evening when they were less likely to attract a very high number of viewers. Cynics may suspect that terrestrial television has included a small number of art programmes, often shunted into late night spots, to attract cultural esteem and to deflect criticisms that television was saturated with undemanding entertainment.

Criticism and reviews of the arts on terrestrial television have had a smaller role than in broadsheet newspapers or on radio. From 1964 until 1972 BBC2's *Late Night Line-up*, originally called just *Line-up*, discussed topical matters from the arts world. Granada's *Cinema* ran from 1964 until 1975 and reviewed recent cinema releases and interviewed cinema celebrities, a formula followed more or less by the BBC's *Film 71*, which has run from 1971 though with changes to its title. In recent years the BBC2 current affairs programme *Newsnight* has held a studio discussion of recent events in the art world, but this occurs only once a week, whereas the Radio 4 equivalent, *Front Row*, is broadcast every weekday evening. Criticism and interviews, in addition to performing bands, were regular features of BBC2's pop music *Disco 2*, which became the *Old Grey Whistle Test* in 1971 and ran until 1988. No series concerned with ballet or opera lasted for so many years.

Television and the Presentation of the Arts

Apologists for arts television have claimed that it is a vehicle of art education, that it promotes understanding and appreciation of art. Kenneth Clark, a director of the National Gallery, the first chairman of the ITA and the writer and presenter of the BBC's much-acclaimed history of fine art *Civilisation*, first broadcast in 1969, argued that in many ways television was superior to books in stimulating appreciation of the visual arts because 'a combination of words and music, colour and movement can extend human experience in a way that words cannot do'.[12] A long-established television technique of presenting visual art was for a leading critic to provide a commentary. Some presenters such as the nun Sister Wendy on painting or the poet John Betjeman on architecture, though authorities on their subject, gave the impression that their unusual personalities as much as the content of their programmes were being used to attract viewers. While television can deepen appreciation of painting and can demonstrate the techniques that artists employed to achieve their effects, seeing a painting on television will almost always be inferior to looking at the original. Even the most sensitive of colour broadcasts cannot match the subtleties of hue and tone that are noticeable when one views an original painting. The effects created by the size of paintings, especially very large canvases, cannot be captured by the relatively small television screen.

Watching ballet or modern dance on television is a different experience from watching a live performance in a theatre. There has been debate about whether television should film a production being performed in a theatre or whether a production should be performed in a television studio. Brendan McCarthy, a producer of television dance programmes, has pointed out that choreographers and dancers have usually preferred their work to be seen on a theatre stage. Very few 'big name' choreographers have designed pieces for performance on television. As the choreographer Christopher Bruce says, 'In live theatre *you* are the camera.' With televised studio productions, dancers have found it difficult to adjust to the demands of having a performance broken into separate parts to obtain what may work best in televisual terms. Bruce recalled that the filming for television of *Pierrot Lunaire* in 1979 was 'tough going. Stopping and starting is very hard on dancers.' Peter Wright, who has worked with the Stuttgart Ballet and in television, agreed that dancers could never give of their best if 'you are going to break it down and re-do it, in order to make it work for the camera'. Bruce has refused to rework his dances for television, his policy being 'this is the work, shoot it'. Yet often with televised dance there was a trade-off between a 'nice shot for television' and doing justice to the aims of the choreographer. One choreographer complained that he felt 'short-changed' when his work was televised because usually it was recorded too cheaply with few cameras and little editing time.

Dance appeared on terrestrial television less often in the 1990s. In part this was because programme schedulers believed that other types of programme would bring in larger audiences or could be made more cheaply, but Melvyn Bragg also explained that, although the standard of dancing could be very high, the lack of figures with iconic status like those in opera had meant that it was 'inevitable that dance has a lower profile'.[13] In the late 1990s there was a trend by television to screen shorter, more experimental dance works in the hope that these could undermine preconceptions about the nature of dance and 'show that there are young people in the ballet world, doing slightly off-the-wall stuff – not just girls in tutus and boys in blouses'.[14]

Television presentations of opera have often been criticised. Televised operas have usually been a direct relay of a stage performance, or a production created for television, or an adaptation of a work made originally for the stage. By the 1980s the latter had become the most common kind of operatic broadcast. In 1988 the critic Michael Kennedy argued that all forms of televised opera had suffered from the poor quality of television sound, though this may not have been obvious to those whose only acquaintance with opera had been through television. For him television was unsuited to grand ensembles, but its close-ups meant that it worked best with solos and duets.[15] In the 1950s and 1960s for some productions the singers and orchestra were in different studios, which can hardly have improved the overall quality of a broadcast. A writer in the *Financial Times* in 1988 condemned the practice taken from cinema of singers miming to a recorded soundtrack as 'a herring of the rosiest hue . . . A dainty moue on screen more or less synchronised with a fortissimo top C from the loudspeakers simply won't wash.'[16]

The visual nature of television probably explains why readings from novels or poetry have been unusual on television. *Jackanory*, the children's programme which the BBC broadcast on weekday late afternoons from 1965 to 1996, consisted of an actor reading a story with minimal visual effects. Its longevity suggests that schedulers have perhaps underestimated the potential of television as a medium for the reading of literary works. Novels by Austen, Dickens, Hardy and Trollope have been made into television costume dramas and been advertised as major artistic television events, although a novel of great literary merit does not necessarily translate into artistically outstanding television. Very few television programmes have shown poetry readings, though poets have been profiled in television arts magazines. Television made

Pam Ayres nationally known, but this was through light entertainment and not arts programmes, and the literati have largely ignored her work.

In the thirty years up to 1982, no series about books ran for more than thirteen weeks, though some had more than one series. Melvyn Bragg thought that the content of four or five half-hour television book programmes was equivalent to only two *Sunday Times* book pages.[17] In 1975 he had said that few people came into television wanting to make programmes about books.[18] The first television book programme was probably *To Read*, broadcast from Manchester in 1959/60.[19] *Read All About It*, presented by Melvyn Bragg, had series each year from 1975 to 1978 and concentrated on paperback books. Other book programmes on terrestrial channels have included *Burning Books*, *Speaking Volumes*, *Bookstand*, the *Book Programme*, *It's All About Books*, *Book Four*, *Cover to Cover*, *Bookmark* and *Book Choice*, but none attracted more than minority audiences. No satellite or cable channel has been dedicated to books. Programmes on classical music and the visual arts have outnumbered those about writers or books on the Performance, Artsworld and BBC4 channels. In 2003 BBC2 broadcast *Battle of the Books*, in which audiences listened to discussions about the merits of books and voted on which they preferred. Books and authors were the subject of discussion programmes such as *Late Night Line-up*, and profiles of writers and their work were the subjects of arts magazine programmes.

One reason for the small number of programmes about books may have been the difficulties of adapting a print medium to television. Stuart Cosgrove, producer of Channel 4's *Burning Books*, spoke in 1993 about the 'laziness on the part of directors and producers'. 'Pop videos and film come ready-made', he pointed out, 'with a visual bank of information – just string the clips together and you have a programme. It's much harder to make books come alive on television.'[20] In the early 1980s Melvyn Bragg wrote of 'the gut feeling of many in the educated classes that books and television cannot mix and, indeed should not mix' and the 'terror that television – in its monster potential – represents the end of a print era'. In 1985 he wrote that people had been brought up to believe that 'what you read is always more important than what you see on the screen'.[21] Bragg was convinced that television extended appreciation of a writer's work. He argued that an interview of Harold Pinter, interspersed with extracts from his plays, showed his 'replies/non-replies, his sudden starts and endings, his speech rhythms' and gave 'a terrific sense of the man . . . in a more complete way than you might get in print'.[22]

Television and Drama

Drama has always formed a vast proportion of television output. In 1937, its first full year of broadcasting, BBC television screened 123 transmissions of plays, though some of these were repeats and only two were written specifically for television.[23] All the classic plays originally written for the stage have been performed on television and, as only theatres in the big cities have usually produced such plays since the Second World War, television must have increased the opportunities for many to watch this form of drama. Shakespeare's verse dramas have been broadcast – between 1978 and 1984 the BBC broadcast all thirty-seven of Shakespeare's plays – but productions of other plays in verse have been rare. Whether television adaptations of Shakespeare have been successful is debatable. The actors have been highly competent and close-ups may make soliloquies more effective, but television studios are not suited to crowd scenes, and before the 1980s trade union pressures often discouraged outdoor filming. By the end of the twentieth century relatively few television productions of classic plays were being broadcast. All the major cinema film versions of classic plays made have been shown at some time on television and many are available as videocassettes. Television dramas that have attracted the largest audiences, such as soap operas and crime series, have rarely received critical acclaim.

Discussion of how far the general run of television drama should be regarded as high art and whether its quality has improved over time leads back to the subjective nature of artistic judgements. While the very big names of the acting profession have preferred to work in live theatre or cinema rather than television, the oversupplied labour market for actors and the relatively high pay for television acting have intensified competition for work on television. This has perhaps been all the more fierce as television has reduced opportunities for employment in live theatre and contributed to the decline of cinema film production in Britain. Before video recordings became widespread in the early 1960s, almost all television drama was broadcast live and rehearsal time was often limited. While live performances could go wrong – in 1958 the actor Gareth Jones collapsed and died during the transmission of the play *Underground* – some actors contend that the immediacy of live performances gives acting a sharper and fresher edge. On the other hand, mistakes can be edited out of recorded performances and a scene shot from several angles to find what works best. Competition for work on television among actors has meant that the standard of acting in television drama has been high. In the 1990s, when it was often alleged that the quality of television had declined, the standard of acting was hardly ever criticised.

Playwrights have never found it easy to have their work produced. Writers with established reputations for stage work have rarely written specifically for television, and relatively few television writers have achieved widespread critical acclaim for their work in television. The hours of televised drama demand an enormous number of scripts each week and, while there has always been fierce competition to write for television, run-of-the-mill television drama probably calls more for the ability to present scripts on time and to conform to the style of a series' format than for great creative originality. As with acting, it has probably been the case that television has presented viewers with work that has been carefully crafted and has passed a quality threshold rather than with what is highly original. The standard of writing for everyday television drama seems to compare more than favourably with that of B feature films produced in Britain between 1930 and 1960, though this, of course, is an expression of opinion.

A few dramas written specifically for television have been accorded the status of high art. Dennis Potter's *Vote, Vote, Vote for Nigel Barton*, *Pennies from Heaven* and *The Singing Detective*, Alan Bennett's series of monologues *Talking Heads*, Alan Bleasdale's *Boys from the Blackstuff* and *The Monocled Mutineer*, Jack Rosenthal's *Another Sunday and Sweet FA*, *The Evacuees*, *Bar Mitzvah Boy* and *The Knowledge* were all regarded as having demonstrated how television drama could be considered an art form in its own right and are widely accepted as among the high points of British culture in the second half of the twentieth century. None of them, however, was among the twenty most popular programmes of the year or even the month in which they were first broadcast. The drama series that lasts for several episodes has been explored more by television than by other art forms. The early cinema developed the cliff-hanging serial as a means of persuading audiences to return the following week, though these have never been regarded as classics of the cinema, and radio had experimented with drama series before television, but series were rarely produced for the live theatre. Much of the work of Potter, Bennett and Bleasdale was produced as series. Plays written originally for television have hardly ever been remade for television with different directors and casts, perhaps because so much television drama is concerned with contemporary issues. The only dramas seen on television with different directors and actors have been plays written for the theatre. Different television adaptations of classic novels have usually had different scripts. Situation comedies, however, have sometimes been adapted for showing in another country with a different cast of actors. *All in the Family*, an American adaptation of the British situation comedy *Till Death Us Do Part*, was even broadcast by the BBC in Britain between 1971 until 1975.

The single-production play was a staple of television until the 1980s but has now largely disappeared from television. ITV's *Armchair Theatre* ran from 1956 until 1974 and included Harold Pinter's first television play. Emphasis in many of its plays on the more seamy everyday issues led to its being nicknamed 'Armpit Theatre'. The BBC's *The Wednesday Play* ran from 1964 until 1970 when it became *Play for Today*, which lasted until 1984. These encouraged experimental writing and those which received most attention were David Mercer's *And Did Those Feet?*, Dennis Potter's *Vote, Vote, Vote for Nigel Barton*, Nell Dunn's *Up the Junction*, Jim Allen's *The Lump* and *Rank and File*, Jeremy Sandford's *Cathy Come Home* and *Edna, The Inebriate Woman*, and Jack Rosenthal's *Bar Mitzvah Boy*. The BBC's *Play of the Month* ran from 1965 to 1979 and from 1982 to 1983, but included some plays written originally for the theatre. Cost has been a major reason for the disappearance of the single-production play. Drama has always been one of the most expensive of television genres and, because sets could be used more than once and permitted other economies of scale, one hour of a series has usually been cheaper than one hour of a single play. Series provided more opportunities to build audiences. Madeleine Macmurraugh-Kavanagh claims that in the 1960s the BBC was already considering concentrating on drama serials, which could reuse the sets and had the advantage for writers of providing a more regular income than payment for a single play. She also emphasises that in the 1960s the BBC, desperate to find audiences that matched those of ITV, was moving from an ethos of providing 'what the audience needs' to that of what 'the audience wants'.[24] The greater competitiveness of television in the 1990s intensified pressures against single-production plays. By the early 1990s, a television producer of successful series said of single productions that 'the Director of Programmes finds it risky, and the Director of Advertising Sales hates them; they'd rather have an on-going success'.[25] As cinema films are self-contained productions, the screening on television may have met in part any desire among viewers to see single-production dramas.

Has Television Stimulated Interest in the Arts?

Assessments of whether television has stimulated interest in the arts are complicated by the difficulties of defining and measuring interest. Television's capacity to create interest by introducing viewers to an art form about which they knew little perhaps reached its peak when there was only one television channel. Since the start of ITV there has almost always been an alternative programme to an arts broadcast. Watching a television arts programme may have reinforced a suspicion among many viewers that they disliked or could not understand a particular art form. Probably many, and perhaps a majority, who watch an art programme are likely to have been interested already in the form of art covered by the programme. Data collected by the British Market Research Bureau in 1995–6 and 1996–7 suggest television had little capacity to create interest in art. Of those who did not attend artistic events, nearly 19 per cent claimed to watch plays on television, but less than 10 per cent watched television programmes about ballet, contemporary dance, opera, classical music, jazz, art galleries or exhibitions.[26]

'High' arts broadcasts have never attracted large audiences by the standards of television, but they compare very favourably with the numbers who attend artistic events in person. In 1988 the total audience for twenty-eight operas broadcast by BBC2 and Channel Four was about 11 million. The audience of 800,000 for one televised Mozart opera, a small audience by the standards of terrestrial television at that time, was three times higher than the annual total of those who attended all operas performed at the Royal Opera House in that year. In 1988/9 the number of seats sold for the 547 performances given in the UK by the Royal Opera, English National Opera, Opera North and Welsh National Opera companies was around 950,000.[27] It can be argued that these figures show that, but for the opportunities that television provides to watch opera, the numbers who see opera would be far smaller. This would also be true for ballet, contemporary dance and classical music concerts.

In the 1980s and 1990s a few opera singers became nationally known largely through television, such as Kiri Te Kanawa following her singing at the Charles-Diana wedding and the three tenors José Carreras, Placido Domingo and Luciano Pavarotti, who sang the operatic theme tune for the 1990 soccer World Cup. More recently television has helped Lesley Garrett become known to a very wide public. The dancers Fonteyn and Nureyev were well known to the British public, though they rarely appeared on television. In the 1990s the celebrity of the dancers Deborah Bull and Darcey Bussell was enhanced by their television appearances. The tiny number of televised modern dance programmes probably explains why no choreographers or performers of modern dance are instantly recognisable by the general public. Until the mid- to late 1980s television had made stars of a small number of performers who continued the variety-hall style of dancing such as Lionel Blair and Roy Castle, but dance routines formed only part of their television work. Dance routines, of course, have long been a part of televised pop music shows. Ice dancing, though usually televised as part of sports programmes, has borrowed extensively from ballet and contemporary dance. The leading British ice dancers, especially those who won gold medals at the Winter Olympics, such as John Curry, Robin Cousins, and Jayne Torvill and Christopher Dean, were probably better known to the public than any classical or modern dancers. Television had only a minor part in creating the fame of Barbirolli, Sargent and Beecham, perhaps the three best-known British orchestral conductors in the third quarter of the twentieth century, but their careers were well established before television became a mass interest. In the last quarter of the twentieth century Sir Simon Rattle has probably been the best-known British conductor but, while he has appeared on television, he is perhaps not a household name. Television contributed to the celebrity of the flautist James Galway, the cellist Jacqueline Du Pré, the violinist Nigel Kennedy and the percussionist Evelyn Glennie, but it is hard to think of, say, a classical brass instrumentalist who has become nationally known through television.

The growth of television in the late 1940s and early 1950s coincided with a period of expansion for classical music and the theatre. By the mid-1950s there were ten permanent symphony orchestras compared with three in the early 1920s and a hundred permanent repertory companies compared with around thirty in 1930.[28] But by the late 1950s worries about ticket sales suggest that television could have been discouraging theatre attendances. The annual report of the Arts Council noted that during the year ending in March 1959 most provincial theatres were not half-full and that twelve of 'exemplary quality' had been hit especially hard.[29] From the mid-1980s the Arts Council produced more comprehensive figures for the numbers attending arts events. The numbers attending plays, opera, ballet, classical music, art galleries and exhibitions in 1990/1 were higher than in 1986/7, though the numbers for contemporary dance had dropped. By 1995/6 those attending all of these art forms had fallen below the figures for 1986/7, which suggests that television was not stimulating a desire to attend them.

Had television raised public awareness of the importance of the arts, politicians would probably have been more concerned with the arts. All prominent politicians pay lip-service to the arts, but the post of Minister for the Arts was created only in 1964, the same year as the first Minister for Sport. Since television became a mass interest, the arts have rarely been the subject of intense party political controversy. Support for the arts has never been a key issue at general elections. In 1945/6 the Arts Council gave £136,000 to the arts in Great Britain. In 2000/1 the total grants distributed by Arts Council England alone exceeded £134 million, though this was equivalent to spending less than one penny per day for each person living in England. On the other hand, government expenditure on the teaching of English, art and music in schools and colleges is a form of spending on the arts; and the television licence fee can be regarded as a form of taxation which goes to support the BBC's arts broadcasts. Establishing the National Lottery in 1994 as a means of producing additional finance for the arts may indicate that John Major's Cabinet did not believe that the electorate would have been prepared to pay higher taxes to support the arts. It often seems to be widely believed that the arts are of no great consequence and that interest in them is an expression of elitism or dilettantism. Perhaps linked with this is a feeling that other causes deserve more public funds. Television reporting of artistic events such as Tracy Emin's unmade bed may have raised public suspicions of what is often regarded as cutting-edge art. These factors could have caused politicians to be diffident about advocating greater public expenditure on the arts.

Television, Cinema and the Watching of Film

As television was so similar to watching film and had the advantage that it could be viewed at home, television has often been regarded as the major reason why cinema audiences fell between 1950 and the mid-1980s. Total cinema admissions in Britain dropped from 1,396 million in 1950 to 501 million in 1960. Total cinema admissions continued to fall in almost every subsequent year until 1984, when they reached their lowest level of 54 million. After this came a partial recovery. By 2002 total cinema admissions were 176 million. While television caused cinema audiences to decline, more films began to be watched on television. In the late 1940s and early 1950s, film-makers and distributors were reluctant for films to be shown on television, but by the late 1950s they were realising the financial benefits of allowing selections from their film libraries to be shown by television. Between the early 1950s and the early 1970s, films increased more than any other element as a proportion of the total output of television in Britain.[30] In the early 1950s the BBC had been able to show only twelve American films per year, but in 1957 RKO agreed that the BBC could select for showing 100 of its library of 800 films.[31] In 1960 the BBC and Associated-Rediffusion made a joint deal that permitted them to show fifty-five British films. In 1964 the Cinematograph Exhibitors' Association allowed British-made films to be shown on television; and in 1967 it was agreed that British-made films more than five years old could be shown on television. By 1972 the BBC estimated that it required 200 films to be shown for the first time each year on television.[32] In the late 1980s British Satellite Broadcasting and Sky Television believed that the showing of films, especially those made in Hollywood, would be essential for the expansion of satellite television in Britain. In 1988 BSB paid £85 million for the right to show films of Paramount, Universal, MGM/United Artists and Columbia. Sky paid £60 million to Orion, Touchstone, Warner Brothers and Fox, in which Rupert Murdoch already had a controlling interest.[33]

In 1983 Anthony Smith, then director of the British Film Institute, wrote: 'Thirty years ago, when TV was young, the cinema industry created a *cordon sanitaire* between film and TV media; today it is the needs of TV that guarantee the financial viability of a film.'[34] The expansion of video recording and the realisation by film producers, especially in America, that video sales could be a valuable source of income strengthened further the ties between cinema and television. As William Shawcross pointed out, American film production companies by the late 1980s expected 'to milk a film at various stages: first of all the cinema release; then at video release; then pay-TV release, followed by free-TV release; then library release'.[35] Chapter 3 has discussed the contribution of television to the making of films in Britain.

The numbers of films shown on terrestrial television varied in the 1990s and early twenty-first century. In 1993, 4,646 feature films, excluding 243 that were made for television, were shown, but only 1,910 in 1996.[36] In 2001 the figure was around 2,500. During one February week in 2001, the five terrestrial channels showed forty-nine films, but only thirteen were screened between 7 p.m. and 11 p.m. Virtually all cinema films are shown at some time on television, and video versions of films made in the 1980s and 1990s are available for sale or hire. Videos can also be bought of the better-known films made in earlier decades.

Large numbers have watched films on television. Films shown at Christmas were the single programmes with most viewers in 1976, 1980 and 1981. In 1984 six films figured in the twenty television programmes with most viewers in that year, though four were broadcast in Christmas week.[37] The BARB viewing figures for one February week in 2001 indicate that more were watching films on television than in cinemas and that viewing figures were higher than when cinema visits were at their peak. During this one week in February 2001, around 33.5 million watched films on the five terrestrial channels alone. In addition, watching films on satellite channels accounted for nearly 4 per cent of all television viewing. How many watched films on hired or purchased videos and DVDs each week in 2001 is not known, though over 93 million videos and 24 million DVDs were hired in that year and many of these would have been of films. In 2001 the average weekly number of cinema admissions was nearly 3 million. In 1945, the year when cinema admission peaked, the weekly average had been 30 million.[38] Viewing on television a film made for exhibition in a cinema is probably less aesthetically pleasing than seeing it in a cinema, but in most localities more films of artistic merit are shown each week on television than in cinemas. Television has largely ignored short experimental films, often thought to be at the cutting edge of cinematic art, but these are also hardly ever screened in commercial cinemas.

Television, Literature and Reading

Literature has always been regarded as an art form, but there has long been debate about what types of writing merit consideration as art. Reading is a measure of interest in literature. The *General Household Survey* shows that since the 1960s the expansion of television viewing has not been accompanied by a decline in reading. In 1995 about the same amount of time was spent reading as in 1966. From 1980 to 1997 consumers spent more on books than on admissions to live arts events, cinema admissions, videocassette hire, or purchases of pre-recorded videocassettes, CDs, pre-recorded music cassettes or vinyl records,[39] but between 1981/2 and

1999/2000 the number of books borrowed per reader from libraries dropped by a third. Not all that is read would necessarily be regarded as writing of artistic merit. In 1995 on average each adult spent four hours each week reading books (though the quality of these was not specified) and nearly as much time reading newspapers.[40]

Television has boosted interest in some forms of reading. Sales of classic novels have risen after they have been televised. Covers of their paperback editions often show scenes from television adaptations. Over the past two decades a book has accompanied almost every television series concerned with the arts or history. In 2003 it was claimed that 3 million extra copies of the books mentioned on the BBC series *Britain's Favourite Book* had been sold. Yet many of the books associated with television that sell well, such as those based on cookery programmes, would probably not be considered to have literary merit. The same could also be said of the magazines connected with television which have large circulations. Television probably added to the economic pressures that led to the closure of magazines such as *Time and Tide* in 1979, though other, more specialist magazines pitched at a highbrow readership that were started, such as the *London Review of Books* in 1979 and *Granta*, which was relaunched in 1980 after closing in 1973, have survived.

Television, Radio and the Arts

Much of radio's content has been concerned with the 'high' arts such as classical music, drama and readings of what is taken to be 'quality' literature and, even though radio has no visual element, it has broadcast criticism of plays performed in theatres, ballet, opera, painting and sculpture. The loss of audiences to television did not cause a decline in radio's provision of access to the high arts. The great majority of radio listeners, however, had rejected the attempts of BBC radio to provide them with 'high' culture. By 1948 only two in a thousand people were listening to the Third Programme.[41] The content of Radio 3, which started in 1967, has been very similar to that of the Third Programme, but it too attracted only a relatively small proportion of radio listeners. In September 2000, for instance, it had only 1.2 per cent of the radio audience and only a little over 2 per cent of the total BBC radio audience. Classic FM, the commercial radio station started in 1992 that broadcasts only classical music though often only sections of orchestral works, had fared better. By 1993 about 10 per cent of the population listened to it at some time of the week, and in 2002 it had 6.7 million listeners each week, more than the popular music channels Radio 1, Kiss or Virgin in London.[42] In 2000 the commercial radio station Jazz FM, which broadcasts mainly jazz, had 1.6 per cent of the total radio audience.[43] If pop music is regarded as an art form, arguably television helped it to expand on radio by contributing to the reorganisation of BBC radio and the start of local and commercial radio in the 1960s and 1970s, which resulted in the rise of niche pop music radio stations. Audiences for such radio stations may have been boosted by the limited broadcasting of pop music on television. The rise of cable and satellite television saw the start of niche television pop music channels such as The Box, Smash Hits, VH1, Play UK, Kiss, MTV1, MTV2 and MTV Dance.

Many television dramatists worked first in radio, but how many plays written for radio were later performed on television is not clear. The single-production drama has survived on radio, perhaps because radio does not need sets. Because their sets are used only once, single-production plays have become one of the more expensive forms of television drama. Gillian Reynolds claims that radio is keeping alive the traditions of BBC television's *The Wednesday Play*. Because it relies so much on listeners imagining pictures in their minds whereas television provides the pictures, Reynolds believes that radio has more scope for experimentation.[44] Often the more successful radio playwrights and the more successful situation comedies have gravitated to television. Sir Bill Cotton has recalled that as the Head of Light Entertainment for BBC Television and the Controller of BBC1 he took programmes from radio but did not use radio to test programmes that might be transferred to television. He found that, as television expanded, more performers and writers wanted to move from radio to television.[45] Writing in the *Guardian* in 2002, Rupert Smith conceded that many television series would probably not have been screened had they not first proved themselves on radio, but stressed that the 'idea that executives at the Television Centre are ransacking the corridors of Broadcasting House for decent ideas to nick is no longer true, if it ever was; in fact, radio is recognised as a testing ground for ideas already earmarked for television.' Smith thought that, with less commercial pressure, radio was a 'more liberal, laissez-faire environment', where 'a greater diversity of talent' could flourish. Drama and comedy could 'address a far wider, more challenging range of topics without getting the tabloids up in arms'. Jon Plowman, head of BBC comedy entertainment, had decided to make a television series of the comedy sketch programme *Goodness Gracious Me*, but first gave it a radio run to iron out possible problems. He said, 'it's a way of developing a format for a relatively small amount of money and it's good for the artists, because they get to the confidence of doing six half-hours in front of a live audience, even if they are just mad blue-rinsed old ladies we've pulled in off Regent Street'. The television producer Paul Schlesinger emphasised that differences between radio and television audiences meant some radio programmes did not suit television. 'Radio audiences', he argued, 'understand satire, they don't seem to need huge stars, and they'll swallow amazingly experimental stuff. That's not true of mainstream TV',[46] though political satire was not a form of radio comedy before the success of television's *That Was The Week That Was*. The BBC had several unsuccessful attempts to make a television equivalent to the *News Quiz* before it created *Have I Got News For You?*[47] Not surprisingly most BBC radio shows that have been transferred to television have been broadcast by BBC television, though Channel 4's hit celebrity improvisation comedy *Whose Line Is It Anyway?*, first shown on television in 1988, had started on BBC radio. Very few commercial radio programmes have been transferred to any BBC television channel. Some programmes made originally for television, such as the sitcom *Steptoe and Son*, have been adapted for radio but television programmes hardly ever seem to have been made to establish whether they were suitable for transfer to radio.

Television and the Content and Style of Other Art Forms

Television has made a deep impression on the content and style of other art forms. Given the vast number of novels published each year, some are bound to have been concerned with the world of television, though no novel whose central theme is the television world has received widespread critical acclaim. Television never had more than a minor role in the works of those who are usually regarded as the more prominent British novelists of the second half of the twentieth century. Margaret Drabble's *The Radiant Way* is the only novel with television as an essential part of its structure that Steven Connor discusses in his survey of the novel in Britain from 1950 to 1995.[48] The main character of *Therapy* by David Lodge is a television writer, and the novel centres around his mid-life crisis, marital break-up and desire to return to his roots, though perhaps the novel would have worked as effectively if this character had worked in another medium. *Bridget Jones' Diary*, one of the great hits of the late 1990s which was often accused of stimulating a host of 'chick lit' imitators, also had a main character who worked in television, but here too it is possible that the novel could have worked equally well had the lead character been employed in some other London-based, fashionable occupation. The three television novels by Lis Howell, who has worked as television reporter, presenter, producer and editor, belong to the whodunit genre but provide much background about the power struggles and insecurities of television workers.[49]

Establishing whether the style of novels may have changed because of television is more difficult. Connor argues that television and then computer technology created 'an information revolution which has fundamentally reorganised the ways in which knowledge and experience are transmitted and preserved and narrated. It is not surprising that, under these conditions, novels and novelists have shown themselves uneasy about the influence of the electronic media.' He claims that in *The Passion of New Eve*, Angela Carter uses stylistic devices in an attempt to show that the novel can outdo the capacities of the electronic media.[50] The rise of the cinema in the first half of the twentieth century may have caused novelists to imagine and describe the world in a more visual manner; if this is so, it may have been continued by television. It is possible that television may have caused novelists to view the world in ways of which they are not conscious. Some writers may have cast their novels in a style which they hoped would result in their adaptation for television, especially as the television adaptations have often boosted sales of novels. The more popular television soaps and drama series have spawned novels. Six have been based on *Coronation Street*. Seven books based on characters from *Coronation Street* have also been published.[51] Such novels have hardly ever attracted critical praise.

Opera, ballet and contemporary dance have not been reinvented because of television. Few operas, ballets or modern dance pieces made while television has been a mass interest have had television as their setting. In 1961 Lionel Slater, Head of Music Productions for BBC television, argued that television's impact on opera was 'already . . . not inconsiderable'. Television encouraged clearer enunciation so that each word could be understood. Television was setting 'higher dramatic standards' by exposing such 'absurdities, only too common on the stage' as 'mature, generously built sopranos who have to impersonate youthful heroines' and 'stout, squat tenors', though even forty years later such figures were still seen on the operatic stage.[52] In 1986 it was claimed that the enjoyment of audiences at opera houses had been boosted by the provision of surtitles, an innovation borrowed from televised opera.[53] Relatively few operas have been composed specifically to be performed on television, possibly because of the costs. Benjamin Britten, arguably Britain's most acclaimed operatic composer in the second half of the twentieth century, wrote *Owen Wingrave* for television; but Charlotte Higgins of the *Guardian* claimed that, perhaps because Britten did not own a television set, this 'ended up being more suited to the stage'. In her view Gerald Barry's *The Triumph of Beauty and Deceit* was 'such a disaster on TV' and Jonathan Dove's *When She Died* 'tried to be televisual in form, but didn't really pull it off'.[54] One of the more profound effects of television on opera and dance performance may have been through the rise of video recordings as an aid to rehearsals. The sale of opera and dance videos is an important source of income for opera and dance companies, but it is not clear whether the commercial potential for video sales influenced the choice and style of stage productions.

Very few works composed since the Second World War have become included in the repertoire of symphony orchestras because of television, though the frequent dismissals of Harrison Birtwistle's avant-garde work may have resulted from his work being broadcast on television. Television has made enormous use of classical music and musicians. David Kershaw has pointed out that television has commissioned work from composers and called on music composed originally for other purposes as background music for dramas, programme signature tunes, station opening and closing signals and for commercials. Among commissioned scores for drama series were George Fenton's for *Jewel in the Crown, Bergerac* and *The Trials of Life*. Besides commissioning scores, commercials have also used snatches of classical music.[55] Although television has made extensive use of classical and other forms of music, it is hard to decide whether music composed for television background has a distinctive sound.

Television itself has rarely formed the subject matter for painters and sculptors, although Andy Warhol's pictures of Campbell's soup cans used an image from an American television commercial. Few artists have stated that their work was influenced by television, though the use of videos of the work of prominent artists as teaching aids in art colleges in the 1980s and 1990s may have had some impact on their development. Portraits have been made of prominent figures from the world of television but this is perhaps a measure of their celebrity as much as of their involvement with television.

The design of television sets has required the skills of painters and sculptors, and a high level of draughtsmanship has been needed to produce animated film, though the numbers employed in this field in Britain have never been very great. For much of the twentieth century many painters and sculptors who achieved critical acclaim no longer attempted to produce representational art, a trend which was stimulated in part by the highly accurate representation achievable by photography, moving film and then television. Television video recordings were often part of situation and installation art in the late twentieth century, which in some respects can be viewed as a refinement or even replacement of painting and sculpture, and though often featured in art exhibitions, they were rarely shown on terrestrial television art programmes. The celebrity of the installation artists Tracy Emin and Damien Hirst probably owes something to the reports of their work on television news bulletins.

As cinema audiences declined in Britain and America in the 1950s, film producers, particularly in Hollywood, tried to make films that emphasised the contrasts between watching films in cinemas and watching television. More films were made in colour and the colour quality of cinema film was superior to that of America's colour television in the 1950s. The introduction in the 1950s of the wider cinemascope screens, stereophonic sound and the making of epic films that lasted for up to three hours was intended to demonstrate the qualitative differences between cinema and television. Changes in the content of cinema film made in America and Britain can also be interpreted as attempts to withstand the competition from television. By the 1960s nudity and sexually explicit scenes appeared more often in films than on television. In the 1990s special effects, especially in disaster movies, were intended to attract audiences by providing a visual impact that television could not achieve. The second features or B movies, films intended as little other than a filler for the main feature in an evening at the cinema, and which were often regarded as devoid of quality, were dropped in the face of competition from television. Documentary films disappeared from cinemas as television began to dominate this genre. Television news led to the collapse of cinema newsreels.

Competition from television for audiences did not prevent films that have received artistic acclaim from being made. In each decade since the 1950s British films have been made which became regarded as classics of cinematic art. The late 1950s and the early 1960s have been considered a golden age for film production in Britain. *Saturday Night and Sunday Morning*, *The Loneliness of the Long Distance Runner*, *This Sporting Life* and *A Kind of Loving* were acclaimed for being the first convincing cinematic portrayals of working-class life in England. The dramas *The Bridge on the River Kwai* and *Lawrence of Arabia*, set in wartime, also received critical accolades. Distinguished pictures continued to be made in Britain after this but they tended to be fewer and further apart. Film production in Britain declined after the rise of television but this was more marked after the 1950s. One hundred and one films were made in Britain in 1949, 150 in 1954 and 122 in 1959. This figure had dropped to 24 in 1981, 53 by 1984 and to 30 in 1989 but by 1996 had reached 128.[56] Film production in Britain had always suffered from under-investment and it is probable that declining cinema audiences added to this. Chapter 3 has discussed the contribution of the BBC, ITV companies and Channel 4 to film production in Britain. Television concerns had made or been co-producers of such acclaimed films as *On Golden Pond*, *My Beautiful Launderette*, *Another Time Another Place*, *A Room with a View*, *Rita, Sue and Bob Too*, *Four Weddings and a Funeral*, *Secrets and Lies*, *The Madness of King George*, *The Crying Game*, *Trainspotting*, *East Is East*, *Iris* and *Billy Elliot*.

Jane Stokes has analysed more than 100 cinematic films made in the United States and Britain in which television is crucial to the development of the plot.[57] Only a few were fictional explorations of the world of television. The American comedy *Tootsie*, released in 1982 and directed by Sydney Pollack, was possibly the most acclaimed of the films based on a television studio. This featured Dustin Hoffman who could not get work as an actor but became a television soap opera star when he impersonated a woman. *The Killing of Sister George*, made in 1968, examined how being written out of a British soap opera caused an actor's personal life to disintegrate and was one of the first films to present a lesbian love triangle. Some American films emphasised corruption in television. Sidney Lumet's *Network*, for instance, described by Stokes as 'One of the most startlingly vitriolic assaults on television the cinema industry has ever made', showed television executives as obsessed with audience ratings. In *Power*, Lumet considered how political campaign managers manipulated television and other media. Robert Redford's *Quiz Show*, released in 1994, was based on television quiz shows that were rigged in the 1950s to boost audience ratings. So many films have been made in Britain and America that Stokes may have underestimated the number that have been concerned with television but, as it is unlikely that she has overlooked any prominent films that feature television, it would seem that television has not figured largely as a subject for cinematic film.

Cinema has profited from those who developed their talents in television. Television has been a springboard for those who wished to work in film. British directors such as Mike Leigh, Ken Russell, and John Schlesinger worked in television before concentrating on cinema. Dennis Potter and Alan Bennett, often regarded as the most aesthetically successful of television dramatists, also wrote for films though never turned their backs on television. Yet the very big names among British film actors, such as Michael Caine, Richard Burton, Albert Finney, Tom Courteney, and Alan Bates have made only rare appearances on television and the stage rather than television has been their pathway to leading film roles. Dudley Moore, however, became a Hollywood star on the basis of his television work. During the last two decades female cinema stars such as Judi Dench and Julie Walters have continued to appear regularly on television. Nearly all of those who starred in the *Carry On* films continued working in television. Television programmes have been the basis for feature films. Feature films were made of the television situation comedies *Steptoe and Son*, *Dad's Army* and *On the Buses*. The Monty Python team made three cinema films. Tony Hancock's starring roles in *The Rebel* and *The Punch and Judy Man* followed his television success. Possibly films based on television series were made in the hope that television celebrity would boost box-office receipts.

The television world has rarely been the subject matter of plays written for the stage. Stage versions of television series such as the sitcoms *Are You Being Served?* or *Dad's Army*, like the staging of plays with actors who had become household names through working on television, were perhaps attempts to use television celebrity to fill theatres. In the 1950s and 1960s there were complaints that television was using acting and writing talent from the theatre but putting little back into the theatre. Many critically acclaimed theatre plays were also shown on television, though sometimes these were the cinematic versions of them. The range of plays produced for the stage has varied so much that it is hard to be sure whether television has influenced writing for the theatre. In 1961 John Elliott of the BBC Drama Department argued that the changes to British theatre in the 1950s had used techniques developed by television. Television had broken the three-act pattern for plays. By taking attention off scenery and focusing it on actors, television, he claimed, had helped 'to break up the old theatrical moulds, and even if it is not marching "shoulder to shoulder" with the new movements, it is thoroughly mixed up in them'. While conceding that 'the real cutting edge of creative drama still exists in the theatre than in the studio', Elliott contended that the 'spadework' of the theatre's 'pure gold' of writers and directors such as Pinter, Mortimer, MacWhinnie and Tony Richardson had been done in radio and television.[58] With the rise of the BBC *The Wednesday Play* and later the work of television dramatists such as Dennis Potter, Troy Kennedy Martin, Alan Bleasdale and Alan Bennett, one could have argued that the television studio was as much at the cutting edge of drama as the theatre.

The curriculum of the most prestigious drama colleges has remained very much a preparation for acting in the theatre, which could reflect a conviction that those who are equipped to act in a theatre would be able to meet the demands of television acting. It is sometimes claimed that, when those whose previous acting experience has all been on television have to act in a live theatre, they sometimes have difficulty with voice projection and using the whole body rather than just the face to create a character. Some were reputed to have found it difficult to keep giving the same performance night after night in a theatre. Timothy West, an actor with vast experience of the theatre, film and television, has argued that television 'fights shy' of 'heightened or poetical language' and that using unfamiliar language naturally could be acquired only through working in the live theatre.[59] Olivier wrote in 1986 that he was sorry about standing aloof from television for so long and hoped that more 'classically-trained stage actors should appear regularly on the box, explore its possibilities like I explored film's, and create classical television roles'.[60] Before the widespread use of video recordings in the 1960s, most television drama was live and this may have needed acting techniques more like those needed for theatre performances. The writer and arts broadcaster Mark Lawson has argued that in the very recent past reality television shows such as *Big Brother* have allowed television audiences to observe everyday behaviour and that this is leading to a more understated style of acting that approximates to the image of reality in such shows. This, in turn, may affect the performances of actors in theatres. The sitcom *The Office*, sometimes called a mockumentary because it imitates so successfully the appearance of fly-on-the-wall documentaries, is perhaps an example of how reality television has influenced television acting.

Television Comedy as an Art Form

Comic plays, particularly the half-hour situation comedy, have been a staple of television since the late 1950s. One can argue that the half-hour situation comedy represents a peak of British television achievement. It originated with radio, though it was also influenced by variety-hall sketches. It has already been mentioned that many television situation comedies were adapted from successful radio programmes but there has been less traffic in the opposite direction. Ninety-minute cinema film versions of some of the more widely praised television situation comedies have been made, but the general critical opinion has been that they worked less well than their shorter television form.

Within the British artistic establishment, television situation comedy has not always been given great recognition. Despite the wit and observation of character of situation comedy writers such as Roy Clarke, Johnny Speight, Alan Simpson and Ray Galton, David Croft and Jimmy Perry, John Cleese and Ben Elton, their work is rarely compared to the 'big names' of the British stage comedy like Sheridan or Wilde. Some may think that situation comedy is trivial and ignores deeper social issues; but this criticism could be levelled against Wilde's comedies of manners. Many situation comedies have dealt with major social issues or at least showed how individuals can be victims of social and economic change. Much of the humour of, say, *Hancock's Half Hour*, *Only Fools and Horses* and *The Likely Lads* centred on how the class structure frustrated social aspirations. Racial tensions associated with Britain's imperial decline were the underlying theme of *Till Death Us Do Part*.

The visual element of television gave a distinctive quality to television situation comedy, but this developed slowly. In the 1950s and 1960s few of the jokes in situation comedy depended entirely on the visual. Facial gestures were very much part of the comic appeal of Tony Hancock; but Galton and Simpson claimed that they did not have to change their style of writing when Hancock moved from radio to television. The settings and clothing of *Steptoe and Son* set the scene for this situation comedy but, as with other situation comedies, most of the humour derived from the interplay of characters, and this was achieved very largely through dialogue. Visual gags were found more often in the 1950s and 1960s in comedy sketch shows such as *It's A Square World* starring Michael Bentine, which started in 1960, and Spike Milligan's *Q*, which had six series between 1969 and 1982. Visual effects were a key part of the sketches of Marty Feldman's *It's Marty*, which was first broadcast in 1968. For some viewers Feldman's unusual facial features were a constant visual joke, but he also devised and acted in sketches such as 'The Loneliness of the Long Distance Golfer', which included Feldman playing golf shots from the roof of a train and from a women's bath. Feldman also contributed to *At Last the 1948 Show*, in many ways the forerunner of *Monty Python's Flying Circus*. The Ministry of Silly Walks, one of the most celebrated of *Monty Python* sketches, was dependent on its visual effect. Les Dawson was only one of many who continued the music hall tradition of men dressed as women, a form of comedy that needed men to be seen in frocks. Visual effects had been part of the American situation comedy *The Monkees*, first shown in Britain in 1966, which was loosely modelled on the British pop group the Beatles. *The Goodies*, which had eight series between 1970 and 1980, was probably the first highly successful situation comedy in which visual humour was essential. In one episode a blancmange played tennis. In another a giant domestic cat terrorised London. Visual jokes became a main element of situation comedy in the 1980s with *The Young Ones*, which involved the anarchic life of a group of male students living together, and in 1990s series such as *Mr Bean* and *Bottom*. Even in the 1990s and early twenty-first century, dialogue rather than visual effects has been the basis of most television situation comedy. Before the development of video recording film, the fear that something could go wrong with a live comedy show may have discouraged the use of visual humour. The sets required for much visual humour may have made it prohibitively expensive. It may also have been thought that humour that develops from characters and dialogue is more sophisticated and has more appeal to adult viewers.

If situation comedies are accepted as an art form, then it can be claimed that television has brought this form of art to very large numbers. Harbord and Wright have shown that *Steptoe* in 1964 and *To The Manor Born* in 1980 were the only situation comedies to win the biggest audiences of all television programmes in any particular year between 1955 and 1994. On the other hand, 1966 and 1967 were the only years after 1957 when no situation comedy was among the twenty programmes with most viewers. From the 1970s usually around four situation comedies were among the twenty programmes each year with most viewers. In the 1970s and 1980s television schedulers may have thought that situation comedies were a means of attracting relatively large audiences. The nature of the situation comedies that tended to be most popular with viewers, however, weakens the case for regarding situation comedies as exposing large numbers of viewers to a form of artistic expression. Those with most viewers were often not those that received the most lavish praise. Much television situation comedy can be formulaic. In 1975 *Man about the House* and *Are You Being Served?* both appeared four times in the twenty programmes with most viewers each month in 1975, whereas *Porridge* and *Dad's Army*, which received far more critical acclaim, appeared only once.

The shorter comic sketch, which probably originated with Victorian music hall, can also be defined as a form of artistic expression that was brought to a mass audience by television. Before the Second World War, weekend evening viewing on television included variety-hall sketches and the techniques required for these later fed into the development of television situation comedy. The expansion of television in the 1950s contributed to the collapse of variety halls, a process begun by cinema, but at the same time leading comedians whose careers had begun in the halls, such as Arthur Askey and Arthur Haynes, were performing sketches on their television variety shows. In the 1970s and 1980s the shows of Morecambe and Wise were largely a series of sketches that continued the variety-hall sketch tradition. The television work of Benny Hill, whose television series in Britain ran from 1955 until the late 1980s, consisted almost exclusively of short sketches. These were very much based on the 'nudge, nudge', 'wink, wink' style of variety-hall humour and the sauciness of the British seaside postcard, and Hill's sketches often involved little more than a single joke. Many of Hill's sketches were entirely visual, with no dialogue, which may explain why he was the television comedian whose work had the strongest following abroad. In the 1970s and 1980s he may have been the best-known television comedian throughout the world but, perhaps because of the sexist and sexual nature of his comedy, and possibly the retelling of the same gag, he received very little critical praise. In the late 1960s the much-acclaimed *Monty Python's Flying Circus*, which often included jokes whose appreciation required a high level of formal education, extended the sketch format by having gags that ran into different sketches and making extensive use of visual effects that could not be achieved on a theatre stage. In the late 1990s *Goodness Gracious Me!*, the comedy series with an Asian cast, was using the comedy sketch format.

Television, the Arts and British Life

Television, it can be claimed, has enriched the artistic life of Britain. High-art programmes have formed only a small proportion of the total output of television and, except for film, have rarely attracted the largest of television audiences, but they provided the opportunities to see artistic work that has been considered to be of the highest quality. Probably the people who have watched arts programmes have tended to be already interested in art, yet even those who have no time for high art on television are exposed on a regular basis to acting of a high quality. Soaps and drama series, the most popular forms of television, are often derided but, except for *Crossroads* in the 1960s and 1970s, the standard of acting has not been condemned. If television itself is accepted as an art form, one can argue that viewers have been presented with high-quality television camera work and design, though these are often taken for granted. The development of the drama series and the half-hour situation comedy were not created by television, but television brought them to new levels of achievement.

There is also a debit side to television's involvement with the arts. It drew audiences from the cinema and, probably though to a lesser extent, from the theatre and concert halls. It exploited the creative talent of radio. By its nature television is a medium of spectatorship. It has provided opportunities to consume art but, except for those whose work is shown on television, it has done relatively little to encourage others to create art. Programmes concerned with how to create art have been far fewer than those concerned with cooking, gardening or interior decoration, though some would argue that these are forms of art. Television's role in the artistic life of Britain could already have passed its peak. The next decade may well see more channels dedicated to the arts. Indeed, there may even be channels devoted to each art form, as has already happened with popular music. This may delight devotees of an art form but it could also result in the ghettoisation of art on television, of arts television never having the opportunity to reach those who had previously shown little interest in it. The great artistic achievement of television could be that it has provided access to the arts. The irony of the near future could be that television will have more art to be accessed but few will be taking advantage of it.

Chapter 9

TELEVISION AND SPORT

Sport on Television

S ports events have always been a major part of television broadcasting. Television coverage of sport has always been far more extensive than that of the cinema, the other great visual medium of the twentieth century. The BBC's first outside television broadcast was a test transmission of a golf demonstration on 5 October 1936.[1] The Wimbledon tennis championships were first televised live in 1937. In 1938 the England–Scotland football international, the FA Cup Final and the Boat Race were televised. In June 1954, a month that included live broadcasts of test-match cricket, soccer's World Cup, Ascot, Wimbledon and the Royal Horse Show, sport constituted a third of all BBC television output. In June 1962 sport formed more than a fifth of all BBC television broadcasts and 15 per cent of ITV broadcasting.[2] The 1970 soccer World Cup coincided with the general election. In the first week of the election campaign, the BBC transmissions of the World Cup were four times longer than those of the election. In the week of the election the BBC broadcast thirty-one hours of football and ITV nineteen.[3] In the 1970s and 1980s the number of hours of sports broadcasts grew as the total hours of television broadcasting expanded. In 1988/9 sports broadcasts formed more than 13 per cent of the output of BBC1, 16 per cent of BBC2, 8 per cent of ITV and 9 per cent of Channel 4.[4] In the 1990s the introduction of round-the-clock television and the rise of cable and satellite television saw a massive expansion of sports broadcasts. Between 1995 and 2000 the total hours of sports broadcasts rose from 11,000 hours to 35,000. In 2000 they comprised nearly 10 per cent of all television broadcasting.[5] Sport has also been a frequent item in news bulletins.

Television has never given all sports equal coverage. In the 1980s and early 1990s the sports televised most often were horse racing, cricket, football, snooker, tennis, golf and rugby union. In Olympic years the Olympic Games would have to be added to this list. Despite their large numbers of participants, angling, badminton, squash, netball and hockey have been rarely televised. Blood sports have hardly ever been included in televised sports programmes. What sports have been broadcast has depended on the level of pre-existing interest, the costs of televising events including the sums needed to pay for broadcasting rights, and whether a sport can provide 'good television'. In 1975 John Bromley, head of sport for London Weekend Television, explained that for a sport to make 'good television', which involved attracting what schedulers regarded as a satisfactory number of viewers, a sport event needed rules that were simple and easily understood by viewers, could be televised without too much extra work and cost, and was capable of drawing a reasonable number of spectators to the venue where it was held.[6] A year later Tony Preston and Tony McCarthy, also from ITV, made more or less the same points, but added that the playing area should not be so large as to make it difficult to televise the action and that an element of skill created good television.[7] It has always been easier for some sports to meet these criteria than for others. Squash and badminton may have been screened rarely because viewers find it hard to follow the ball or the shuttlecock.

Garry Whannel has pointed out that 'sport is a reliable, rather than a spectacular winner of audiences'.[8] The BBC Research Department estimated that in 1987 sports broadcasts accounted for over 28 per cent of the time spent viewing BBC1, 34 per cent on BBC2, 21 per cent on ITV and 16 per cent on Channel 4.[9] In 1975/6, the BBC had an average weekly audience of 13 million for *Superstars*, a programme in which stars from different sports competed against each other in a series of athletic events, 10.5 million for *Match of the Day* and 9 million for *Sportsnight*, respectable rather than impressive audiences.[10] BARB figures for the week ending 4 March 2001, a week of no remarkable sporting activity, show that, when there were no big sports events, sport did not figure among the programmes with most viewers. The sports quiz, *A Question of Sport*, with 6.4 million viewers, was BBC1's twenty-seventh most popular programme. No broadcast of a sport event was among the thirty BBC2, ITV or Channel 4 programmes with most viewers. The three BSkyB sport channels accounted for 4.7 per cent of all television viewing, more than the combined total for all the Sky film channels. Sports broadcast most often have not always been those with most viewers. In 1992 horse racing constituted 13.7 per cent of all sports broadcasting, but provided only 9.9 per cent of the viewers for all sports programmes.[11]

Only occasionally has sport delivered very large audiences. Because the BBC and ITV used different methods of audience measurement before 1981, it is not certain what sport broadcast had the highest UK audience. The BBC calculated that England winning the World Cup in 1966 had been watched on the BBC by 26 million and on ITV by 4 million. The highest number of viewers for a sports broadcast in the period when the BBC and ITV used the BARB audience statistics was nearly 24 million for the BBC1 coverage of Torvill and Dean in the 1994 Winter Olympics. Harbord and Wright calculated that two sports broadcasts were among the twenty programmes with most viewers each year only in four years between 1955 and 1994. Some sports events held in Britain attracted very large television audiences worldwide. Four hundred million are thought to have watched the 1966 football World Cup Final and 350 million the men's final of the Wimbledon tennis tournament in 1987.[12]

The biggest events of the sporting calendar have attracted most viewers. In the winter of 1971/2, the number of viewers for rugby league transmissions, broadcast most Saturdays, averaged between 3.3 million and 3.7 million, but the Rugby League Cup Final had a television audience of between 4.5 million and 5.2 million.[13] In 1985, 18.5 million stayed up until 0.23 a.m. to watch the final frame of the World Professional Snooker Championship, the largest audience for any BBC2 programme and the highest audience up to that time for any television programme screened after midnight.[14] The highest number of viewers for any Channel 5 broadcast in 2001 was the 5.6 million who watched the England versus Albania soccer World Cup qualifying match, but this formed only 24 per cent of all those who were watching television in Britain at the time of the broadcast.[15]

The appeal of sport to particular social groups has made it attractive to programme schedulers. Sport is one television genre watched by more men than women. In 1988, men never formed more than 60 per cent of the audience for any televised sport, and more women than men watched athletics, equestrian sport other than horse racing, gymnastics, ice-skating and tennis, all sports in which television carried extensive coverage of competitions for women.[16] Sport has also been an effective method in attracting viewers from social classes A and B. More than 20 per cent of the viewers for rugby and skiing were from social classes A and B. In 1995 nine out of ten men from social classes A, B and C1 were reported to have watched the coverage of the rugby union World Cup.[17] In the early 1990s it was

thought that BSkyB spent so much on buying the rights for sports broadcasting because this was the most effective method of reaching young men.

Television stimulated interest in some sports. In the 1950s show jumping
achieved a national following through television exposure, though interest in
this had been aroused by Britain's only gold medal at the 1952 summer
Olympics being won for show jumping. In the 1980s Channel 4's coverage of
minority sports created a cult following for sports so unfamiliar to Britain as
American football and sumo wrestling. In 1985/6 American football had 3
million viewers per week in Britain. In 1987 the weekly audience for sumo
wrestling was 1 million.[18] The regular screening of live rugby league matches
from the 1950s helped the nature of the game and its leading clubs and
players to be become known for the first time outside its north of England
heartlands. The televising of snooker made possible by colour television
revived snooker as a spectator sport.

The Varieties of Television Sport Programmes

Most television sports coverage has consisted of live transmissions of sports
events or edited versions of them hours after they took place. This reflects, no
doubt, the form of sport material that those interested in sport have wanted. In
1937 the BBC had broadcast *Sporting Magazine*, a monthly programme, and
Television Sports Magazine in 1946.[19] The BBC launched *Sportsview*, hosted by
Peter Dimmock, in 1954, a midweek sports magazine with features on different
sports and sport performers though sometimes a whole programme was devoted
to a live or recorded broadcast of one sport. This ran until 1968 when it was
replaced by *Sportsnight*, but the programme format remained broadly similar. In
1958 the BBC started *Grandstand*, a live sports programme lasting for almost the
whole of Saturday afternoon. It included previews of the afternoon's sport,
recordings of sports events from the previous week, live coverage of more than
one sport and a results service. Its format has changed little and it is now the
longest-running live sports programme in the world. The BBC broadcast short
highlights of football and other sports on Saturday evenings in the 1950s, but
its *Match of the Day*, with a longer recording of one match, began on BBC2 in
1964. It acquired more viewers when it was transferred to BBC1 in 1966. The
establishment of BBC2 allowed the BBC to have blanket coverage of test-match
cricket and Wimbledon. Lord Briggs has argued that sports coverage boosted
viewing numbers for BBC2.[20] ITV did not have a nationally screened equivalent

to *Sportsview*, although in 1963 thirteen regional sport magazine and sport news programmes were broadcast by ITV companies.[21] *World of Sport*, ITV's Saturday afternoon rival to *Grandstand*, did not start until 1965. In 1976 and 1977 it had more viewers than *Grandstand*[22] but was scrapped in 1985. Sports magazine programmes have not featured extensively on Channel 4 or Channel 5. Discussion and preview sport programmes have been shown on the cable and satellite dedicated sport channels.

Investigative sports journalism has never been particularly strong on British television, possibly because the makers of television sports programmes, like newspaper and radio sports journalists, could not afford to antagonise sports organisations by drawing attention to disreputable aspects of sport. Explorations by television of sporting scandals have usually been presented in current affairs programmes. The allegations in 2002, for instance, that the Jockey Club had been too dilatory in investigating accusations of trainers and jockeys having connections with bookmakers were screened on the BBC's *Panorama* and not a sports programme. News such as speculation about injuries to players and demands from players for higher wages or transfers that has made up so much of the reporting on sport by the popular press has not been pursued by television. Television has no equivalent to the tabloid press coverage in the 1980s and 1990s of the private lives and particularly the sexual exploits of prominent sports personalities, though these are mentioned on the sports quiz *They Think It's All Over* and form the basis of the fictional drama series *Footballers' Wives*.

Fictional dramas based on sport have provided only a very tiny part of the output of television. *United!*, a soap opera based on a fictional Second Division football club broadcast twice weekly by the BBC, started in 1965 but never challenged the popularity of Granada's *Coronation Street* and was dropped in 1967. In 1972 Jack Rosenthal's play *Another Sunday and Sweet FA*, about a referee of a Sunday morning football match, captured the nuances of recreational soccer. In 1989 and 1990 *The Manageress* featured a woman as the manager of a Football League club, an event not yet mirrored in professional league football. In 1998 the BBC broadcast *Playing the Field*, a series about a women's football team in South Yorkshire, but most storylines revolved around the romances, family tensions and work problems of the players. Sport has surfaced only occasionally in *Coronation Street* and *EastEnders*. One major way in which these soaps have not represented accurately everyday life is their ignoring of sport.

Sport has been the basis of television humour, though rarely of situation comedies. The BBC broadcast *Quizball*, in which teams of players and celebrity supporters of league clubs answered general knowledge and football questions, from 1966 to 1972; it had an air of jollity with an expectation that contestants would make humorous remarks. *A Question of Sport*, screened by the BBC since 1970, had a similar format of prominent sports players answering questions on sport, and appealed more to viewers. While light-hearted banter has always been part of the programme, its comic element became more prominent over time. The broadcast in 1987 on which Princess Anne appeared had 19 million viewers, making it the television programme with the third-highest number of viewers for that year.

In the 1990s sport comedy programmes exploited other television comedy shows. *They Think It's All Over*, first broadcast by the BBC in 1995, appears to be modelled on the satirical current affairs programme *Have I Got News For You*. In *They Think It's All Over* leading sports players have been expected to be the butt of satirical humour, but this has been mixed with laddish culture that stresses the sexual adventures and divergence from the clean-cut image of sports stars. *Fantasy Football League*, hosted by the alternative comedians Frank Skinner and Alan Baddiel, had many similarities with the late-night chat shows and also took a laddish, irreverent view of football. Most attempts to use sport in humorous quiz shows have been examples of the self-referential element of so much television. Clips used in them have been invariably taken from television sports broadcasts.

Most viewers would probably agree that technological developments have caused the pictorial quality of the live and recorded broadcasting of sports programmes to improve. In the 1930s and 1940s broadcasts of outdoor events relied on fixed camera positions which could swivel to track movement across an arena but had only limited facilities for close-ups. Multiple cameras were used rarely. Boxing featured prominently among sports televised in the 1940s and 1950s because its action was restricted to a relatively small area and could be covered by a fixed camera. Before the introduction of video recording film in the late 1950s, televised recordings of sport could give the impression that an event had been played in a snowstorm. Video recording tape not only improved the quality of recordings and encouraged more programmes of recorded sport but also made possible playbacks of decisive and controversial incidents.

The first sports event to be screened in colour on British television was the Wimbledon tennis championship in 1967. Colour made sports broadcasts more of a spectacle but, perhaps because there was some blurring of performers in long-distance shots, colour, in conjunction with more sophisticated zoom cameras, led to more close-ups in broadcasts of outdoor sports, which did not always indicate whereabouts on the field the action was taking place. From the 1970s a main development in the pictorial presentation of sport on television has been the increase in the number of cameras used and their positioning. The BBC began having cameras at both ends of cricket grounds only after it had screened highlights of test matches recorded by Australian television, which had cameras at both ends. To stress the novelty and superiority of its exclusive televising of league soccer in 1988, ITV's publicity emphasised that instead of the usual four or five cameras it would have ten, including one inside each goal.[23] Channel 4's coverage of test-match cricket has included close-up views from cameras inside the stumps, electronic animations to establish whether LBW decisions were correct, and highly sensitive microphones and graphics that could establish whether the ball had made the faintest of contacts with the bat. Even in the earliest days of televised sport the television viewer probably had a better view of the action than that of any spectator present at an event.

Televised sports events have always had oral commentaries, but different sports have called for different styles of commentary. The sense of excitement conveyed by Murray Walker's motor-racing commentaries would probably be inappropriate for a more leisurely paced sport such as golf. Assumptions about viewers' knowledge of a sport influenced the nature of commentaries. In the 1950s and 1960s Eddie Waring's rugby league commentaries often stressed that a goal was worth two points, but cricket commentators rarely explained the LBW rule. Having former players to provide expert analysis became more common in the 1960s and is now standard practice for almost all sports broadcasts. Former players have been used increasingly as commentators, though the leading commentators on soccer in recent years – Brian Moore, Barry Davies, John Motson and Clive Tyldesley – did not play the game at the highest level. Some commentators, such as Eddie Waring in rugby league, Harry Carpenter in boxing and Dan Maskell in tennis, became major personalities of their sports between the 1950s and 1980s. Waring's fame probably exceeded that of any rugby league player.[24] Styles of commentary reflected, and perhaps helped to create, the cultural resonances of particular sports. Waring reinforced impressions of rugby league as a north of England sport, and of the north of England as a place where people faced a harsh environment with a cheerful toughness. The upper-class tones of Dorian Williams emphasised showjumping as a sport for toffs.

One clear change in the oral presentation of sport on television has been the involvement of women in the 1980s and 1990s, which can be related to the rise of the women's movement in wider society. Sue Barker, a former top-class tennis player, has introduced the BBC's coverage of Wimbledon and chaired *A Question of Sport*, while Hazel Irvine has presented snooker competitions and introduced the sport section of the Saturday evening news. In the 1970s women former tennis players were providing expert comments on Wimbledon and this was extended to most sports with a strong women's presence in the 1990s. By the 1990s it was also common for former women players in sports played extensively by both sexes to interview male sports stars and to take part in pre- and post-match analysis of matches played by men. Commentary, however, has remained very much a male preserve. On terrestrial television women have hardly ever been the commentators for men's soccer, either rugby code or cricket, or on the panels that analyse matches in these sports.

Television has increased public knowledge of sports. Even enthusiasts for sport have seen some sports only on television. Even those with relatively little interest in sport have probably picked up some knowledge of sports through being in the same room when others watch televised sport. Television has caused the followers of sports to become less insular in their outlook. Before television, awareness of the leading players from overseas varied between sports. Enthusiasts of cricket, athletics, tennis and boxing knew of the leading overseas figures in their sports, whereas until Hungary defeated England at Wembley in 1953 most football fans would probably not have been able to name the leading foreign players or even clubs. The televising of the 1954 World Cup and then the European Cup meant that the leading overseas players were household names within three or four years of England's defeat by Hungary. Television has probably boosted appreciation of sports tactics and skills. Even in the 1950s commentators drew the attention of viewers to playing tactics. In the 1960s Kenneth Wolstenholme repeatedly mentioned how the more attacking style of overlapping full-backs was transforming full-back play in soccer. The conversation of football fans shows that many of them have picked up the terminology of televised sports commentary, though the reactions of football supporters in a pub to the comments of Jimmy Hill show that expert comments have often been taken with a pinch of salt. The introduction of immediate action replays made possible by use of video recording film in the 1960s increased the opportunities for explaining the course of play and for appreciating playing skills.

Television and the Playing of Sport

Recreational sports contests have been almost totally ignored by television and relatively few series on how recreational players can improve their skills have been broadcast. In sports with frequent pauses that permit instant action replays such as cricket, television commentators have often been able to advise younger viewers on how to copy the techniques of top-class players. Television is often accused of having created a nation of couch potatoes, of discouraging children in particular from taking physical exercise and playing sport. While there is no way of knowing whether more would have played sports had there been no television, the expansion of television since the Second World War has been accompanied by higher numbers playing sport, though not every sport has experienced higher numbers of participants.[25] Television has been only one influence on participant numbers. Rising levels of affluence, more sports centres, the playing of sports at schools, newspaper coverage and the loss of playing fields have also affected participation.

Television seems to have encouraged the playing of some sports. By the early 1970s snooker was still played in clubs, but most commercial snooker halls had closed, perhaps partly because of television as a rival leisure interest. The expansion of interest in the game as a televised sport made possible by the introduction of colour transmissions prompted a revival in the playing of snooker and the opening of commercial snooker halls. Steven Barnett has pointed out that the increased television coverage of volleyball in the mid-1980s coincided with an increase in the number of registered players from 4,703 in 1983 to over 24,000 by 1988.[26] Some sports have received very little television coverage while the number of their participants has increased. Between 1960 and 1980 membership of the British Sub-Aqua Club expanded from 4,000 to 28,000. Over the same period the membership of the Royal Yachting Association grew from 11,000 to 65,000.[27] The ETTA, the governing body for table tennis, thought that declining television coverage between 1978 and 1988 was a significant factor in explaining why the number of players dropped from 3.2 million in 1980 to just over 2 million in 1988.[28] The rise in the number of soccer clubs from over 25,000 to over 40,000 between the mid-1960s and the mid-1980s, and an estimated rise in the number of cricket participants from 400,000 to 500,000 between 1973 and 1985, suggest that television had not caused the playing of these sports to decline.[29] Localised studies indicate that the numbers playing cricket in the 1990s were declining. Cricket administrators hardly ever blamed this on the televising of cricket but did see the poor performance of the England team as a major factor. Television highlighted the inadequacies of the national team.

Television and Sport Spectators

Soccer, cricket, speedway and rugby league all had record attendances in the seasons immediately after the Second World War but, while their spectator numbers fell with the spread of television, it does not follow that television was the chief cause of this. Rising affluence in the 1950s probably increased access to a wider range of leisure interests, which included watching television. Administrators of many sports feared that live television broadcasts of sport could cause spectator numbers to fall. By 1950 the Association for the Protection of Copyright in Sports, to which the governing bodies of many sports were affiliated, was concerned about the effects of televised sport on gate receipts. Except for a brief experiment in 1960, the Football League did not agree to the live televising of its matches until 1983. From the start of BBC2, cricket had allowed virtually all of each day's play in test matches to be televised, even though county matches were played at the same time. Many in rugby league complained that live television reduced attendances at other matches, but Bill Fallowfield, the Secretary of the Rugby League, pointed out that television fees brought much-needed income into the game and argued that, had rugby league not been televised live, some other game would have been and this could have hit rugby league attendances and finances even harder.

For most sports, television has not usually caused attendances at their biggest events to fall. The FA Cup Final, the soccer match with the longest history of being broadcast live, has always had a full house. With most sports, it is the lower levels of the first-class competitions that seem to have lost spectators through other sports being televised. Television coverage is free advertising for a sport, but even the recorded coverage of the highest levels of a sport may discourage match attendances at the lower reaches of its professional competitions by increasing spectator awareness of the inferior quality of what is on offer. This could be a partial explanation why average match attendances in the Fourth Division of the Football League fell from 8,000 in 1960 to 4,000 in 1990. Speedway suggests that an absence of television coverage can cause interest, and spectator numbers, in a sport to fall. In the late 1940s and early 1950s, speedway was sometimes called Britain's second most popular spectator sport, but its regular television coverage ceased in the 1970s; however, in the early 2000s satellite television started to screen it. In the 1990s speedway promoters were complaining that speedway in Britain was on its last legs as a spectator sport through being denied the oxygen of television publicity.

Impressionistic evidence suggests that television has affected the behaviour of spectators. The earliest television broadcasts, perhaps influenced by cinema newsreels of sport, included shots of spectators and these have continued to be used to convey the atmosphere of sports events. Television has not so much initiated forms of spectator behaviour as made them more widespread by drawing attention to them. In the early 1960s television was probably a key factor in the spread of unison chanting at football matches. Despite its expanding sociological literature, there is still no satisfactory explanation for the growth of football hooliganism, though the refusal of television to show spectator misbehaviour during match broadcasts indicates a suspicion that televising hooliganism had helped its spread. Closed-circuit television has been used to compile databases of hooligans and to monitor crowd behaviour. The refusal of television to screen pitch invasions by streakers also supports the suspicion that television publicity encourages imitation. The spread of outlandish but harmless forms of spectator behaviour such as painting faces in club colours and the craze in the early 1990s for waving large inflatables owed something to television coverage. Wearing fancy dress at cricket test matches may have been stimulated by a desire to be noticed by television. In 1998 a university lecturer who was ejected from Headingley when dressed as a carrot claimed that he had worn fancy dress at test matches since 1982.[30]

Television and Changes in Sports

No totally new sport has been created to provide a television spectacle. Perhaps the nearest to this was *Gladiators*, first shown on ITV in 1992, which called for physical skills and coordination similar to those demanded in sport. The soccer player John Fashanu and the rugby international Jeremy Guscott were among its presenters. Sports played in Britain have changed their rules in order to boost their televisual appeal. Hardly any sports televised in Britain are played solely in Britain and, where rule changes have been made to attract television audiences, the impetus has come from overseas as much as from Britain. The tie-break was introduced into international tennis tournaments largely to prevent television viewers becoming bored by sets that lasted too long and to ensure that matches did not take so long that they interfered with the schedules of television stations. The penalty shoot-out was introduced in British soccer's knockout competitions after being tried first in international competitions, where it was perhaps thought that the excitement would appeal to television viewers, and to ensure that replay matches would not interfere with the programme of matches arranged for television. An equally important consideration, reducing the physical strain on players of replay matches, may have owed little or nothing to television.

A desire to increase the numbers of spectators who attend events has been at least as powerful a reason for the changes that many sports have made to their rules as hopes of boosting their televisual appeal. Rugby league's limitation of possession to four tackles, though tried first in the televised Floodlit Trophy in 1966 and then changed to six tackles in 1972, was introduced to encourage match attendances as much as to meet the demands of television, and can be regarded as part of the recurring changes made to raise the spectator appeal of the game since its establishment in 1895. Limited overs cricket, which began to be played by the first-class counties in 1963 with the Gillette Cup, was intended to attract television but was also, and very much more, intended to appeal to paying spectators and to bring in sponsorship.

The prospect of television income led British sports to restructure and create competitions. County cricket's limited overs Sunday league, the John Player Trophy, was started in 1969 to bring in sponsorship and to attract spectators, but it is unlikely that it would have been launched without a promise that it would be televised. Similar reasons led to the introduction of the Benson and Hedges Cup, a further limited overs competition, in 1972. Rugby league's Floodlit Trophy would not have started in 1965 but for a BBC commitment to broadcast matches live. Higher gate receipts and television fees seem to have been the main reason for having two touring sides and six rather than five test matches in most English summers. Television revenues, and the sponsorship they could attract, seem to have been the main reason for the start of cricket's World Cup in 1975 and that of rugby union in 1987. When ITV was televising the Dulux Open Snooker competition, the higher costs for filming before 2 p.m. and after midnight led ITV to insist that the starting time be moved from 1 p.m. to 2 p.m. To ensure that play finished before midnight, the second-round matches were reduced to the best of nine instead of eleven frames. The first round, which was not televised, remained the best of eleven frames.[31]

The establishment of English football's FA Carling Premiership in 1992, when the twenty-two First Division clubs left the Football League, was stimulated very largely by their desire for a bigger share of the revenues from televising matches. As an indoor sport, the number of spectators who could attend snooker's major events was always limited, which has meant that the prize and appearance money of snooker has been dependent on television fees and its accompanying sponsorship. The final of the World Professional Championship was reduced from the best of seventy-three frames to the best of forty-nine when the highlights of the final were covered for the first time by television in 1977. By 1980 this had been reduced to the best of thirty-five frames, presumably to suit the demands of television. All of snooker's grand prix events held in Britain have been designed for television and sponsorship. Ice dancing removed the compulsory figures element from its competitions largely because television took little interest in them.[32] As world championship fights have more appeal for television viewers, international professional boxing has devised more world titles. There were 10 world championship fights in 1958 but 124 in 1991.[33]

The relationship with television has caused great conflict between the governing bodies of sports, their leading clubs, players and supporters. In the late 1970s cricket in England and all test-match playing countries was convulsed by the Packer affair. In 1977 the Australian media magnate Kerry Packer, who controlled the Australian television station Channel Nine, established World Series cricket in Australia as a rival to test cricket. In return for what were large sums at the time, thirty-five of the world's leading cricketers agreed to play World Series cricket. Test cricket continued but, as many of the world's best players had joined World Series cricket, many tests were no longer contests between the best players of the countries concerned. In Britain the courts declared that it would be unlawful for the Test and County Cricket Board to follow an International Cricket Conference recommendation and ban the Packer players from county and test-match cricket. This breach in international cricket was healed in 1979, when the Australian Cricket Board made an unexpected volte-face by selling the exclusive television rights for test cricket in Australia to Channel Nine.[34] In negotiations stretching over many months in 1994 and 1995, the Rugby League agreed to establish the Super League, a competition to be played in summer, in return for the money offered by BSkyB; but opposition from some clubs caused proposals for six new clubs to be formed by amalgamations of fifteen clubs to be abandoned.[35] In 1993 the demands of the Rugby Union for England to have a larger share of income from television than Ireland, Scotland and Wales put the Five Nations Championship in doubt.[36]

Television has transformed the finances of sport. In the 1940s and 1950s television got sport on the cheap. The BBC argued that it was not paying for the right to broadcast a sports event but was offering a facility fee, with twenty-five guineas being the usual payment, to compensate for the inconvenience of accommodating television equipment. In the 1950s and 1960s the fees for televising sports events rose but not dramatically. Sport governing bodies had not realised the potential income that could be derived from television, but the limited interest of the ITV companies in sport would have made it hard for them to play off ITV against the BBC. In 1954, the BBC paid £125 per day for the exclusive live coverage of Wimbledon.[37] In the early 1960s daily fees paid by the BBC were £1,600 for a cricket test match, £1,200 for a top show jumping event and less than £600 for Wimbledon.[38]

Fees for televising some sports rose more quickly in the 1970s as governing bodies started to demand higher fees. ITV also showed more interest in screening sport but competition between the BBC and ITV for sports rights was far from cut-throat as ITV showed only intermittent interest in many sports. In the 1960s ITV had broadcast wrestling, a sport which the BBC refused to screen, and many would probably not have regarded wrestling as a sport. ITV's agreement to broadcast gymnastics in 1979 was the first time that it became the sole broadcaster for a sport in which the BBC was also interested. The ITV companies had broadcast football highlights since 1965 but until 1988 acted with the BBC when negotiating the fees for televising football. In 1978 Michael Grade and John Bromley had negotiated the 'Snatch of the Day' when they persuaded the Football League to agree that highlights of league football would be shown only on ITV, but the ITV companies soon resumed their cooperation with the BBC. In effect the BBC and ITV operated a cartel. In return for raising fees in 1983, they were able to persuade the Football League that its matches would be televised live over the next two years.[39] The launch of Channel 4 did not intensify the competition for sport broadcasting rights in the 1980s.

The eagerness of satellite television to pay large sums to broadcast sport live, linked to a more aggressively commercial approach by governing bodies, saw massive escalations in broadcasting fees from the late 1980s. In 1986 the BBC and ITV had paid the Football League £6.5 million to televise live and recorded football over two years. In 1988, worried about losing the televising of football to satellite television, ITV abandoned its understanding with the BBC and agreed to pay £44 million to screen eighteen live matches in each of the next four seasons. In return for televising sixty live matches per year, BSkyB paid £191.5 million in 1992 for a five-year deal, £670 million in 1997 for a four-year deal and £1.1 billion for a three-year deal in 2000. In 1999 ITV paid £250 million for the exclusive right to televise live Champions League matches over the next four years. In 2000 ITV paid £183 million to televise recorded highlights of Premiership matches, while the BBC and BSkyB in a joint deal paid £400 million to televise the FA Cup live. In 2001 ONDigital, the ITV satellite service, paid £315 million to televise live Football League matches.[40] Such high fees were not paid to televise other sports but the more intense competition for broadcasting rights pushed them up. The BBC paid £5 million to broadcast the Wimbledon tennis championship from 1985 to 1989, but had to pay £9 million for the broadcasting rights from 1990 to 1992.[41] In 1994 the BBC and BSkyB paid £58.5 million to televise cricket in England. In 1999 Channel 4 and BSkyB agreed to pay £103 million to broadcast live and recorded cricket over the next four years.[42] In 1992 BSkyB paid more than £3 million for the four-year coverage of live rugby league matches, but in order to persuade rugby league to accept the Super League and playing in summer agreed in 1995 to pay £87 million over five years.[43]

Sport has been a relatively cheap form of broadcasting. In 1970 the average cost of making a one-hour outside broadcast sport programme was about £6,000, far lower than £75,000 for the *Engelbert Humperdinck Show*, £25,000 for *The Wednesday Play*, £15,000 for Harry Worth's comedy show, £8,000 for arts programmes and between £10,000 and £15,000 for *Panorama* and *World in Action*.[44] In the 1970s and early 1980s television sports programmes began to cost more, though not vastly more, but continued to be cheaper than other forms of programmes. By the late 1980s the BBC's costs for a one-hour sports programme had risen to £27,000 per hour but, as these were far lower than the costs of £250,000 per hour for some drama series, sport was still a relatively cheap form of television.[45] In the 1990s higher broadcasting fees caused the costs of sports programmes to rise more quickly than most other programme genres, but in 2001 the cost per hour of a sports broadcast for the BBC was, at almost £128,000 per hour, lower than the figures of £518,000 for drama and £177,000 for entertainment.[46]

In most sports, individuals and organisations competing at the highest level have usually received the highest payments from television; but television income has often been vital for clubs at the lower levels of professional sport. In rugby league, for instance, television income in 1966 was equal to 29 per cent of the gate receipts of the clubs with the lowest match attendances but only 8.8 per cent of the gate receipts for the best-supported clubs.[47] Even between the wars the distribution of test-match profits was essential for the survival of several county cricket clubs. In the early and mid-1990s the finances of all the county clubs would have been in deficit but for the distribution of test-match and one-day international profits, which accounted for around a third of the total income of counties. After 1994 television fees provided about half these sums distributed by the TCCB.[48] In 2001 broadcasting fees and other sums distributed by governing bodies accounted for 16 per cent of the income of the Football League's First Division clubs, 25 per cent of that of the rugby union English Premiership clubs, 43 per cent of that of the first-class county cricket clubs and 35 per cent of that of the Rugby League Super League.[49] While television income has been vital in keeping professional sports clubs afloat, it can be argued that this has encouraged the economics of the madhouse and merely provided many of them with opportunities to continue living beyond their means.

Television fees have helped the poorer clubs to survive but they have also widened the financial gulf between the wealthiest clubs and the rest. Association football in England provides the most extreme example of this. Between 1987 and 1993, the television income of the clubs in the Football League's bottom two divisions fell from 12 per cent to 5 per cent of that of the Premiership clubs. In the 2000/1 season, payments to Premiership clubs from BSkyB and ITV varied from £20.4 million to Manchester United to £8.4 million to Bradford City.[50] In 1998 Manchester United, in a joint venture with BSkyB and Granada, launched MUTV, so becoming the first football club in the world with its own television channel, though it could not screen live in the UK the matches its first team played in the Premiership, the FA Cup or the European club competitions, which were covered by existing agreements with other television stations. By 2000 it had more than 60,000 subscribers. In 2001 Chelsea became the second English football club to establish its own television station. In the financial year 2001/2, the gate receipts for Manchester United, which attracted 67,000 spectators to all its first-team games, were over £42 million, but its various sources of television revenue brought in nearly £52 million.[51] The higher a club's income, the more it can spend on buying and paying players and so the greater are its prospects of success and attracting higher match attendances, advertising, sponsorship and other commercial promotions. Relegation from the Premiership can have catastrophic impacts on a club's television income. When Coventry City was relegated from the Premiership in 2001, its television income dropped from £23 million to £7 million.[52]

Television boosted the income of sport from advertising. Television's coverage of sport was in effect free advertising for sport but television also advertised counter-attractions. By the 1970s it was common to find advertisements placed along the edge of the playing surface in the range of television cameras when an event was to be televised. In the 1990s advertisements were painted onto the playing surface itself. Television encouraged advertisements on players' clothing. In 1983 the Football League chairmen, when negotiating a new deal to televise league football, insisted that the BBC and ITV accept that players could wear shirts bearing advertisements.[53] In 1980 Liverpool FC had claimed that the £50,000 received for advertising Hitachi on its players' shirts could have been trebled had players been allowed to wear these shirts in televised matches.[54] Advertising revenue for Lancashire County Cricket Club between 1991 and 1997 tended to be higher in those years when more days of international cricket were scheduled and televised at its ground. In 1991, when there was only one one-day international match, advertising revenue was nearly £300,000. In 1992, when there was a one-day international and a five-day test match, advertisements brought in almost half a million pounds.[55]

Sponsorship, which can be regarded as a disguised form of advertising whereby commercial bodies try to buy favourable publicity by having their names associated with a sporting organisation or event, has been very much linked with the televising of sport. In 1989 Tony Moore of the Institute of Sports Sponsorship claimed that the sponsorship of sport was driven very largely by television exposure,[56] though there is much sponsorship of recreational sport and of the lowest levels of professional sport that are not televised. In 1993 Peter Radford of the British Athletics Federation (BAF) made clear how sponsorship was related to television coverage. The BAF's income, he explained, came from the televising and sponsorship of 'specially handcrafted events'. If the BAF tried to pay the top British and world athletes less than others paid, 'they would simply not bother to come. If they do not come then our television is not interested in them. If television is not interested in them and does not want to put it on at a good time, the sponsors do not want to come.' Alan Pascoe, who negotiated sponsorship on behalf of sports organisations, had found that 'media exposure is critical to many major sport sponsorships'. A representative from Guinness believed that, when a sports event was to be televised, it pushed up the price of sponsorship.[57]

Banning cigarette advertising on television in 1965 seems to have increased the sponsorship of televised sport by tobacco companies. Sponsorship was a relatively cheap means of keeping tobacco logos and brand names on television. In 1985 the BBC screened 382 hours of tobacco-sponsored sport. In 1989 cigarette logos and brand names were on televised sports programmes for 1,100 minutes. Buying this much advertising time on television would have cost £24 million at cheap rates or £77 million at peak hours. In the early 1990s tobacco companies spent £9 million on sports sponsorship. Nearly two-thirds of those aged between nine and fifteen believed in 1990 that they had seen cigarette advertising on television, even though this had been banned since before they were born.[58]

The growth of sports sponsorship cannot be mapped with total accuracy as details of sponsorship deals were not always released to the public. In 1994 the House of Commons National Heritage Committee, concerned 'at the massive discrepancies in the information supplied to it', was unable 'to decide which figures are the correct ones'.[59] There can be little doubt, however, that it has grown enormously over the last thirty years. In 1971 the Sports Council estimated that sports sponsorship amounted to £2.5 million. IPSOS, the market-surveying specialists, believed that between 1981 and 1999 the annual value of sports sponsorship in the UK had risen from £50 million to £377 million, more than a threefold increase when adjusted for inflation. In 1999 motor sport with £124 million and football with £115 million were the sports with the highest sponsorship income.[60] Both were very far ahead of rugby union, the sport in third place, which received £23 million. Motor sport and football each had a higher income from sponsorship than the combined total for athletics, rugby union and rugby league, golf, horse racing, cricket, tennis and snooker.

The money that flowed into sport from television helped to end amateurism at the highest level of competition and boosted the incomes of top sports players. Cricket scrapped the distinction between amateurs and professionals in 1963. Wimbledon became open to professionals in 1969. In 1982 athletes to all intents and purposes were allowed to accept payment. When rugby union accepted professionalism in 1995 those competing at the highest level of all British sport were being paid openly. One reason why governing bodies agreed to professionalism was a fear that, if they did not do so, alternative televised competitions in which players were paid could be introduced.

In the 1970s, and more particularly the 1980s and 1990s, television was a key factor in the dramatic increases to the earnings of top sports players. Until the last quarter of the twentieth century, television was not bringing sufficient money into sport for it to have a very marked impression on players' earnings. The earnings of top footballers rose after the abolition of the maximum wage in 1961 but this had been brought about by the threat of a players' strike and not television. In the 1970s and the 1980s the rise of snooker as a television sport, and its accompanying sponsorship deals, led to a dramatic rise in prize money. The final and semi-finals of the snooker World Championship were televised for the first time in 1979. The prize money for the winner was £6,000. With snooker's growing popularity as a television sport, this had grown to £15,000 by 1980 and £105,000 in 1989.[61]

In 1992 twenty British sports players had total earnings above £1 million. The boxer Lennox Lewis with earnings of £10.5 million was the highest earner, with the racing driver Nigel Mansell in second place with £7.5 million and the golfer Nick Faldo third with £7 million. The footballers Paul Gascoigne, Gary Lineker and David Platt earned between £2.9 million and £1.2 million but Gascoigne and Platt were playing abroad. The income for Will Carling, the England rugby union captain in what was still an amateur sport, was £425,000, putting him in 47th place in the list of earnings.[62] The earnings of those on this list were not all payments for playing sport but included endorsements and fees for advertising, journalism and interviews. The precise amount that could be attributed directly to television is not clear, but they all played sports in which high fees were paid for television broadcasting rights. In the second half of the 1990s, increased television revenues led to a rapid escalation in the wages paid to footballers by the clubs playing in the English Premiership. The total wage bill for the Premiership clubs rose from £163 million in 1995/6 to £471 million in 1999–2000.[63] In the mid-1990s Eric Cantona, who was thought to have received £15,000 per week from Manchester United, may have been the highest-paid footballer in Britain.[64] By 2002 Roy Keane and David Beckham were each believed to be paid close to £100,000 a week by Manchester United. In 2000 the average annual salary for a footballer in the First Division of the Football League was £175,000, £52,000 in the Second Division and £37,000 in the Third Division.[65]

Leading players were able to augment their incomes by advertising products on television, by endorsing sports equipment and clothing in televised events or by advertising products that were advertised in media other than television but which exploited their television-based celebrity. The footballer Kevin Keegan and the boxer Henry Cooper in the 1970s were probably the first sports stars to be used extensively in television advertisements. They were featured in a television advertising campaign for male toiletries but Keegan also entered into advertising and endorsement contracts with Nabisco, Lyons Maid, Mitre Footballs, Arthur Barker publishers, Harry Fenton suits and Heinz beans. In 1978 his advertising, endorsement and media agreements were thought to have made up more than half of his total earnings, which exceeded £250,000.[66] Reliable statistics about how much sports stars were paid for advertisements and endorsements have been kept obscure, but probably they escalated in line with the wages for playing sport. The *Guardian* believed in 1997 that the England footballer Alan Shearer was paid £1.5 million for playing football but had advertising and endorsements deals worth £5 million.[67]

The higher fees for broadcasting sports events and the escalating payments to sports stars have resulted in part from, and have also encouraged, the rise of sports agents who negotiate on behalf of sports bodies and players. By the mid-1980s two of the world's leading sports agent businesses were the American-based Mark McCormack's International Management Group (IMG) and West Nally. McCormack began representing the golfers Arnold Palmer, Gary Player and Jack Nicklaus in the 1960s, but by the 1980s his British clients had included the British sports personalities Jackie Stewart and Peter Alliss and the broadcaster Michael Parkinson, who was also a sports journalist. By the early 1980s IMG represented the international television rights for Wimbledon, the US Tennis Open, the American National Football League, the American National Basketball Association and many international golf tournaments.[68] West Nally concentrated on representing sporting bodies when negotiating broadcasting television rights and sponsorship for televised sports events. West Nally had a key role in the establishment of the Benson and Hedges cricket competition in 1972.[69] Agencies that negotiate sponsorship and television broadcasting fees for sports organisations charge high commission. McCormack was rumoured to take between 25 per cent and 50 per cent commission on deals he negotiated for his clients. It was alleged in the early 1980s that the sports promotion agency Alan Pascoe Associates (APA) took as commission £25,000 of an £80,000 sponsorship deal with Nike for British athletics. It was also claimed that APA had negotiated a £250,000 deal with Peugeot Talbot to sponsor televised athletics events to be held in Britain but took £90,000 as a service contract from Peugeot Talbot and £44,000 from British athletics as an agency fee.[70]

Television, Sport and Gender

For much of the period since the Second World War, sport has been largely a male cultural domain. More men than women have played and watched sport. The media have concentrated on male sport. Much male involvement with sport has been based on the cooperation or exploitation of women. While men played or watched sport, usually their womenfolk looked after the children and washed the sports kit, though some men stopped playing and watching sport because of opposition from their womenfolk. No doubt for many men the level of male sporting attainment emphasised the differing physical capabilities of men and women and buttressed assumptions of male supremacy in other areas of activity. Sport has often been seen as a means of expressing and consolidating masculine identity but masculinity and femininity now tend to be thought of not as fixed categories but rather as amalgams of culturally conditioned characteristics that differ over time and between social contexts. Garry Whannel has shown that in recent decades male sports stars may represent dedication and self-discipline or the self-indulgent hedonism of the new laddism that can be interpreted as a reassertion of a traditional working-class male culture reacting against the rise of feminism.[71]

A strong case can be made for seeing sport, and particularly the playing of sport, as encouraging the emancipation of women. The sporting achievements of women boosted their confidence in their physical capabilities and extended the range of activities thought suitable for women. The playing of physically demanding sports by women helped to undermine male beliefs that women were too frail to hold their own against men in the professions and in other forms of employment which had been dominated by men.[72] Yet television reflected and helped to reinforce notions that sport was essentially a male cultural space. Most televised sport has been male sport. Sports played almost exclusively by women, such as netball, have rarely been screened. Where both sexes play a sport, the male variant has generally been given more coverage. The Wimbledon tennis championships are one of the few sports events in which television gives equal coverage to the male and female competitions. Following the booming interest in gymnastics stimulated by the 1972 Olympics, women's gymnastics has been screened probably more often than men's gymnastics. Women's swimming has also been televised as often as men's swimming. In the last two decades women's athletics has been televised on more or less the same scale as men's athletics, but in the 1950s it was men's athletic events that predominated. Despite the growth in the numbers of women playing soccer and both rugby codes in the last quarter of the twentieth century, the women's forms of these sports have had minimal exposure on terrestrial television. For much of the period since the 1960s, cricket has been the team ball sport that has been screened live for most hours. Before the 1990s little women's cricket was televised and then it usually consisted of edited highlights. It has been mentioned already that more men, but not overwhelmingly more, than women watch most sports on television.

Television gave greater coverage to women's sport in the last quarter of the twentieth century. As the press also paid more attention to women's sport in this period, television may have been reflecting an expanding interest in women's sport among the general public and was linked to the rise of the women's movement. Television's capacity to present the movement and action of sport has probably stimulated interest in some sports played by women in a way that the press, by having to rely on words, could never have done. The written word alone could not have captured the appeal of women's gymnastics or ice dancing. The show jumper Pat Smythe was probably the first woman sports player to become a national celebrity through television.

She was one of the leading British show jumpers in the 1950s when television was acquainting the general public with show jumping. In the late 1950s and 1960s television coverage of the international successes of the tennis player Christine Truman, the swimmer Anita Lonsborough and the athlete Ann Packer made them nationally known. In the 1980s and 1990s the ice dancer Jayne Torvill enjoyed massive popularity because of the television coverage of her successes in the Olympics and skating world championships. Some women sports players from overseas, such as the leading women tennis players and the Soviet gymnasts Olga Korbut and Nellie Kim, became household names in Britain through television. It has already been mentioned how few women have been employed as sports commentators. Behind-the-scenes roles in sports television such as producers, camera operators and sound technicians have tended to be dominated by men, reflecting, no doubt, a wider assumption that such jobs were the 'natural' province of men.

Feminists have often contended that male discourse reinforces stereotypes of women as sex objects, though of course in the last two or so decades women have made more overt comments about male sexual attraction. Because of its physicality, sport has strong links with sexuality. The trim but muscular athletic figure has come to be regarded as the ideal of physical beauty for men and women. Sport on television tended to reflect rather than cause changes in how the sexuality of sport has been perceived. Before the 1970s the television presentation of sport in Britain did not often stress the physical attractions of female sports players but rather created the impression that successful female athletes represented the homely charms of the girl next door. Male sporting commentary often adopted a condescending tone towards women playing televised sport. Often they were described as 'girls'. Sporting success was depicted as masculinising women and referred to in terms which suggested that women with high levels of determination and physiques that indicated great physical strength were not conforming to what were considered the 'natural' standards of feminine attractiveness. Highly successful east European athletes were described as 'swimming like men' or having the strength and competitiveness of men, although references to British women athletes having a will to win similar to that of men could be phrased as a compliment. Perhaps influenced by the women's movement, commentators described women athletes as 'girls' less often in the 1980s and 1990s, but 'honey' shots or views of attractive young women spectators were often used in broadcasts of summer sports. In the 1980s and 1990s women newspaper journalists did mention the sexual attraction of leading male sports players more often but women sports commentators on television have rarely referred to the physical attraction of male sports stars, though changes to the hair styles of male footballers are discussed.

Television and the Cultural Role of Sport

Since the Second World War the role of sport in British popular culture seems to have grown. Press coverage of sport is greater than fifty years ago. Consumer spending on sport is higher. More books were published on sport in the 1990s than in the 1950s. Women have become more knowledgeable about sport and play and watch sport in greater numbers. Sport figures extensively in advertising. Sports clothing has become a form of everyday fashion. Television has been very much involved with this expanding role of sport in popular culture. Much of the press commentary on sport is based on what people see of sport on television. The more extensive television coverage of sport in the 1990s in many respects resulted from the expanding number of channels, but it seems unlikely that so many of these would have been established and retained had there not been a sufficiently strong desire to watch televised sport. Without sport, BSkyB may not have attracted sufficient viewers to survive. How far television has stimulated interest in sport cannot be measured. Many aspects of life are more important than sport, yet without doubt television has given an air of importance, perhaps an exaggerated one, to sport. Perhaps television has led to sport becoming too big for its boots.

Chapter 10

CONCLUSION

This book has tried to assess the social and cultural significance of television in Britain. It has examined whether and how far cultural institutions, attitudes and behaviour have been influenced by television. A recurring theme has been that conclusions about the social and cultural impacts of television have to be drawn with caution. None the less, it is hoped that this book has shown that a very strong case can be made for the claim that some aspects of life in Britain have been changed by television.

One of the most obvious cultural and social effects of television is that television has become a major interest for the great majority of people living in Britain. Empirical evidence shows that since around 1960 only work and sleep have consumed more time than watching television. Television viewing has become *the* major leisure interest. This in itself is a change of great cultural significance. We do, however, need to know more about the nature of viewing and whether this has changed over time. Statistics of television viewing have equated viewing with being in the presence of a television receiver that is switched on, but studies of the nature of viewing, admittedly few in number, suggest that many viewers perform other tasks while watching television and that some pay very little attention to what they watch. The practice in recent years for making advertisements sound louder than programmes themselves suggests that advertisers assume that many people pay only fitful attention to what is being broadcast. Some may claim that leisure interests are of no great importance, and are trivial when set against the worlds of work and politics. One reply to this is that the way people choose to spend their free time reveals much about their values. It can also be argued that what is experienced in leisure time helps to shape cultural assumptions and consequently behaviour.

The time spent watching television has reduced the time available for other leisure activities, though some of these, such as knitting or glancing at a newspaper, could be combined with television viewing. Television has competed, often successfully, with other leisure interests for time. It was almost certainly the major reason why cinema admissions dropped so sharply between the early 1950s and the mid-1980s. By the end of the 1950s, watching television had replaced listening to radio as the main form of evening leisure in the home. In addition much can be said for the view that television has not so much transformed leisure but been a new medium for pursuing pre-existing leisure interests. Few forms of cultural expression have been created by television, though some, such as soap operas, half-hour situation comedies and the drama serial, have been extended and taken in new directions by television. Many more people watch films on television than in the cinema. More watch sports events on television than in the stadium. Television rather than live theatre provides drama. While television has arguably been merely a new means of delivering existing cultural forms, does the experience of watching, say, a football match on television, differ from that of attending the match in person? Usually, attending a football match is a more social event, an experience shared in the company of many others. What one sees on television is accompanied by a commentary and, perhaps more subtly, the television viewer has less control over what he or she sees than the viewer at the stadium. The verbal and cultural packaging of an event on television may make its viewing a quite different experience from observing it through another medium.

This book has argued that television has been a major contributor to changes in many, though not all, cultural institutions. Cultural forms are never static but change over time. While it would be absurd to claim that television caused all the changes in the organisation, content and style of cinema and radio, by transforming their social contexts it influenced the way they developed in the second half of the twentieth century. By competing with newspapers for the time of readers and for advertising revenue, television was very likely a leading cause of the decline in the circulation of newspapers, though different management strategies might have helped newspapers to compete more effectively with television. Over time newspapers have given more space to television material. As radio and television provide accounts of what is happening in the world faster than newspapers, this seems to be a crucial reason why broadsheet newspapers have increased their commentary on news events. The money coming into sport, or rather into some sports, from television in the 1980s and 1990s in particular facilitated the greater commercialisation of spectator sport and the creation of new competitions. Many sports changed their rules to enhance their televisual appeal.

It is hard to argue convincingly that television has had a profound effect on the 'high' arts. Arts programmes have formed only a tiny part of television output and may well have been watched primarily by those already interested in the arts. Little dance and opera has been designed specifically for television. Television has given work to many writers and broadcast plays written originally for the stage; but, except for dramatic adaptations of classic novels, television has devoted relatively little attention to the novel and poetry, though this could be related to the nature of television as a visual medium. Television styles of acting do not seem to have had a strong impact on theatre acting. Television has broadcast classical music and pop music, though far less than radio. Programmes about painting, sculpture and architecture have formed only a small part of television, which is surprising given their visual nature. As so much of creativity is thought to come from the artist's subconscious, it is never easy to be sure of the influences on an artist's work; but few composers and visual artists have claimed that their work was influenced by television. Television has been an important patron of the arts. It has provided work for writers and actors, designers, composers and musicians, but has commissioned relatively few symphonic works, ballets, modern dances, operas, paintings or architecture. Indeed, television has had something of a parasitical relationship with other art forms. Art programmes have rarely attracted large audiences by television standards, though their viewers have often far outnumbered those who go to artistic events in theatres or galleries, and television has increased opportunities to view art.

Politicians have determined the organisational and financial structures of television in Britain, but, as was shown in Chapter 4, television has rarely been a major topic of party political controversy. By the 1960s, television was becoming one of the major media of political information and, while it was supposed to be politically neutral, its selection and presentation meant that it could never be wholly impartial. Little of the political information broadcast by television was very different from that which could be obtained from radio or newspapers, though television allowed viewers to see the body language and personal manner of politicians. By the 1960s, parliamentary politicians had realised that they had to be effective performers on television, and television became the battleground on which general elections were fought. How far television has influenced voting preferences is still not clear.

Television may do more to strengthen than to change existing views. It is also unclear whether television has caused politicians to be held in lower esteem or contributed to the lower turnouts at recent elections. Arguably, television has affected little more than the presentation of politics, though this, of course, could help to determine the outcome of general elections. Much of political life has remained the same despite the rise of television. Parliamentary politics are still dominated by the Labour and Conservative parties. Managing the economy and international relations were major concerns of Westminster long before the rise of television. During the television age, growing political attention has been focused on education, the National Health Service and social security, and while television has ventilated concerns about these subjects, the experiences of everyday life have probably been far more important in maintaining their political significance. Television coverage can give political significance to an issue, such as piles of uncollected rubbish in the streets during the strikes in 1979 or the Ethiopian famine in 1984, but seems to have less capacity to shape the political agenda in the long term.

Chapter 3 has shown that the measurable impacts of television on the British economy have not been very great. The coming of commercial television provided a new outlet for advertising, and television has played a key role in the expansion of advertising—though other forms of advertising may have expanded more had television not existed. The sale and renting of television receivers and of video players became big business; but none of the giants of the electrical goods market survived by selling television sets alone. Perhaps the most significant impacts of television on the economy cannot be calculated. Those who bought advertising time on television must have expected that it would benefit their businesses; but such effects are impossible to quantify. There has been much talk of the rise of a consumerist culture in Britain during the second half of the twentieth century. While many television programmes have celebrated materialist values, this does not prove that television led to a greater acceptance of them.

Television has registered social and cultural changes in Britain, though it is not an infallible guide to them. The increasing presence of those who are not white on television indicates that Britain's population has become ethnically varied in the second half of the twentieth century. In very general terms, it can be argued that the social power of women was greater at the end than in the middle of the twentieth century and that this has been reflected in the higher number of women who hold senior positions in television broadcasting and in the more varied roles that women have in front of the camera, even though some areas of television production are still dominated by men. But these changes in television are not necessarily an accurate barometer of social change in Britain. There was a time lag before television began to reflect the growing presence of non-white people or the rise of the women's movement; those who are not white and women had to campaign for more representation on television. The small number of gay and lesbian appearances in television may well under-represent the degree to which homosexual identities are now expressed openly. Retired people feature relatively rarely in television programmes, even though they constitute a growing sector of the population. Assessments of how far television records social and cultural change, of course, must consider different programme genres and how they represent life in Britain. Crime dramas can present a quite different view of life in Britain from documentaries about crime. Rather than registering social and cultural change, television possibly records the changing assumptions of channel controllers, schedulers and producers about the sorts of depictions of life in Britain that they expect will attract the most viewers.

Television and Social Cohesion

This book has provided data with which to evaluate some of the grander claims about the effects of television on British culture. It has often been contended that television was a force for social and cultural cohesion. Before cable and satellite television, it is argued, the vast audiences for the most popular programmes demonstrated that enormous numbers were sharing the same cultural experience. The previous night's programmes, it has been alleged, were a frequent topic of conversation at the workplace. This viewpoint expresses great distaste for cable and satellite television and perhaps a rose-tinted view of the past. By extending the number of channels on such a vast scale, cable and satellite television has been accused of fragmenting the television audience and so undermining the capacity of television to promote social cohesion.

The data presented in this book provide only limited support for the view that television no longer has the capacity to express social cohesion. Age, gender and social class have affected viewing patterns, but not very much.

Arguably, the growth and vast size of television audiences throughout the second half of the twentieth century has emphasised the widespread acceptance of watching television. If viewers had not felt that television viewing was in harmony with their cultural attitudes, it is unlikely that so many would have watched television. Gauntlett and Hill found in the 1990s that marginalised people in modern society watched more television, which can be interpreted as an attempt on their part to feel included in mainstream society.[1] Audiences have fragmented since the early 1980s, but not to a vast extent. In 1981 BBC1, BBC2 and ITV had a monopoly of television viewing. In 2000 they still accounted for around two-thirds of all television viewing, although the ITV share had dropped from nearly 50 per cent to below 30 per cent. Fewer programmes had more than 10 million viewers in 2000 than in the 1980s; but audiences for the most popular programmes were not very much smaller. Even when the television audience was less fragmented, not all viewers were watching the same programmes. In 1983, for instance, BARB programme viewing figures show that, when ITV was screening *Coronation Street*, the programme that regularly drew most viewers, the audience for a sitcom on BBC1 could be more than half that for *Coronation Street*. As has been said many times already, it does not follow that all viewers drew the same meanings from the same programmes. They may have done so, but it is hard to prove this.

Television has been involved with what seem to have been great outbursts of national unity. In the 1950s the monarchy was often seen as a symbol of national cohesion. The 40 per cent of the population that watched the coronation on television in 1953 perhaps helped to consolidate support for the monarchy. Television seems to have been a key factor in creating the public mood, some might say hysteria, that surrounded Princess Diana's funeral in 1997. International sporting competitions provide television with opportunities to celebrate patriotism, but televised matches against England can also give vent to anti-English sentiment in Scotland and Wales. Moreover, televised sporting contests between teams from different towns may have enhanced inter-town rivalries and also those between regions. The establishment of Welsh and Gaelic language channels was intended to keep alive languages threatened by the rise of English and the means of retaining cultural diversity within the United Kingdom. Until the 1990s, ITV, the channel with most viewers, was organised on a regional basis in England and Scotland. This regional element of ITV was largely forced on the ITA by the geographical location of its transmitters in the mid-1950s, but by the 1960s regionalism was defended as a strength of the ITV system. All ITV licence holders had to carry a proportion of local programmes, which can be seen as an expression of local identities, but at peak hours the ITV companies usually all showed the same programmes. In the 1990s takeovers between ITV companies weakened their regional element. BBC1 broadcasts regional news bulletins but BBC2 and Channels 4 and 5 have always been primarily national services, which may mean that television ought to be seen as an expression of national culture. The audiences for local cable services have been very small and there are few regional satellite channels.

The greater numbers of cable and satellite channels provide more opportunities for minority groups to express their identities and in this way could be doing more to weaken than to uphold a common culture. The accessibility of Asian language television for those of Asian descent may be helping them to retain their distinctive identities. Yet, at the same time, the growing number of appearances by those who are not white on terrestrial television has been motivated in part by a desire to promote ethnic harmony and so disarm racial prejudice. More programmes and satellite channels for gays and lesbians may be enabling them to emphasise their distinctive lifestyles, but at the same time such programmes could also stress the diversity of homosexual lifestyles.

How far television may have been an expression of a common culture in Britain is related to the issue of class divisions and class consciousness. Historians and social analysts have debated whether Britain in the last quarter of the twentieth century became a classless society. Usually talk about the death of class has been taken to mean that there is no longer a fierce antagonism between what were called the working class and the bourgeoisie and that class is no longer the predominant form of identity to which most people subscribe. Not all historians, however, have accepted that confrontationist class ideologies were the dominant forms of social consciousness in Britain before the last three or so decades. Levels of skill, religion, gender and regional loyalties divided the working class. The very limited degree of support for militant socialism and the failure of Labour to win clear majorities at general elections other than in 1945 and 1966 suggested that, while most working-class people were aware of how their incomes and lifestyles differed from those of the middle and upper classes, their degree of hostility to other classes was not so very great. In the last two or three decades the so-called death of class has been related to the decline of the manufacturing industry and blue-collar employment, the spread of higher education and the importance of ethnicity and gender in determining senses of identity. The Labour Party won two successive general elections after transforming itself into classless New Labour.[2]

Consciousness of class is an expression of culture, of how people imagine their position and that of others in the social world. All classes have watched television and the preceding discussion has shown that television events can provoke a sense of national belonging that transcends social divisions. But much television has emphasised differences in the lifestyles of what have been called the upper, middle and working classes. Documentaries about the aristocracy and the super-rich have been relatively common. Most television commercials have been for everyday commodities, though many are also for goods which only the well-to-do can afford. The hardships of the least privileged have often been the subject of soaps and other drama series. Until the last two decades much television situation comedy played on class distinctions. Yet one can argue that the general trend of television has been to weaken class consciousness. The main emphasis in television has been on the individual, and individuality is the antithesis of the collective outlooks that have been seen as the hallmark of class. A similarity of values and lifestyle is a defining aspect of class, but television, and television drama in particular, has accentuated differences between those with similar incomes and more or less the same social situation. Television has depicted heroes and rogues in all classes. Its overall effect has perhaps been to suggest that people should be judged as individuals and not as members of a class, and when this is done the whole notion of class consciousness is jettisoned. Television has also stressed the importance of gender, ethnicity and generation as forms of cultural identities and as such may have been weakening, or reflecting a weakening of, the potential of class to be a dominant form of social consciousness. In the 1990s the rising number of channels may have heightened television's capacity to express a wider variety of lifestyles, though clearly it would be helpful if more data were revealed to the public about the social background of those who watch each channel. If situation comedy is a barometer of how society is perceived, it would seem that people in Britain were aware that they lived in a stratified society but that the relations of those from the different segments of this society were characterised more by tolerance than by antagonism.

The Quality of Television

A common complaint in the 1990s was that television had been dumbed down, that the more intense competition for audiences had resulted in more programmes that made few intellectual demands on viewers and dragged down the quality of programmes. It can be argued that, given the extent of television viewing, a deterioration in the quality of programmes would result in a deterioration in the quality of life for a large proportion of the population. Many who disliked the managerial style of John Birt and his attempts to impose a more cost-conscious culture on the BBC argued that these were inimical to creativity and meant that talent could no longer be nursed. Objective measures of quality are hard, if not impossible, to devise. In all decades the bulk of television's output has been dismissed as rubbish. In the early 1960s the Pilkington Report condemned the quality of much commercial television. It is possible that what one judges to be the gold of the past stays in the mind longer than the dross. This book has drawn attention to content analyses of news programmes that have shown that the proportion of political items and background material has declined since the early 1990s. Changing the times of *Panorama* and scrapping other current affairs programmes can be seen as a downgrading of political coverage, but twenty-four-hour news programmes on cable and satellite television mean that there is now more news coverage than in the past. What has perhaps occurred is that terrestrial news programmes are no longer force-feeding viewers a diet of heavy political news, though some television journalists argue that including human-interest items in news bulletins is a strategy to ensure that viewers also see more 'serious' items.

How far the quality of other television genres has declined is debatable. Arts magazine programmes declined in the 1990s but have revived in the past two or three years. The launch of cable and satellite arts channels could mean that more arts programmes are being broadcast than ever before, but this may be used as an excuse to limit their numbers on terrestrial television. The single-performance play has all but disappeared on television and little televised drama now seems to have the exploratory nature of *The Wednesday Play* from the 1960s and 1970s or the social criticism of *Boys from the Blackstuff* in the early 1980s. In the 1990s the numbers of cinema films being broadcast were higher than ever. The increased competition for audiences may have raised the quality of some programme genres. Most sports enthusiasts would probably agree that increased competition between broadcasters in the 1990s stimulated the use of more camera angles and electronic devices to analyse play and resulted in more informative and varied pictures of sporting events.

Television and Visual Culture

Devotees of print and radio have claimed that television has strengthened the visual element in modern culture. Again this is a claim that is difficult to evaluate. The term 'visual culture' is not easy to define. It has already been mentioned that watching television replaced radio as the main form of domestic evening leisure in the 1950s and television contributed to the closure of some newspapers. Yet the printed word has remained important in modern culture. Illiteracy is still a cultural and economic handicap. Although the number of books borrowed from libraries fell in the 1980s and 1990s, book purchases rose. In the mid-1990s people on average were spending an hour a day reading, though this was about only a third of the time spent viewing television. The increased number of pictures in newspapers, perhaps as a means of persuading readers to read an accompanying story, may be an indication of a growing emphasis on the visual, but it may be due more to changes in the technology of printing photographs and the economics of newspaper publishing than to television. Impressionistic evidence suggests that advertisements on hoardings and in newspapers and magazines make more use of pictures than was the case thirty or forty years ago, but this could be because they have to attract attention instantly. There seems to be more stress on personal appearance now than in the 1950s. Men appear to be more fashion-conscious. This can be linked with what seems to be a growing concern with style and image, though some would probably regard this as appearance being given priority over substance. Such trends may be signs of a more visually aware culture, but it is hard to be sure of how far television has been responsible for this. The concern with fashion can be seen as the product of higher levels of affluence and the functioning of a post-industrial economy, although of course television could have a key role in popularising lifestyles and their associated purchases. It is to be hoped that this book will have indicated that grand claims for the influence of television need to be treated with circumspection.

The Need for Further Research

This book has also brought to light those areas of television history that are crying out for more detailed research. What television reveals about social relations comes through its programmes, but relatively little is known about the culture of those who have made programmes. Much can be learned from the autobiographies of those who worked in television, and Bakewell and Graham, Tunstall and Cottle have provided valuable collections of interviews,[3] but there is still a pressing need for a history that indicates in what respects, and for what reasons, the culture of programme makers changed over time. As the nature of programmes has always been determined by finance, economic history of television is needed, but before this could be written more research would have to be conducted into the financial history of the BBC, each of the ITV companies, Channels 4 and 5, and cable broadcasters and BSkyB. There is an equal need for an economic and cultural history of the independent television production sector in Britain. Textual analysis is a vital, and thankfully growing, area of research into television, though much of this has concentrated on drama and news bulletins. Textual analyses with a historical dimension of televised sport – for instance, deconstructing the language and visual imagery – could unearth much about how television has represented different sports in different styles. Most television researchers would value studies that made more accessible the scattered data on the social backgrounds of viewers for different programme genres and how these may have changed over time. Most students of television would have little difficulty in adding to this list of issues requiring further research.

We can never know what life in Britain would have been like without television. Because television has conquered the entire developed world, comparisons cannot be drawn with developed societies that have no television. There is also no means of establishing whether the nature of television programmes and the scale of television viewing will change in the next few decades. What one can say is that television viewing has been so extensive in the past half-century that those wishing to understand British society and culture cannot ignore it. What this book has shown is the complexity of making sense of television. Watching television is easy: understanding it is not.

NOTES

Chapter 1

1. For critical commentaries on their work, see M. Jay, *Adorno* (London: Fontana, 1984), S. Jarvis, *Adorno: A Critical Introduction* (Cambridge: Polity, 1996), R.W. Witkin, *Adorno on Popular Culture* (London: Routledge, 2003) and P.M.R. Stirk, *Max Horkheimer: A New Interpretation* (Hemel Hempstead: Harvester, 1992).
2. J.G. Blumler, 'The Social Character of Media Gratifications', in K.E. Rosengren, L.A. Wenner and P. Palmgreen (eds), *Media Gratifications Research: Current Perspectives* (London: Sage, 1985); J.D. Halloran, *The Effects of Mass Communication, with Special Reference to Television* (Leicester: Leicester University Press, 1964); J.D. Halloran, 'Introduction: Studying the Effects of Television' and 'The Social Effects of Television', in J.D. Halloran (ed.), *The Effects of Television* (London: Panther, 1970).
3. N. Postman, *Amusing Ourselves to Death: Public Discourse in the Age of Show Business* (London: Methuen, 1987).
4. I. Hargreaves, *Journalism: Truth or Dare?* (Oxford: Oxford University Press, 2003), p. 107.
5. S. Hall, 'Encoding and Decoding in the TV Discourse', in S. Hall (ed.), *Culture, Media, Language: Working Papers in Cultural Studies, 1972–79* (London: Hutchinson, 1981).
6. J. Tulloch, *Watching Television Audiences: Cultural Theories and Methods* (London: Arnold, 2000).
7. J. Curran, 'The New Revisionism in Mass Communications Research: A Reappraisal', in J. Curran, D. Morley and V. Walkerdine (eds), *Cultural Studies and Communication* (London: Arnold, 1996), p. 268; G. Philo, *Seeing and Believing* (London: Routledge, 1990).
8. Key texts in feminist film theory have included C.E. Brunsdon, 'Identity in Feminist Television Criticism', *Media, Culture and Society*, 15 (1993), 309–20; C. Gledhill, 'Pleasurable Negotiations', in D. Pribham (ed.), *Female Spectators* (London: Verso, 1988); L. Mulvey, 'Visual Pleasure and Narrative Cinema', *Screen*, 16, no. 3 (1975), 6–18; T. Modleski, *Loving with a Vengeance: Mass-Produced Fantasies for Women* (New York: Methuen, 1984). For a review of feminist theories and their relevance to the study of television, see L.M. Mumford, 'Feminist Theory and Television Studies', in C. Geraghty and D. Lusted (eds), *The Television Studies Book* (London: Arnold, 1998).

9. *Listener*, 22 May 1986.

10. E. Cashmore, . . . *And There was Televi̇si̇on* (London: Routledge, 1994).

11. P. Scannell, *Radio, Television and Modern Life: A Phenomenological Approach* (Oxford: Blackwell, 1996).

12. A. Briggs, *The History of Broadcasting in the United Kingdom*, vols III, IV and V (Oxford: Oxford University Press, 1995), *The BBC: The First Fifty Years* (Oxford: Oxford University Press, 1985); B. Sendall, *Independent Television in Britain: Volume 1: Origin and Foundation, 1946–62* (London: Macmillan, 1982), *Independent Television in Britain: Volume 2: Expansion and Change, 1958–68* (London: Macmillan, 1983); J. Potter, *Independent Television in Britain: Volume 3: Politics and Control, 1968–80* (London: Macmillan, 1989), *Independent Television in Britain: Volume 4: Companies and Programmes, 1968–80* (London: Macmillan, 1989); P. Bonner and L. Aston, *Independent Television in Britain: Volume 5: ITV and the IBA 1981–92: The Old Relationship Changes* (London: Macmillan, 1998).

13. C. Horrie and S. Clarke, *Fuzzy Monsters: Fear and Loathing at the BBC* (London: Heinemann, 1994).

14. R. Snoddy, *Greenfinger: The Rise of Michael Green and Carlton Communication* (London: Faber and Faber, 1996); W. Kay, *Lord of the Dance: The Story of Gerry Robinson* (London: Orion Business, 1999).

15. M. Leapman, *Treachery? The Power Struggle at TV-am* (London: Allen and Unwin, 1984).

16. A. Briggs and J. Spicer, *The Franchise Affair: Creating Fortunes and Failures in Independent Television* (London: Century, 1986); A. Davidson, *Under the Hammer: The Inside Story of the 1991 ITV Franchise Battle* (London: Heinemann, 1992).

17. P. Chippingdale and S. Franks, *The Rise and Fall of British Satellite Broadcasting* (London: Simon & Schuster, 1991).

18. C. Horrie and A. Nathan, *Li̇ve TV* (London: Simon & Schuster, 1999).

19. J. Trenaman and D. McQuail, *Television and the Political Image: A Study of the 1959 General Election* (London: Methuen, 1961); J.G. Blumler and D. McQuail, *Television and Politics: Its Uses and Influences* (London: Faber and Faber, 1968). The monographs on British general elections by David Butler and others discuss the role of television and other media.

20. P. Goodwin, *Television under the Tories: Broadcasting Policy: 1979–1997* (London: BFI, 1998).

21. M. Cockerell, *Live from Number 10: The Inside Story of Prime Ministers and Television* (London: Faber and Faber, 1988).

22. C. Seymour-Ure, *Prime Ministers and the Media: Issues of Power and Control* (Oxford: Blackwell, 2003).

23. Glasgow University Media Group, *Bad News* (London: Routledge, 1976), *More Bad News* (London: Routledge, 1980) and *Really Bad News* (London: Writers and Readers, 1982); S. Barnett and I. Gaber, *Changing Patterns in Broadcast*

News (London: Voice of the Listener & Viewer, 1993); S. Barnett, E. Seymour and I. Gaber, *From Callaghan to Kosovo: Changing Trends in British Television News 1975–1999* (Harrow: University of Westminster, 2000); I. Hargreaves and J. Thomas, *New News, Old News* (London: ITC, 2002).

24. J. Harrison, *Terrestrial TV News in Britain: The Culture of Production* (Manchester: Manchester University Press, 2000).

25. J. Curran and J. Seaton, *Power without Responsibility: The Press and Broadcasting in Britain* (London: Routledge, 1997); C. Seymour-Ure, *The British Press and Broadcasting since 1945* (Oxford: Blackwell, 1997).

26. Hargreaves, *Journalism.*

27. J. Seaton (ed.), *Politics & the Media: Harlots and Prerogatives at the Turn of the Millennium* (Oxford: Blackwell, 1998).

28. R. Collins, N. Garnham and G. Locksley, *The Economics of Television: The UK Case* (London: Sage, 1988).

29. C. Geraghty, *Women and Soap Opera: A Study of Prime Time Soaps* (Cambridge: Polity, 1991).

30. G. Cumberbatch, S. Woods, C. Stephenson, M. Boyle, A. Smith and S. Gauntlett, *Ethnic Minorities on Television: A Report for the ITC* (Birmingham: Aston University Communications Research Group, 1996); G. Cumberbatch, S. Gauntlett, M. Richards and V. Littlejohns, *Top 10 TV: Ethnic Minority Group Representations on Popular Television* (Communications Research Group for the Commission for Racial Equality, 2000).

31. S. Bourne, *Black in the British Frame: Black People in British Film and Television 1896–1996* (London: Cassell, 1998); J. Pines, *Black and White in Colour: Black People in British Television since 1936* (London: BFI, 1992); S. Cottle and P. Ismond, *Television and Ethnic Minorities: Producers' Perspectives: A Study of BBC In-house, Independent and Cable TV Producers* (Aldershot: Avebury, 1997).

32. T. Daniels and J. Gerson (eds), *Black Images in British Television: The Colour Black* (London: BFI, 1989).

33. T. Daniels, 'Programmes for Black Audiences', in S. Hood (ed.), *Behind the Screens: The Structure of British Broadcasting* (London: Lawrence & Wishart, 1994).

34. H. Carpenter, *Dennis Potter: A Biography* (London: Faber and Faber, 1998).

35. G. Brandt (ed.), *British Television Drama* (Cambridge: Cambridge University Press, 1981); R. Millington and R. Nelson, *Boys from the Blackstuff: The Making of a TV Drama* (London: Comedia, 1986).

36. J. Bignell, S. Lacey and M. Macmurraugh-Kavanagh (eds), *British Television Drama: Past, Present and Future* (Basingstoke: Palgrave, 2000).

37. See, for example, G. McCann, *Dad's Army: The Story of a Classic Television Show* (London: Fourth Estate, 2001).

38. J. Stokes, *On Screen Rivals: Cinema and Television in the United States and Britain* (London: Macmillan, 1999).

39. H. Carpenter, *The Envy of the World: Fifty Years of the BBC Third Programme and Radio* (London: Weidenfeld and Nicolson, 1996).

40. G. Whannel, *Fields in Vision: Sport, Television and Cultural Transformation* (London: Routledge, 1992); S. Barnett, *Games and Sets: The Changing Face of Sport on Television* (London: BFI, 1990).

41. G. Whannel, *Media Sport Stars: Masculinities and Moralities* (London: Routledge, 2002).

42. J. Hill, Sport, *Leisure and Culture in Twentieth-Century Britain* (Basingstoke: Palgrave, 2002).

Chapter 2

1. A. Briggs, *The History of Broadcasting in the United Kingdom: Volume II: The Golden Age of Wireless* (London: Oxford University Press, 1965), pp. 611, 620.

2. *BBC Handbook 1987* (London: BBC, 1987), p. 161.

3. *Social Trends 10* (London: HMSO, 1980), p. 33; *Social Trends 21* (London: HMSO, 1991), p. 101; *Social Trends 26* (London: HMSO, 1996), p. 119.

4. *ITV 1965* (London: ITA, 1965), p. 28; C. Seymour-Ure, *The British Press and Broadcasting since 1945* (Oxford: Blackwell, 1997), p. 167.

5. *Keynote Market Report 2000: Cable & Satellite TV* (n.p.: Keynote, 2000), p. 31.

6. *Social Trends 12* (London: HMSO, 1982), p. 111.

7. *Social Trends 22* (London: HMSO, 1992), p. 178.

8. Seymour-Ure, *British Press and Broadcasting*, p. 166; *Social Trends 10* (London: HMSO, 1980), p. 227.

9. *Guardian*, 1 February 2002; *BFI Film and Television Handbook 2001* (London: BFI, 2000), p. 34.

10. *Social Trends 1* (London: HMSO, 1970), p. 80.

11. *Social Trends 26* (London: HMSO, 1996), p. 217.

12. *Broadcast*, 22 September 1980.

13. *Listener*, 22 May 1986.

14. S. Hood, *A Survey of Television* (London: Heinemann, 1967), p. 30.

15. *Social Trends 9* (London: HMSO, 1979), p. 179.

16. Seymour-Ure, *British Press and Broadcasting*, p. 174; R. Caines, *Key Note: Broadcasting in the UK: 1995 Market Report* (Hampton: Key Note, n.d.), p. 77.

17. For further details of the numbers from each social class viewing each channel, see Seymour-Ure, *British Press and Broadcasting*, p. 174.

18. *Report of the Committee on Broadcasting 1960: Volume I: Appendix E: Memoranda Submitted to the Committee (Papers 1–102)* (London: HMSO, 1962), Cmnd. 1819, p. 90.

19. *ITV 1965*, p. 27.

20. *Social Trends 19* (London: HMSO, 1989), p. 163.

21. www.barb.co.uk/monthly/terrestrial (accessed 13 March 2001).

22. *BBC Annual Report and Accounts 1960–1961* (London: BBC, 1961), p. 157; *Television Mail*, 3 June 1960.

23. *Report of the Committee on Broadcasting* (London: HMSO, 1977), Cmnd. 6753, p. 464.

24. *Broadcast*, 22 February 1974.

25. *Monopolies and Mergers Commission: The British Broadcasting Corporation and the Independent Television Publications Limited* (London: HMSO, 1985), Cmnd. 9614, p. 10.

26. *Guardian*, 2 April 2001.

27. NRS Top Line Results July 1996–June 1997: Women's Weekly and Fortnightly Periodicals, Women's Monthly, Bimonthly and Quarterly Periodicals, www.nrs.c.uk/topline (accessed 16 March 2001).

28. Seymour-Ure, *British Press and Broadcasting*, p. 158; *Report of the Committee of Broadcasting 1960: Volume I: Appendix E: Memoranda Submitted to the Committee (Papers 1–102)* (London: HMSO, 1962), Cmnd. 1819, pp. 15–16, 89; A. Briggs, *The History of Broadcasting in the United Kingdom: Volume V Competition* (Oxford: Oxford University Press, 1995), p. 158.

29. *ITC Annual Report 2000*, www.itc.org.uk/ann_ann_report (accessed 25 February 2002).

30. *ITC Annual Report 2000*, www.barb.co.uk/monthly/terrestrial (accessed 13 March 2001).

31. Briggs, *History of Broadcasting in the United Kingdom: Volume II*, pp. 612, 620.

32. A. Briggs, *The History of Broadcasting in the United Kingdom: Volume IV: Sound and Vision* (Oxford: Oxford University Press, 1995), pp. 225, 230.

33. *Daily Mirror*, 2 January 1980, 5 January 1990.

34. *Social Trends 25* (London: HMSO, 1995), p. 102.

35. *Guardian*, 7 January 1999; www.barb.co.uk/viewingsummary/weeklyreports (accessed 17 July 2002).

36. D. Gauntlett and A. Hill, *Television, Culture and Everyday Life* (London: Routledge and BFI, 1999), p. 30.

37. Gauntlett and Hill, *Television, Culture and Everyday Life*, pp. 108–9.

38. P. Coleman, 'Ageing and Life History: The Meaning of Reminiscence in Late Life', in S. Dex (ed.), *Life and Work Analyses: Qualitative and Quantitative Developments* (London: Routledge, 1991), p. 130.

39. Gauntlett and Hill, *Television, Culture and Everyday Life*, p. 30.

40. R. Silvey, *Who's Listening? The Story of Audience Research* (London: Allen & Unwin, 1974), p. 165.

41. G.W. Goldie, *Facing the Nation: Television and Politics 1936–1976* (London: Bodley Head, 1977), pp. 18–19.

42. B. Sendall, *Independent Television in Britain: Volume 1: Origin and Foundation, 1946–62* (London: Macmillan, 1982), p. 14.

43. D. Attenborough, *Life on Air: Memoirs of a Broadcaster* (London: BBC, 2002), pp. 17–18.

44. Interview with Sir Bill Cotton, 21 May 2003.

45. B. Cotton, *Double Bill: 80 Years of Entertainment* (London: Fourth Estate, 2000), pp. 52–3.
46. *The Times*, 20 December 1950.
47. *Daily Mirror*, 22 March 1950.
48. *Listener*, 2 November 1961.
49. M. Bose, *Michael Grade: Screening the Image* (London: Virgin, 1992), p. 279.
50. J. Sergeant, *Give Me Ten Seconds* (London: Pan, 2001), p. 81.
51. *Guardian*, 19 November 2001.
52. M. Grade, *It Seemed like a Good Idea at the Time* (London: Macmillan, 1999), p. 172.
53. *Observer*, 1 April 2001.
54. *Variety*, 10 December 1990.
55. *Report of the Committee on Broadcasting 1960*, p. 54.
56. R. Hoggart, *An Imagined Life (Life and Times, Volume III: 1959–91)* (Oxford: Oxford University Press, 1993), p. 70.
57. *Daily Telegraph*, 25 October 1999.
58. *Observer*, 16 April 2000.
59. *Guardian*, 8 February 2003.

Chapter 3

1. *Out of the Box: The Programme Supply Market in the Digital Age: A Report for the Department for Culture, Media and Sport* (Taunton: David Graham & Associates, n.d.), pp. 52–4.
2. M. Hussey, *Chance Governs All: A Memoir by Marmaduke Hussey* (London: Macmillan, 2001), pp. 204, 231.
3. BBC, *The Annual Report & Accounts 1986–87* (London: BBC, 1987), p. 37.
4. R. Caines (ed.), *Key Note: Broadcasting in the UK: 1995 Market Report* (London: Key Note, n.d.), p. 20.
5. *BBC Annual Report & Review 2000–01*, www.bbc.co.uk/info/report2001 (accessed 2 August 2002).
6. *BBC Annual Report and Accounts 2002–03*, www.bbc.co.uk/info/report2003 (accessed 18 November 2003).
7. www.top1000.co.uk (accessed 10 March 2002).
8. B. Sendall, *Independent Television in Britain: Volume 2: Expansion and Change, 1958–68* (London: Macmillan, 1983), pp. 79–81.
9. A. Briggs, *The History of Broadcasting in the United Kingdom: Volume V: Competition* (Oxford: Oxford University Press, 1995), p. 11.
10. *National Board for Prices and Incomes Report No. 156: Costs and Revenues of Independent Television Companies* (London: HMSO, 1970), p. 19; *Report of the Committee on the Future of Broadcasting* (London: HMSO, 1977), Cmnd. 6753, p. 180.
11. G. Beadle, *Television: A Critical View* (London: Allen & Unwin, 1963), pp. 62–3.

12. *Granada Annual Report and Accounts 2001*, p. 44, www.granadatv.co.uk (accessed 18 July 2002).

13. D. Forman, *Persona Granada: Some Memories of Sidney Bernstein and the Early Days of Independent Television* (London: Deutsch, 1997), p. 245.

14. C. Jenkins, *Power behind the Screen: Ownership, Control and Motivation in British Commercial Television* (London: MacGibbon & Kee, 1961), p. 150; *The Granada Television Area & The Market* (n.p.: Granada, n.d.), p. 55; for a chronology of company acquisitions and sales by the Granada Group, see Media Groups Profile: Granada Chronology, www.caslon.co.au/mediaprofiles/granada2.htm (accessed 18 July, 2002).

15. Forman, *Persona Granada*, pp. 248–50.

16. *Guardian*, 23 September 2002.

17. *Key British Enterprises 2002: Britain's Top 50,000 Companies: Volume 4 British Business Rankings* (High Wycombe: D&B, 2002), pp. 126, 380.

18. R. Collins, N. Garnham and G. Locksley, *The Economics of Television: The UK Case* (London: Sage, 1988), pp. 63–4; *Creative Industries: Mapping Document 2001, Radio and Television*, table 5, www.culture.gov.uk/creative/telet_05.htm (accessed 6 September 2001); *Out of the Box*, p. 39; D, Graham and Associates, *Building a Global Market: British Television in Overseas Markets* (n.p., n.d.), pp. 14–17.

19. Collins, Garnham and Locksley, *Economics of Television*, p. 73.

20. *Out of the Box*, p. 9–10.

21. D. Graham and Associates, *Building a Global Audience* (n.p., n.d.), pp. 27, 38.

22. *Creative Industries: Mapping Document 2001*.

23. A. Briggs, *The History of Broadcasting in the United Kingdom: Volume IV: Sound and Vision, 1945–1955* (Oxford: Oxford University Press, 1995), p. 204.

24. *BBC Handbook 1972* (London: BBC, 1972), p. 185.

25. P. Goodwin, *Television under the Tories: Broadcasting Policy 1979–1997* (London: BFI, 1998), p. 158.

26. *BBC Report and Accounts 1993–94* (London: BBC, 1994), p. 75; *Guardian*, 7 January 1999; www.top1000.co.uk (accessed 10 March 2002).

27. *ITV 1965: A Guide to Independent Television* (London: ITA, 1965), p. 160, 172; *Television & Radio 1980: Guide to Independent Television and Independent Local Radio* (London: IBA, 1980), p. 199.

28. *Televisual Franchise Supplement*, Autumn 1991.

29. See www.top1000.co.uk.

30. *Key Note Market Report 2000: Cable & Satellite TV* (n.p.: Key Note, 2000), p. 12.

31. *Out of the Box*, pp. 11, 30, 34; *ITC Annual Report 2000*, www.itc.org.uk/ann_ann_report (accessed 25 February 2002).

32. *Skillset Freelance Survey 2000–2001: November 2001*, www.skillset.org/uploads/docs (accessed 3 March 2003).

33. K. Geddes and G. Bussey, *The Setmakers: A History of the Radio and Television Industry* (London: BREMA, 1991), pp. 351–2.

34. National Economic Development Office, *Annual Statistical Survey of the Electronics Industry* (London: HMSO, 1972), p. 23.

35. Geddes and Bussey, *Setmakers*, ch. 6 provides a detailed account of the collapse of British-owned television receiver manufacturing.

36. *Ibid.*, p. 398.

37. *Ibid.*, p. 407.

38. *Ibid.*, pp. 407, 418, 427.

39. *Brema 56th Annual Report*, 19 April 2001, Review of 2000–01, www.brema.org.uk (accessed 4 December 2001).

40. *Brema 56th Annual Report*, 19 April 2001, Review of 2000–01.

41. Cabinet Office Information Technology Advisory Panel, *Cable Systems* (London: Cabinet Office, 1982), p. 7.

42. Goodwin, *Television under the Tories*, ch. 5.

43. *Key Note Market Report 2002: Cable & Satellite TV* (n.p.: Key Note, 2002); P. Fisher and S. Peak (eds), *The Guardian Media Guide 2002* (London: Matthew Clayton, 2001), pp. 192–3.

44. A. Milne, *DG: The Memoirs of a British Broadcaster* (London: Coronet, 1989), p. 113.

45. Goodwin, *Television under the Tories*, ch. 4. For a detailed analysis of British government policy to cable and satellite broadcasting in the 1980s, see M. Palmer and J. Tunstall, *Liberating Communications: Policy-Making in France and Britain* (Oxford: Blackwell, 1990).

46. C. Seymour-Ure, *The British Press and Broadcasting since 1945* (Oxford: Blackwell, 1991), p. 123.

47. *Advertising Association Information Centre: Statistics*, www.adassoc.org.uk/inform/stats.html (accessed 2 February 2002); *Advertising Statistics Yearbook 2001* (Henley-on-Thames: Advertising Association/NTC Research/A.C. Nielsen-MMS, 2001), p. 14.

48. *Advertising Association Information Centre: Student Briefing No. 6: Facts and Figures on Advertising Expenditure*, www.adassoc.org.uk/inform/in6.html (accessed 2 February 2002).

49. *Advertising Statistics Yearbook 2001*, p. 183.

50. *Advertising Association Information Centre: Student Briefing No. 6*.

51. *Advertisers Annual 2000–2001* (London: Hollis, 2000), p. 42.

52. *Ibid.*, p. 42.

53. *Advertising Statistics Yearbook 2001*, p. 20.

54. P. Barwise and A. Ehrenberg, *Television and its Audience* (London: Sage, 1988), pp. 167–72.

55. R. Caines (ed.), *Key Note: Broadcasting in the UK*, p. 117.

56. R. Dickason, *British Television Advertising: Cultural Identity and Communication* (Luton: University of Luton Press, 2000), discusses the cultural referents of television advertising. Changes in the style of television advertisements are also considered in B. Henry (ed.), *British Television Advertising: The First 30 Years* (London: Century Benham, 1986).

57. *National Board for Prices and Incomes Report No. 156: Costs and Revenues of Independent Television Companies* (London: HMSO, 1970), Appendix E, p. 56.

58. *Advertisers Annual 2000–2001*, p. 29.

59. *The Granada Television Area*, p. 20.

60. *Brown & White Goods Retailing UK*, www.browneyedsheep.com/brown&whitegoodsretail.htm (accessed 3 March 2002), p. 1.

61. *Guardian*, 24 May 1990.

62. British Film Institute, *Film and Television Handbook 2004* (London: BFI, 2003), p. 52.

63. National Economic Development Office, *Industrial Report by the Electronics EDC on the Economic Assessment to 1972* (London: NEDO, n.d.), 25–6.

64. Geddes and Bussey, *Setmakers*, pp. 331–4.

65. *Ibid.*, p. 381.

66. *Ibid.*, pp. 381–3.

67. *The Granada Television Area*, pp. 3, 20, 35.

68. *Brown & White Goods Retailing UK*, p. 1.

69. *TV and Video Rental April 1994*, www.accountingweb.co.uk/common/keynote/vcr (accessed 4 April 2002).

70. *Brown & White Goods Retailing UK*, p. 1.

71. *Independent*, 18 December 1999.

72. *Granada PLC Annual Report and Accounts 2001*, www.granadatv.co.uk (accessed 18 July 2002), p. 21.

73. BBC Online Network, 10 March 1999, www.bbc.co.uk/hi/English/business/the_company_file (accessed 4 April 2002).

74. www.top1000.co.uk (accessed 10 March 2002).

75. *Financial Times*, 21 June 1978, 16 August 1978, 18 December 1981; *Sunday Times*, 13 April 1980; *Daily Mail*, 28 February, 26 June 1981; *Guardian*, 26 June 1981; *Daily Mail*, 1 November 1981, 15 January, 20 March, 21 April, 1982. Q. Falk and D. Prince, *Last of a Kind: The Sinking of Lew Grade* (London: Quartet, 1987), provides a detailed narrative of Grade's involvement with film-making. H. Davies, *The Grades: The First Family of British Entertainment* (London: Weidenfeld and Nicolson, 1981), discusses Grade's film-making career but was published before Grade was forced to relinquish control of ACC.

76. S. Harvey, 'Channel 4 Television: From Annan to Grade', in S. Hood (ed.), *Behind the Scenes: The Structure of British Broadcasting* (London: Lawrence & Wishart, 1999), pp. 123–4.

77. *Guardian*, 25 April 2003.

78. Thames Television Press Release, 1 May 1987; *Sunday Times*, 3 May 1987. M. Alvarado and J. Stewart, *Made for Television: Euston Films Limited* (London: BFI, 1985), discusses the economics of Euston Films and reviews its major films.

79. *BBC Films* http://cgi.bbc.co.uk/bbcfilms/info (accessed 23 February 2003).

80. C. Barnett, *The Audit of War* (London: Macmillan, 1986); M.J. Wiener, *English Culture and the Decline of the Industrial Spirit* (Cambridge: Cambridge University Press, 1981). For commentaries on the debate about culture and the decline of industrialism, see N. McKendrick, '"Gentlemen and Players" Revisited: The Gentlemanly Ideal and the Professional Ideal in English Literary Culture', in N. McKendrick and R.R. Outhwaite (eds), *Business Life and Policy: Essays in Honour of D.C. Coleman* (Cambridge: Cambridge University Press, 1986), B. Collins and K. Robbins (eds), *British Culture and Economic Decline* (London: Weidenfeld and Nicolson, 1990) and J. Raven, 'Viewpoint: British History and the Enterprise Culture', *Past & Present*, 122 (November 1989), pp. 178–204.

81. *Guardian*, 3 February 2003.

Chapter 4

1. *The Times*, 29 April 1955, 31 August, 19 September 1959.

2. G.W. Goldie, *Facing the Nation: Television and Politics 1936–1976* (London: Bodley Head, 1977), pp. 40, 45.

3. G. Cox, *Pioneering Television News: A First Hand Report on a Revolution in Journalism* (London: John Libbey, 1995), p. 22.

4. A. Goodwin and G. Whannel (eds), *Understanding Television* (London: Routledge, 1990), p. 43.

5. J. Harrison, *Terrestrial TV News in Britain: The Culture of Production* (Manchester: Manchester University Press, 2000), ch. 1.

6. J. Harbord and J. Wright, *40 Years of British Television* (London: Boxtree, 1995).

7. *The Times*, 30 September 1975.

8. R. Day, *. . . But with Respect: Memorable Television Interviews with Statesmen and Parliamentarians* (London: Weidenfeld and Nicolson, 1993), pp. 296–7.

9. Cox, *Pioneering Television News*, p. 172.

10. Goldie, *Facing the Nation*, p. 66.

11. S. Barnett, E. Seymour and I. Gaber, *From Callaghan to Kosovo: Changing Trends in British Television News 1975–1999* (Harrow: University of Westminster, 2000).

12. Harrison, *Terrestrial TV News*, p. 106.

13. Ibid.

14. J. Blumler and D. McQuail, *Television in Politics: Its Uses and Influence* (London: Faber and Faber, 1968), pp. 42–3.

15. A. Goodwin, 'TV News: Striking the Right Balance?', in A. Goodwin and G. Whannel (eds), *Understanding Television* (London: Routledge, 1990), p. 42.

16. C. Varlaam, R. Pearson, P. Leighton and S. Blum, *Skill Search: Television, Film and Video Industry Employment Patterns and Training Needs: Part 1: The Key*

Facts (Falmer: Institute of Manpower Studies, University of Sussex, 1989), p. 59.

17. D. McQuail, *Media Performance: Mass Communication and the Public Interest* (London: Sage, 1992), pp. 192–3.

18. Quoted in J. Curran and J. Seaton, *Power without Responsibility: The Press and Broadcasting in Britain* (London: Routledge, 1997), p. 170.

19. Goodwin, 'TV News', p. 53, gives the source for Curran's comment as I. Connell, 'More Bad News', *Marxism Today* (August 1980). Goodwin's chapter reviews responses to the work of the Glasgow University Group.

20. Goodwin, 'TV News', p. 42.

21. Ibid., pp. 52–3.

22. S. Hood, *A Survey of Television* (London: Heinemann, 1976), p. 109.

23. J. Sergeant, *Give Me Ten Seconds* (London: Pan, 2002), p. 124.

24. B. Ingham, *Kill the Messenger* (London: HarperCollins, 1991), pp. 353–4, 356.

25. T. Shaw, *Eden, Suez and the Mass Media: Propaganda and Persuasion during the Suez Crisis* (London: Tauris, 1996), pp. 122, 150.

26. M. Cockerell, *Live from Number 10: The Inside Story of Prime Ministers and Television* (London: Faber and Faber, 1988), pp. 45–51; H. Grisewood, *One Thing at a Time: An Autobiography* (London: Hutchinson, 1968), pp. 195–203.

27. Cockerell, *Live from Number 10*, ch. 8.

28. Ibid., p. 116.

29. Ibid., pp. 296–8; *Sunday Times*, 18 August 1985.

30. C. Horrie and S. Clarke, *Fuzzy Monsters: Fear and Loathing at the BBC* (London: Heinemann, 1994), pp. 62, 168.

31. Cockerell, *Live from Number 10*, pp. 310–14.

32. Ibid., p. 315; M. Hussey, *Chance Governs All: A Memoir* (London: Macmillan, 2001), pp. 213–17; A. Milne, *DG: The Memoirs of a British Broadcaster* (London: Hodder & Stoughton, 1988), pp. 198–202.

33. J. Campbell, *Margaret Thatcher. Volume Two: The Iron Lady* (London: Cape, 2003), p. 568.

34. For a detailed account of these two programmes and the reactions to them, see R. Bolton, *Death on the Rock and Other Stories* (London: W.H. Allen, 1990).

35. J. Cole, *As It Seemed To Me: Political Memoir* (London: Weidenfeld & Nicolson, 1995), p. 54.

36. P. Ferris, *Sir Huge: The Life of Huw Wheldon* (London: Michael Joseph, 1990), pp. 91–3.

37. Cockerell, *Live from Number 10* (London: Faber and Faber, 1988), ch. 3.

38. Goldie, *Facing the Nation*, p. 172.

39. Cockerell, *Live from Number 10*, p. xiii.

40. D.E. Butler and R. Rose, *The British General Election of 1959* (London: Macmillan, 1960), pp. 81, 83–4.

41. Cockerell, *Live from Number 10*, ch. 7.

42. Ibid., p. 226.
43. Sergeant, *Give Me Ten Seconds*, p. 234; Cockerell, *Live from Number 10*, p. 287.
44. Cole, *As It Seemed To Me*, p. 290.
45. Cockerell, *Live from Number 10*, pp. 248, 263.
46. Quoted by Day, *But with Respect*, p. 288.
47. *Listener*, 12 December 1968.
48. Day, *But with Respect*, pp. 5–6.
49. Cox, *Pioneering Television News*, p. 78.
50. *Guardian*, 11 November 2000.
51. *Guardian*, 8 August 2000.
52. *Guardian*, 11 November 2000.
53. J. Paxman, *Friends in High Places: Who Runs Britain?* (London: Penguin, 1991), p. xvi.
54. John Naughton's profile of Jeremy Paxman, http://molly.open.ac.uk/Personal-pages/Pubs/Profiles/ (accessed 20 January 2003). This profile had originally appeared in the *Observer*.
55. *Guardian*, 16 July 2001.
56. Day, *But with Respect*, p. 2.
57. Quoted in H. Carpenter, *That Was The Satire That Was* (London: Gollancz, 2000), pp. 205–6.
58. *Ibid.*, p. 207.
59. Cockerell, *Live from Number 10*, p. 86.
60. Carpenter, *That Was The Satire*, p. 256.
61. Ibid., p. 271.
62. Ibid., p. 238.
63. *Guardian*, 8 April 2002.
64. For a more detailed discussion of the pros and cons of tabloid television and newspapers, see I. Hargreaves, *Journalism: Truth or Dare?* (Oxford: Oxford University Press, 2003), ch. 3. S. Livingstone and P. Lunt, *Talk on Television: Audience Participation and Public Debate* (London: Routledge, 1994), analyses the nature of television audience participation shows.
65. D. Lyon, *Surveillance Society: Monitoring in Everyday Life* (Buckingham: Open University, 2001), p. 63.

Chapter 5

1. For the circulation figures for all categories of British newspapers for every year from 1945 to 1994, see C. Seymour-Ure, *The British Press and Broadcasting since 1945* (Oxford: Blackwell, 1997), p. 17; the figures for 2003 are based on the data available on the Audit Bureau of Circulations website for the period October 2002 to March 2003, www.abc.org.uk (accessed 10 May 2003).

2. *Royal Commission on the Press 1961–1962 Report* (London: HMSO, 1962, Cmnd. 1811), p. 170.

3. Seymour-Ure, *British Press and Broadcasting*, pp. 16, 274–7.

4. J. Curran and J. Seaton, *Power without Responsibility: The Press and Broadcasting in Britain* (London: Routledge, 1997), p. 91.

5. J. Curran, *Media and Power* (London: Routledge, 2002), p. 101.

6. Seymour-Ure, *British Press and Broadcasting*, p. 143; *Advertising Association Information Centre: Statistics*, www.adassoc.org.uk/inform/stats.html (accessed 2 February 2002).

7. These figures have been calculated from the statistics found in the *Advertising Statistics Yearbook 2001* (Henley-on-Thames: Advertising Association, 2001), pp. 3, 4, 14–17, 153–5.

8. Curran and Seaton, *Power without Responsibility*, p. 103.

9. J. Curran, 'The Impact of Television on the Audience for National Newspapers, 1945–68', in J. Tunstall (ed.), *Media Sociology: A Reader* (London: Constable, 1974), pp. 104–22; P.J. Humphreys, *Mass Media and Media Policy in Western Europe* (Manchester: Manchester University Press, 1996), p. 36.

10. *Monopolies and Mergers Commission: The British Broadcasting Corporation and the Independent Television Publications Limited* (London: HMSO, 1985, Cmnd. 9614), pp. 10, 13.

11. BBC Audience Research Department, *The People's Activities: Statistics of What People Are Doing Half Hour by Half Hour from Six Thirty a.m. until Midnight* (n.p.: BBC, 1965), p. 2, 3.

12. www.rab.co.uk (accessed 17 July 2003).

13. Annual issues of *Social Trends*; C. Seymour-Ure, *The British Press and Broadcasting since 1945* (Oxford: Blackwell, 1997), pp. 166–7.

14. B. Sendall, *Independent Television in Britain: Volume 1: Origin and Foundation, 1946–62* (London: Macmillan, 1982), ch. 11.

15. *Ibid.*, p. 187.

16. *Broadcast*, 22 October 1979.

17. R. Fulford, *The Sixth Decade 1946–1956* (n.p.: BET, 1956), pp. xv–xxi.

18. Seymour-Ure, *British Press and Broadcasting*, table 4.9; A. Smith, *The Age of the Behemoths: The Globalization of Mass Media Firms* (New York: Priory, 1991), pp. 37–8; www.channel5.co.uk (accessed 6 December 2002).

19. Sendall, *Independent Television*, pp. 185–93; J. Potter, *Independent Television in Britain: Volume 3: Politics and Control, 1968–80* (London: Macmillan, 1989), p. 49.

20. P. Bonner and L. Aston, *Independent Television in Britain: Volume 5: ITV and the IBA: The Old Relationship Changes* (London: Macmillan, 1998), pp. 155–6; *Financial Times*, 7 June 1986.

21. *Report of the Committee on Broadcasting, 1960* (London: HMSO, 1962) Cmnd. 1753, p. 182–3.

22. *Royal Commission on the Press: Minutes of Oral Evidence, Vol. I* (London: HMSO, 1962), Cmnd. 1812, pp. 220, 627.

23. *Guardian*, 9 November 1992.

24. *Guardian*, 27 October 1993.

25. *Media Week*, 7 January 1994; *UK Press Gazette*, 10 January 1994.

26. *Guardian*, 14 January 1994.

27. *Financial Times*, 21 May 1996.

28. Mintel Internatonal, *Mintel Leisure Intelligence: Cable and Satellite TV* (London: Mintel International, 2001), p. 5; *Key Note Cable & Satellite TV Market Report 2002* (n.p.: n.d.), p. 13.

29. *Broadcast*, 11 September 1998.

30. *Variety*, 24 June 1996.

31. C. Horrie and A. Nathan, *L¿ve TV* (London: Simon & Schuster, 1999), provides a detailed account of L!ve TV up to 1997.

32. P. Chippindale and S. Franks, *Dished! The Rise and Fall of British Satellite Broadcasting* (London: Simon & Schuster), pp. 14–15.

33. *Guardian*, 28 March 1995.

34. A. Davidson, *Under the Hammer: The Inside Story of the 1991 ITV Franchise Battle* (London: Heinemann, 1992), p. 133.

35. Details of these companies were collected from *Kompass Industrial Trade Names Register 2002/2003*, vols 3 and 4 (Sutton: Reed Business Information, 2002).

36. Interview with Sir Paul Fox, 6 June 2003.

37. *Royal Commission on the Press: Minutes of Oral Evidence*, pp. 220, 627.

38. *Royal Commission on the Press 1961–1962 Report*, p. 78.

39. *Daily Express*, 24 June 1992; *UK Press Gazette*, 29 June 1992.

40. *Listener*, 24 July 1969.

41. For a history of the pirate radio stations, see R. Chapman, *Selling the Sixties: The Pirates and Pop Music Radio* (London: Routledge, 1992).

42. *The Times*, 1 July 1967.

43. Interview with Gillian Reynolds, 24 July 2003. Reynolds has pointed out that she is not totally convinced of the truth of Wilson's account.

44. *The Times*, 16 August 1967.

45. *The Times*, 12 October 1967.

46. *Guardian*, 7 June 2003.

47. A. Briggs and J. Spicer, *The Franchise Affair: Creating Fortunes and Failures in Independent Television* (London: Century Hutchinson, 1986), p. 159.

48. J. Tunstall, *Television Producers* (London: Routledge, 1993), pp. 197–8; interview with Michael Grade, 6 August 2003.

49. Fox interview, 6 June 2003.

50. J. Tunstall, *Producers*, pp. 12–13, 198.

51. Interview with Sir Bill Cotton, 21 May 2003.

52. A. Neil, *Full Disclosure* (London: Pan, 1997), p. 62.

Chapter 6

1. Freshminds, *Employment in Film and Television in the UK: A Report on the Position of Women within the Industry Prepared for Women in Film and Television* (London: Freshminds, 2003), pp. 7–8.
2. J. Arthurs, 'Women and Television', in S. Hood (ed.), *Behind the Scenes: The Structure of British Broadcasting* (London: Lawrence & Wishart, 1999), pp. 87–8, 90.
3. *Employment in Film and Television in the UK*, pp. 7–16.
4. *Televisual*, February 2002.
5. M. Bose, *Michael Grade: Screening the Image* (London: Virgin, 1992), p. 161.
6. J. Tunstall, *Television Producers* (London: Routledge, 1993), p. 176.
7. G. Dougary, *The Executive Tart and Other Myths: Media Women Talk Back* (London: Virago, 1994), pp. xi, 7–8; J. Arthurs, 'Spot the Difference, London, 14 March 1991', *Screen*, 32/4 (1991), pp. 447–51.
8. Tunstall, *Producers*, p. 180; *Independent*, 18 February 1992.
9. S. Lambert, *Channel Four: Television with a Difference?* (London: BFI, 1982), p. 173.
10. Tunstall, *Producers*, p. 180.
11. Political and Economic Planning, *Women in Top Jobs: Four Studies in Achievement* (London: Allen & Unwin, 1971), p. 167.
12. *Employment in Film and Television*, p. 9.
13. Tunstall, *Producers*, pp. 175, 178, 183.
14. Dougary, *Executive Tart*, p. 5–7.
15. Arthurs, 'Spot the Difference', p. 448.
16. *Spare Rib*, no. 23.
17. Arthurs, 'Spot the Difference', p. 449.
18. M. Hussey, *Chance Governs All: A Memoir by Marmaduke Hussey* (London: Macmillan, 2001), p. 205.
19. Dougary, *Executive Tart*, pp. 45, 68.
20. *Evening Standard*, 10 June 1993.
21. J. Hallam, 'Power Plays: Gender, Genre and Lynda La Plante', in J. Bignell, S. Lacey and M. Macmurraugh-Kavanagh (eds), *British Television Drama: Past, Present and Future* (Basingstoke: Palgrave, 2000), p. 140.
22. I. Shubik, *Play for Today: The Evolution of Television Drama* (London: Davis-Poynter), pp. 82–3.
23. Quoted by B. Gunter, *Television and Gender Representation* (London: John Libbey, 1995), pp. 20, 27, 37.
24. S. Hood, *A Survey of Television* (London: Heinemann, 1967), p. 108.
25. *Women in Top Jobs*, p. 187.
26. *Evening Standard*, 10 June 1993.
27. F. Muir, *Comedy in Television* (London: BBC, 1966), p. 12.
28. Tunstall, *Producers*, pp. 205–6.

29. Dougary, *Executive Tart*, pp. 3, 11.

30. *IBA Annual Report and Accounts 1974–75* (London: IBA), p. 50.

31. *Second Report from the Select Committee on Nationalised Industries: Report, together with Minutes of Proceedings of the Committee, Appendices and Index, Session 1971–72* (London: HMSO, 1972), p. 156.

32. Hood, *Survey of Television*, p. 159.

33. D. Gauntlett and A. Hill, *TV Living: Television, Culture and Everyday Life* (London: BFI, 1999), pp. 39, 241.

34. For a discussion of conflicting interpretations of the soap operas and their appeal for women, see L.S. Mumford, 'Feminist Theory and Television Studies', in C. Geraghty and D. Lusted (eds), *The Television Studies Book* (London: Arnold, 1998).

35. J. Obelkevich, 'Consumption', in J. Obelkevich and P. Catterall (eds), *Understanding Post-War British Society* (London: Routledge, 1994); *Independent on Sunday*, 8 March 1998.

36. *Guardian*, 3 February 2003.

37. *Guardian*, 25 November 2002.

38. *News Chronicle*, 12 May 1960.

39. *Daily Express*, 10 October 1966.

40. For a full discussion of this, see J. Potter, *Independent Television in Britain: Volume 3: Politics and Control, 1968–80* (London: Macmillan, 1989), ch. 8.

41. *Guardian*, 13 September 1999.

42. *Daily Star*, 12 November 1983.

43. Quoted in Gunter, *Television and Gender Representation*, p. 105.

44. *Content and Analysis: Briefing Update No. 7* (London: Broadcasting Standards Commission, 2001), pp. 15–19.

45. *The Times*, 1 October 1997.

46. *The Times*, 27 April 2000.

47. W. Wyatt, *The Fun Factory: A Life in the BBC* (London: Aurum, 2003), p. 210.

48. *Daily Telegraph*, 20 June 1996.

49. *Sunday Times*, 2 February 1992.

50. *Sunday Times*, 5 November 1995.

51. *Daily Telegraph*, 15 November 1995.

52. *Sunday Times*, 24 April 1984.

53. M. Tracey, *A Variety of Lives: A Biography of Sir Hugh Greene* (London: Bodley Head, 1983), p. 235.

54. Quoted by A. Smith (ed.), *British Broadcasting* (Newton Abbot: David & Charles, 1974), pp. 186–7.

55. Quoted *ibid.*, pp. 187–8.

56. Tracey, *Variety of Lives*, pp. 240–3.

57. *The Times*, 8 February 1973.

58. *Report of the Committee on the Future of Broadcasting* (London: HMSO, 1977), Cmnd. 6753, p. 257.

59. *Broadcast*, 27 August 1999.

60. Tracey, *Variety of Lives*, p. 241.

61. *Second Report from the Select Committee on Nationalised Industries: Report, Together with Minutes of Proceedings of the Committee, Minutes of Evidence, Appendices and Index: Session 1971–72* (London: HMSO, 1972), p. 274.

62. Potter, *Independent Television in Britain*, p. 13.

63. *Daily Telegraph*, 2 December 1998.

64. *The Times*, 2 September 2000.

65. *Broadcast*, 7 May 1999.

66. *Broadcast*, 5 March 1999.

67. *Broadcast*, 7 May 1999.

68. A.M. Hargrave, *Sex and Sensibility* (London: Broadcasting Standards Commission, 1999), p. 13.

69. *Broadcast*, 7 May 1999.

70. *The Economics of the Programme Supply Chain: A Summary Report for the Department of National Heritage* (Chris Goodall & Co. and David Graham & Associates, n.p., n.d.), pp. 3–4.

71. For further details of this report, see K. Howes, *Broadcasting It: An Encyclopaedia of Homosexuality on Film, Radio and TV in the UK* (London: Cassell, 1993), p. 35.

72. *Briefing Update No. 9: The Representation of Minorities on Television: A Content Analysis* (London: Broadcasting Standards Commission, 2001), pp. 12–13.

73. www.home.cc.umanitoba.ca/~wyatt/tv-characters.html (accessed 12 August 2003).

74. J. Birt, *The Harder Path: The Autobiography* (London: Time Warner, 2002), p. 180.

75. *The Times*, 24 June 1999.

76. *Guardian*, 17 February 2001.

77. *Capital Gay*, 5 August 1994.

78. *Sunday Times*, 30 January 1994.

79. *Pink Paper*, 19 November 1993.

80. W. Wyatt, *The Fun Factory: A Life in the BBC* (London: Aurum, 2003), p. 157.

81. *Sun*, 13 February 2003; *Daily Mail*, 14 February 2003; *Gay Times*, April 2003.

82. Interview with Michael Grade, 6 August 2003.

83. *Capital Gay*, 20 April 1995.

84. C. Geraghty, *Women and Soap Opera: A Study of Prime Time Soaps* (Cambridge: Polity, 1991), pp. 159–63.

85. C. Horrie and A. Nathan, *Live TV* (London: Simon & Schuster, 1999), p. 434.

86. *Gay Times*, 21 February–5 March 1980.

87. *Capital Gay*, 7 October 1988.

88. *Listener*, 3 March 1988.

89. *Gay Times*, November 1996.

90. *Gay Times*, August 1991.

91. *Gay Times*, April 2001.

92. P. Tatchell, *The Battle for Bermondsey* (London: Heretic, 1983).

93. S. Jeffery-Poulter, *Peers, Queers, and Commons: The Struggle for Gay Law Reform from 1950 to the Present* (London; Routledge, 1991), pp. 136–8, 173–4, 203, 257–8.

94. *Ibid.*

95. Quoted by Howes, *Broadcasting It*, p. 35.

96. *Capital Gay*, 19 November 1993.

97. *Daily Mail*, 15 October 1987.

98. Hargrave, *Sex and Sensibility*, pp. 84–5.

99. *Gay Times*, November 2002, pp. 85–6.

100. S. Harvey, 'Channel 4 Television: From Annan to Grade', in S. Hood (ed.), *Behind the Screens: The Structure of British Broadcasting* (London: Lawrence & Wishart, 1999), p. 118; J. Isaacs, *Storm over 4: A Personal Account* (London: Weidenfeld and Nicolson, 1989), p. 59.

101. Quoted in M. Grade, *It Seemed like a Good Idea at the Time* (London: Macmillan, 1999), p. 356.

102. M. Whitehouse, *A Most Dangerous Woman?* (Tring: Lion, 1982), pp. 14–15.

103. *Guardian*, 17 July 2003.

104. *Broadcasting Standards Commission: Bulletin No. 1.*

105. Hargrave, *Sex and Sensibility*, pp. 3–5; *Broadcast*, 27 August 1999.

106. Gunter, *Television and Gender Representation*, ch. 6.

Chapter 7

1. For summaries of historical and more recent debates about the nature of race and racism, see M. Bulmer and J. Solomon (eds), *Racism* (Oxford: Oxford University Press, 1999) and K. Malik, *The Meaning of Race: Race, History and Culture in Western Society* (London: Macmillan, 1996).

2. M. Anwar, *Who Tunes In To What? A Report on Ethnic Minority Broadcasting* (London: Commission for Racial Equality, 1978), pp. 27–8.

3. *Sun*, 20 January 1988.

4. K. Ross, 'In Whose Image? TV Criticism and Black Minority Viewers', in S. Cottle (ed.), *Ethnic Minorities and the Media* (Buckingham: Open University Press, 2000), p. 145.

5. *Guardian*, 12 November 2002.

6. *Broadcast*, 11 July 1983.

7. C. Ehrlrich, *The Ehrlrich Report* (London: BBC, 1986), p. 3.

8. *Voice*, 4 July 1989.

9. *Time Out*, 28 September 1988.

10. S. Cottle and P. Ismond, *Television and Ethnic Minorities: Producers' Perspectives: A Study of BBC In-house, Independent and Cable TV Producers* (Aldershot: Avebury, 1997), pp. 72, 94.

11. *Guardian*, 13 January 2003.
12. S. Malik, *Representing Black Britain: A History of Black and Asian Images on British Television* (London: Sage, 2002), p. 76.
13. T. Daniels, 'Programmes for Black Audiences' and P. Keighron and C. Walker, 'Working in Television: Five Interviews', in S. Hood (ed.), *Behind the Screens: The Structure of British Broadcasting* (London: Lawrence & Wishart, 1999), pp. 77, 206.
14. *Independent*, 8 December 1999.
15. *Time Out*, 28 September 1988.
16. *Guardian*, 13 January 2003.
17. A.M. Hargrave (ed.), *Multicultural Broadcasting: Concept and Reality* (London: BBC, BSC, ITC and the Radio Authority, 2002), pp. 78–9.
18. *Free Press*, July–August, 1990.
19. G. Cumberbatch, S. Woods, et al., *Ethnic Minorities on Television: A Report for the ITC* (London: ITC, 1996); Hargrave, *Multicultural Broadcasting*, Appendix 1, summarises the data for 1997–2001. These two reports drew their data from different samples. Cumberbatch and Woods analysed all programmes broadcast between 5.30 p.m. and midnight for four weeks in four separate months. Hargrave looked at programmes broadcast during the same hours over a fortnight. These differences do not prevent meaningful comparisons being made between their data.
20. Atwell's career is analysed in S. Bourne, *Black in the British Frame: Black People in British Film and Television 1896–1996* (London: Cassell, 1998), ch. 7.
21. Adams' career is discussed in *ibid.*, ch. 5.
22. *Observer*, 12 January 1964.
23. J. Pines (ed.), *Black and White in Colour: Black People in British Television since 1936* (London: BFI, 1992), pp. 10, 13, 31, 80.
24. Malik, *Representing Black Britain*, p. 136.
25. Pines, *Black and White in Colour*, p. 204.
26. Y. Alibhai-Brown, 'Sold Out by Media Wallahs', *New Statesman and Society*, 28 January 1994.
27. Pines, *Black and White in Colour*, p. 171.
28. *Ibid.*, p. 100.
29. C. Geraghty, *Women and Soap Opera: A Study of Prime Time Soaps* (Cambridge: Polity, 1991), p. 33.
30. Malik, *Representing Black Britain*, p. 148; Pines, *Black and White in Colour*, pp. 196–7.
31. S. Bourne, 'Coming Clean: Soap Operas', in T. Daniels and J. Gerson (eds), *Black Images in British Television: The Colour Black* (London: BFI, 1989), p. 123.
32. *New Society*, 16 November 1978.
33. H.V. Kershaw, *The Street Where I Live* (London: Book Club Associates, 1981), pp. 170–1.
34. *Daily Mail*, 10 July 1987.

35. Malik, *Representing Black Britain*, pp. 148–9.
36. *Ibid.*, p. 103.
37. *Time Out*, 25 June–1 July 1976.
38. *Daily Mail*, 7 May 1977; *Guardian*, 6 June 1981.
39. Quoted in *Birmingham Post*, 1 December 1983.
40. 'Changing the Face of Broadcasting', *Connections* (Winter, 2000–1), p. 6.
41. *Guardian*, 13 January 2003.
42. *The Times*, 24 November 1976.
43. Alibhai-Brown, 'Sold Out by Media Wallahs'.
44. *Leicester Mercury*, 27 April 1968.
45. *Broadcast*, 16 May 1977.
46. Malik, *Representing Black Britain*, p. 42.
47. *The Times*, 11 April 1988.
48. Malik, *Representing Black Britain*, p. 180.
49. *Ibid.*, pp. 87–9.
50. *Sunday Telegraph*, 2 February 1969; *Daily Telegraph*, 3 February 1969.
51. *Wolverhampton Express and Star*, 10 January 1979.
52. *Bradford Telegraph and Argus*, 7 February 1979.
53. *Star*, 8 November 1989.
54. *Broadcast*, 10 August 1984.
55. Pines, *Black and White in Colour*, p. 160.
56. *Ibid.*, p. 176.
57. *Ibid.*, pp. 155, 180.
58. Malik, *Representing Black Britain*, pp. 65–9.
59. *Ibid.*, p. 71.
60. For examples of ethnic minority responses to negative stereotyping, see Ross, 'In Whose Image?', pp. 142–6.
61. *Daily Telegraph*, 3 May 1972.
62. *Star*, 3 September 1985.
63. *Daily Sketch*, 26 June 1969; *Broadcast*, 25 October 1982.
64. *Listener*, 26 June 1975.
65. *Sun*, 21 August 1976.
66. *Guardian*, 3 February 2003.
67. *Guardian*, 3 October 1975; *Broadcast*, 13 October 1975.
68. P. Gilroy, *The Black Atlantic: Modernity and Double Consciousness* (London: Verso, 1993).
69. *Asian Times*, 8 May 2001.

Chapter 8

1. Quoted by R. Middleton, 'The "Problem" of Popular Music', in S. Banfield (ed.), *The Blackwell History of Music in Britain: Volume 6: The Twentieth Century* (Oxford: Blackwell, 1995), p. 27.

2. A. Sinfield, *Literature, Politics and Culture in Postwar Britain* (Oxford: Oxford University Press, 1989), p. 176.

3. R. Hoggart, *The Way We Live Now* (London: Pimlico, 1996), pp. 59, 93–5.

4. B. Ford (ed.), *The Cambridge Guide to the Arts in Britain: Volume 9: Since the Second World War* (Cambridge: Cambridge University Press, 1988).

5. A. Sinclair, *Arts and Cultures: The History of the 50 Years of the Arts Council of Great Britain* (London: Sinclair-Stevenson, 1995), pp. 311, 348.

6. Industry News from DOCtv, www.docos.com/news/Previous...Artsworld (accessed 17 July 2002); 'Artsworld To Cease Transmissions', www.artsworld.com/company-information/final-release (accessed 17 July 2002).

7. For a discussion of the evolution and variety of television arts programmes up to the early 1990s, see J.A. Walker, *Arts TV: A History of Arts Television in Britain* (London: John Libbey, 1993).

8. *Guardian*, 14 June 1999.

9. *Guardian*, 10 May 2003.

10. *Guardian*, 30 June 2003.

11. *Guardian*, 19 May 2003.

12. Quoted in A. Briggs, *The History of Broadcasting in the United Kingdom: Volume V: Competition* (Oxford: Oxford University Press, 1995), p. 19.

13. B. McCarthy, 'Vision Scenes', *Dance Now*, 11/2 (2002), 25–30.

14. *Ibid.*, p. 29.

15. *Daily Telegraph*, 12 December 1987.

16. *Financial Times*, 5 October 1988.

17. *Sunday Times*, 14 November 1982.

18. *Bookseller*, 19 July 1975.

19. *Sunday Times*, 15 August 1993.

20. *Sunday Times*, 18 July 1993.

21. *Sunday Times*, 14 November 1982, 29 December 1985.

22. *Sunday Times*, 29 December 1985; *Evening Standard*, 25 January 1986.

23. I. Shubik, *Play for Today: The Evolution of Television Drama* (London: Davis-Poynter, 1975), p. 33; G.W. Goldie, *Facing the Nation: Television and Politics 1936–1976* (London: Bodley Head, 1977), p. 33.

24. M. MacMurraugh-Kavanagh, 'The BBC and the Birth of *The Wednesday Play*, 1962–66: Institutional Containment versus "Agitational contemporaneity"', in J. Thumin (ed.), *Small Screens, Big Ideas: Television in the 1950s* (London: I.B. Tauris, 2002).

25. J. Tunstall, *Television Producers* (London: Routledge, 1993), p. 123.

26. *Artstat: Digest of Arts, Statistics and Trends in the UK 1986/87–1997/98* (London: Arts Council of England, 2000), p. 105.

27. A. Feist and R. Hutchison (eds), *Cultural Trends in the Eighties* (London: Policy Studies Institute, 1990), pp. 40–1.

28. *The Arts Council of Great Britain: Tenth Annual Report 1954–5* (London: Arts Council, n.d.), pp. 6–7.

29. *The Arts Council of Great Britain: Fourteenth Annual Report 1958–9* (London: Arts Council, n.d.), p. 6.

30. Briggs, *Competition*, p. 953.

31. *Appendix to the Committee on Broadcasting (Papers 1–102)* (Cmnd. 1819) (London: HMSO, 1962), p. 317.

32. Briggs, *Competition*, pp. 187–8, 953.

33. W. Shawcross, *Rupert Murdoch: Ringmaster of the Information Circus* (London: Pan, 1993), pp. 450–1.

34. British Film Institute, *British Film Institute: Film and Television Yearbook* (London: BFI, 1983), p. 207.

35. Shawcross, *Murdoch*, p. 451. For a detailed study of the economic difficulties of the British cinema in the 1950s, see J. Spraos, *The Decline of the Cinema: An Economist's Report* (London: Allen & Unwin, 1962).

36. British Film Institute, *BFI Film and Television Handbook 1994* (London: BFI, 1993), p. 52; British Film Institute, *BFI Film and Television Handbook 1996* (London: BFI, 1995), p. 57.

37. For lists of the television programmes attracting most viewers for each year between 1955 and 1994, see J. Harbord and J. Wright, *40 Years of British Television* (London: Boxtree, 1995).

38. British Film Institute, *BFI Film and Television Handbook 2004* (London: BFI, 2003), pp. 39, 52; *Kinematograph Year Book 1949* (London: Kinematograph Publications, n.d.), p. 50.

39. Feist and Hutchison, *Cultural Trends in the Eighties*, p. 2; *Artstat*, p. 98.

40. *Social Trends 25* (London: HMSO, 1995), p. 216; *Social Trends 32* (London: HMSO, 2002), p. 213.

41. H. Carpenter, *The Envy of the World: Fifty Years of the BBC Third Programme and Radio 3* (London: Weidenfeld and Nicolson, 1996), pp. 48, 84.

42. *Ibid.*, p. 345; *Guardian*, 5 August 2002.

43. RAJAR Quarterly Summary September 2000, www.rajar.co.uk/summarytable.cfm (accessed 16 March 2001).

44. Interview with Gillian Reynolds, 24 July 2003.

45. Interview with Sir Bill Cotton, 21 May 2003.

46. *Guardian*, 12 August 2002.

47. Interview with Gillian Reynolds.

48. S. Connor, *The English Novel in History 1950–1995* (London: Routledge, 1996), pp. 29, 67.

49. These are *After the Break* (London: Hodder and Stoughton, 1995), *The Director's Cut* (London: Hodder and Stoughton, 1996) and *A Job To Die For* (London: Hodder and Stoughton, 1997).

50. Connor, *The English Novel*, p. 37.

51. For the titles of those published before 2000, see D. Little, *40 Years of Coronation Street* (London: Granada Media, 2000), p. 277. K. Hardy, *Coronation Street: The Epic Novel: Four Decades of Life on The Street* (n.p.: Granada Media), was published in 2003.

52. *Listener*, 2 November 1961; *Guardian*, 2 November 2003.

53. *Listener*, 25 September 1986.

54. *Guardian*, 1 May 2003.

55. D. Kershaw, 'Film and Television Music', in Banfield (ed.), *Blackwell History of Music in Britain*, ch. 7.

56. J. Stokes, *On Screen Rivals: Cinema and Television in the United States and Britain* (London: Macmillan, 1999), p. 40; British Film Institute, *BFI Film and Television Handbook 2001* (London: BFI, 2000), p. 30.

57. Stokes, *On Screen Rivals*.

58. *Listener*, 2 November 1961.

59. J. Caughie, 'What Do Actors Do When They Act?', in J. Bignell, S. Lacey and M. Macmurraugh-Kavanagh (eds), *British Television Drama: Past, Present and Future* (Basingstoke: Palgrave, 2000), p. 172.

60. L. Olivier, *On Acting* (London: Weidenfeld and Nicolson, 1986), pp. 228–30.

Chapter 9

1. BBC, *BBC Annual 1937* (London: BBC, n.d.), p. 151.

2. Independent Television Authority, *Independent Television Programmes: Facts and Figures* (London: ITA, 1962), p. 7.

3. M. Shulman, *The Least Worst Television in the World* (London: Barrie & Jenkins, 1973), p. 111.

4. S. Barnett, *Games and Sets: The Changing Face of Sport on Television* (London: BFI, 1990), p. 46.

5. *ITC Annual Report 2000: Commercial Television in the UK: An Overview*, www.itc.org.uk/about/ann_report_20/commercial.asp?saection=about (accessed 25 February 2002), pp. 2, 6, 7.

6. Annual Conference of Sports Administrators, Central Council for Physical Recreation, 1975, quoted by G. Whannel, *Fields in Vision: Television, Sport and Cultural Transformation* (London: Routledge, 1992), p. 78.

7. 'Women in Sport and Recreation', Central Council for Physical Recreation seminar, 1976, quoted by Whannel, *Fields in Vision*, p. 78.

8. Whannel, *Fields in Vision*, p. 194.

9. BBC Broadcasting Research Department, quoted in T. Moore, 'Presentation', *British Society of Sports History Bulletin*, 9 (1990), p. 79.

10. BBC, *BBC Handbook 1977 Incorporating the Annual Report and Accounts 1975–6* (London: BBC, 1976), p. 48.

11. *House of Commons Session 1993–94: National Heritage Committee: Fourth Report: Sports Sponsorship and Television Coverage. Volume I: Report and Minutes of Proceedings: House of Commons Session 1993–94*, 289–I (London: HMSO, 1994), p. 10.

12. J. Harbord and J. Wright, *40 Years of British Television* (London: Boxtree, 1995), p. 41; N. Wilson, *The Sports Business* (London: Piatkus, 1988), p. 37.

13. BBC Archives: Audience Research Viewing Barometers 1 April 1971–31 March 1972: R9/37/7.

14. T. Smith and D. Taylor (eds), *Benson and Hedges Snooker Year* (London: Pelham, 1987), pp. 17, 107.

15. Channel 5 Report for 2001, www.channel5.co.uk (accessed 6 December 2002).

16. Moore, 'Presentation', p. 83.

17. *Guardian*, 10 July 1995.

18. *Independent on Sunday*, 5 December 1993; Moore, 'Presentation', p. 83.

19. G. Whannel, '"Grandstand", the Sports Fan and the Family Audience', in J. Corner (ed.), *Popular Television in Britain: Studies in Cultural History* (London: BFI, 1991), p. 183.

20. A. Briggs, *The History of Broadcasting in the United Kingdom: Volume V: Competition* (Oxford: Oxford University Press, 1995), p. 413.

21. Independent Television Authority, *Independent Television Programmes: Facts and Figures January to March 1963* (London: ITA, 1963), p. 16.

22. J. Potter, *Independent Television in Britain: Volume 4: Companies and Programmes 1968–80* (London: Macmillan, 1990), p. 282.

23. Barnett, *Games and Sets*, p. 62.

24. For further details of Waring's status in rugby league, see J. Williams, '"Up and Under": Eddie Waring, Television and the Image of Rugby League', *Sports Historian*, 22/1 (2002), 115–37.

25. For details of the fluctuating numbers playing different sports, see R. Holt and T. Mason, *Sport in Britain 1945–2000* (Oxford: Blackwell, 2000), pp. 5–6.

26. Barnett, *Games and Sets*, p. 115.

27. Holt and Mason, *Sport in Britain*, p. 6.

28. Barnett, *Games and Sets*, p. 114.

29. Holt and Mason, *Sport in Britain*, p. 5; J. Williams, 'Cricket', in T. Mason (ed.), *Sport in Britain: A Social History* (Cambridge: Cambridge University Press, 1989), p. 126.

30. *Wisden Cricketers' Almanack 1998* (Guildford: John Wisden, 1998), p. 400.

31. I. Morrison, *The Hamlyn Encyclopedia of Snooker* (London: Hamlyn, 1985), p. 134.

32. Whannel, *Fields in Vision*, pp. 80–1.

33. *Independent on Sunday*, 5 December 1993.

34. For an account of the Packer affair, see T. McDonald, 'The Packer Intrusion', in E.W. Swanton, G. Plumptre and J. Woodcock (eds), *Barclays World of Cricket: The Game from A to Z* (London: Guild, 1986), pp. 383–90.

35. For a detailed chronology of the moves leading to the launch of the Super League, see R. Fletcher and D. Howes (eds), *Rothmans Rugby League Yearbook 1995–96* (London: Headline, 1995), pp. 9–14.

36. *Independent on Sunday*, 5 December 1993.

37. Quoted by G. Whannel, 'Notes on the Economics of Television Sport 1946–1990', *British Society of Sports History Bulletin*, 9 (1990), 61.

38. Whannel, *Fields in Vision*, p. 43.

39. *The Times*, 16 July 1983.

40. M. Cave and R.W. Crandall, 'Sports Rights and the Broadcast Industry', *Economic Journal*, 111 (2001), F16; *Media Guardian*, 25 February 2003, http://media.guardian.co.uk/broadcast (accessed 27 February 2003).

41. Whannel, *Fields in Vision*, p. 61.

42. *Wisden Cricketers' Almanack 1995* (Guildford: John Wisden, 1995), p. 1330; *Wisden Cricketers' Almanack 1999* (Guildford: John Wisden, 1999), p. 1425.

43. R. Fletcher and D. Howes (eds), *Rothmans Rugby League Yearbook 1992–93* (London: Headline, 1992), pp. 16, 27; Fletcher and Howes, *Rothmans Rugby League Yearbook 1995–96*, pp. 9, 14.

44. C.F. Pratten, *The Economics of Television* (London: PEP, 1970), p. 26.

45. M. Clarke, *Teaching Popular Television* (Northants: Heinemann, 1987), pp. 150–1; Whannel, 'Notes on the Economics of Television Sport', p. 71.

46. *BBC Annual Report 2002*, p. 8.

47. W. Fallowfield to the Rugby League Council, 4 February 1966, Rugby League Television File, Rugby League Archives.

48. For details of the income and expenditure of the county clubs, see *Cricketer*, July 1991, p. 20, June 1992, p. 12, June 1993, p. 15, June 1994, p. 17, June 1995, p. 9, June 1996, p. 16, June 1997, p. 20.

49. *Guardian*, 29 November 2002.

50. G. Crawford and J. Williams, *British Football on Television* (Leicester: Sir Norman Chester Centre for Football Research, University of Leicester, 2002), pp. 4, 10, 11 (Fact Sheet 8), www.le.ac.uk/snccfr/resources/factsheets/fs8.html (accessed 5 September 2002).

51. *Guardian*, 1 October 2002.

52. J. Williams and S. Neatrour, *The 'New' Football Economics* (Leicester: Sir Norman Chester Centre for Football, University of Leicester, 2002), p. 8 (Fact Sheet 10), www.le.ac.uk/fo/resources/factsheets/fs10.html (accessed 6 September 2002).

53. *The Times*, 6 May, 16 July 1983.

54. *The Times*, 29 March 1980.

55. Details of the Lancashire CCC balance sheets were provided in the annual issues of the *Lancashire Cricket Yearbook* until 1998.

56. Moore, 'Presentation'. The article in the *British Society of Sports History Bulletin* consists only of tables and other statistical data which Tony Moore presented at the annual conference of the British Society of Sports History in 1989.

57. *House of Commons National Heritage Committee: Fourth Report: Sports Sponsorship and Television Coverage*, pp. 44, 52, 131.

58. *Ibid.*, pp. 285–68.

59. *Ibid.*, p. xxx.

60. The History of Sponsorship, www.sponsorship-advice.org/student.htm (accessed 29 August 2002).

61. I. Morrison, *Snooker Records: Facts and Champions* (Enfield: Guinness, 1989), p. 48.

62. *Guardian*, 29 April 1994.

63. Williams and Neatrour, *The 'New' Football Economics*, p. 10.

64. *Guardian*, 18 April 2000.

65. *Guardian*, 18 April 2000, 29 November 2002.

66. *Sunday Times*, 15 October 1978, 16 November 1980, quoted in G. Whannel, 'The Alliance: Notes on Television and the Remaking of British Sport 1965–85', *Leisure Studies*, 5 (1986), p. 133.

67. *Guardian*, 24 April 1997.

68. Whannel, 'The Unholy Alliance', pp. 134–5. S. Aris, *Sportsbiz: Inside the Sports Business* (London: Hutchinson, 1990) and Wilson, *Sports Business*, discuss the connections between television, the rise of agents and the commercialisation of sport in Britain and America during the 1970s and 1980s.

69. Whannel, *Fields in Vision*, p. 80.

70. Whannel, 'Notes on the Economics of Television Sport', p. 69.

71. G. Whannel, *Media Sport Stars: Masculinities and Moralities* (London: Routledge, 2002), chs 11 and 12.

72. For detailed appraisals of theoretical studies of sport and gendered identities, see J. Hargreaves, *Sporting Females: Critical Issues in the History and Sociology of Women's Sports* (London: Routledge, 1994), M. Polley, *Moving the Goalposts: A History of Sport and Society since 1945* (London: Routledge, 1998), ch. 4, and Whannel, *Media Sport Stars*. All of these works also trace how the relationship between sports and gender changed over time.

Chapter 10

1. D. Gauntlett and A. Hill, *TV Living: Television, Culture and Everyday Life* (London: Routledge and BFI, 1999), chs 4 and 5.

2. D. Cannadine, *Class in Britain* (London: Penguin, 2000), discusses how the treatment of class by historians has changed over time.

3. J. Bakewell and N. Garnham, *The New Priesthood: British Television Today* (London: Allen Lane, 1970); J. Tunstall, *Television Producers* (London: Routledge, 1993); S. Cottle and P. Ismond, *Television and Ethnic Minorities: Producers' Perspectives: A Study of BBC In-House, Independent and Cable TV Producers* (Aldershot: Avebury, 1997).

INDEX